ROUTLEDGE LIBRARY EDITIONS:
TRANSPORT ECONOMICS

Volume 25

THE WORLD AIRCRAFT INDUSTRY

THE WORLD AIRCRAFT INDUSTRY

DANIEL TODD AND JAMIE SIMPSON

Routledge
Taylor & Francis Group
LONDON AND NEW YORK

First published in 1986 by Croom Helm Ltd

This edition first published in 2017
by Routledge
2 Park Square, Milton Park, Abingdon, Oxon OX14 4RN

and by Routledge
605 Third Avenue, New York, NY 10017

Routledge is an imprint of the Taylor & Francis Group, an informa business

British Library Cataloguing in Publication Data
A catalogue record for this book is available from the British Library

ISBN: 978-0-415-78484-9 (Set)
ISBN: 978-1-315-20175-7 (Set) (ebk)
ISBN: 978-1-138-63273-8 (Volume 25) (hbk)

THE WORLD AIRCRAFT INDUSTRY

DANIEL TODD and
JAMIE SIMPSON

CROOM HELM
London & Sydney

AUBURN HOUSE PUBLISHING COMPANY
Dover, Massachusetts

Croom Helm Ltd, Provident House, Burrell Row,
Beckenham, Kent BR3 1AT

Croom Helm Australia Pty Ltd, Suite 4, 6th Floor,
64-76 Kippax Street, Surry Hills, NSW 2010, Australia

British Library Cataloguing in Publication Data

Todd, Daniel
The world aircraft industry.
1. Aircraft industry
I. Title II. Simpson, Jamie
338.7'62913 HD9711.A2

ISBN 0-7099-2486-0

Auburn House Publishing Company,
14 Dedham Street, Dover,
Massachusetts 02030

Library of Congress Cataloging in Publication Data

Todd, Daniel.
The world aircraft industry.
Includes bibliographical references.
1. Aircraft industry. I. Simpson, Jane. II. Title.
HD9711.A2T63 1986 338.4'762913334 85-26751
ISBN 0-86569-141-X

1986 Todd, Daniel, Auburn House Publishing Company,
14, Dedham Street, Dover, Massachusetts 02030

Printed and bound in Great Britain
by Billing & Sons Limited, Worcester.

CONTENTS

TABLES

FIGURES

ACKNOWLEDGEMENTS

The authors wish to thank the University of Manitoba Research Grants Committee for backing their preliminary interest in the area of aerospace and its implications for national and regional development. This book is an outgrowth of those first cursory explorations and has benefited from the discussions held with industry and government representatives which were made possible through the original project.

The second of us, Simpson, wishes to express his gratitude to his family and Tara. The two of us are indebted to Marjorie Halmarson for her able draughtsmanship.

Chapter One

OVERVIEW OF THE INDUSTRY

In everyday usage the aircraft industry is generally lumped with the 'aerospace' sector. A loose coinage, aerospace embraces aeroengines, avionics (aviation electronics), missiles, and space vehicles in addition to the manufacture of aircraft. Indeed, the aircraft industry in its present form is really focused on the airframe producers, that is to say, the manufacturers of aircraft fuselages and wings who also undertake the installation of power plants and all the other components and systems, manufactured elsewhere, but brought to the airframe plant for final assembly. The aircraft industry is in truth a part-fabricator, part-assembly operation which constitutes perhaps the most visible aspect of the much more amorphous aerospace sector.

It is worth stressing, however, that the aircraft industry is not necessarily the most important part of the aerospace sector notwithstanding its obvious pivotal role. In Canada's case, for example, it is aeroengines and avionics (navigation and flight systems and aircraft flight simulators; to name but two) which are looked upon to counter the country's balance of payments deficit in finished aircraft.[1] Between one quarter and one third of Britain's entire aerospace exports are aircraft parts and subsystems and it is easy to make a case for the view that it is this component of the aerospace sector which accords the UK its greatest comparative advantage.[2] Not only does it underwrite the airframe industry, but it enables Britain to enjoy a level of aerospace infrastructure not available to other European nations. Arguably, UK components producers have displayed the greatest success of any foreign aerospace enterprises in penetrating the vital US market: Lucas Aerospace, to name but one example, has a production plant in New Jersey geared to the provision of electrical systems for US Army helicopters.[3] In truth, the bulk of the aerospace industry falls into the parts, systems, or components category; leaving only a handful of airframe or aeroengine manufacturers (Figure 1.1). Yet, when the diverse range of products of these components or so-called Tier II firms is contemplated - aircraft instruments, supplies and accessories, avionics, communications equipment, computer systems, gears and transmissions, landing gear, navigation systems, satellites, welding and metal finishing and so on - it is evident why aerospace is an equivocal grouping among the set of industrial categories. Clearly, several of the suppliers in question manufacture products that are not unique to the aircraft and missiles sector; thus the obvious query arises as to how far they are truly aerospace enterprises in contrast to, say, telecommunications or vehicles enterprises. Their common focus is, of course, the airframe industry (part of the so-called Tier I of aerospace) to which they supply at least some of their production. In the same vein, the term 'aerospace' is sufficiently broad to cover firms whose prime interest is aircraft overhaul and repair (the Tier III operations). Likewise, these firms are ultimately dependent upon the airframe and aeroengine manufacturers though at one step further removed than the components producers. They are, in short, best viewed as the 'service' aspect of the aerospace sector.

The aim of this book is to concentrate attention on the airframe producers precisely because they are the core of the aerospace sector. Aeroengines are delivered to the plant of the airframe firm for installation, as are the parts emanating from the Tier II enterprises. The only Tier I operation independent of the airframe assembly outcome is that denoted in Figure 1.1 as the Missiles and Space Vehicles group and, arguably, this activity owes as much for its genesis to the automotive and ordnance industries as it does to the aircraft industry.[4] It receives attention in this book only in as much as it comes to bear on the organisation of aircraft enterprises. By the same token, aeroengine firms and Tier II and Tier III operations are the object of peripheral treatment except where they have a direct bearing on the actions of airframe producers. It is hoped, in consequence, to provide an understanding of the activities of the aircraft industry without clouding the issue with concerns which are more germane to electrical or mechanical engineering sectors. Before singling out the airframe producers, however, it is important to review the global distribution of the aerospace sector; the context within which the

Figure 1.1 : The Aerospace Sector

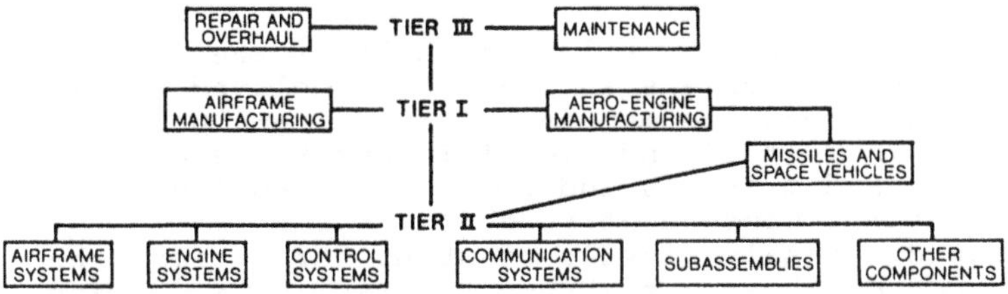

manufacturers of aircraft must function.

GLOBAL DISTRIBUTION

The Advanced-Industrial Countries

By far the largest of the world's aerospace industries, the US industry, employed 1.2 million people (at the end of 1980), utilised 1,150 establishments, and accounted for sales worth $74.7 billion (in 1983). It was responsible for 2.2 per cent of the country's GNP and was consistently the largest manufacturing employer since data were first reported on an aerospace basis in 1959.[5] The industry was a 'star' among American industries on several counts, including its contribution to exports, research and development (R & D), and, not least, its record of accelerating growth. On the first count, aerospace displayed a massive surplus in the balance of payments: in 1980, for example, US aerospace exports amounted to $11.7 billion whereas imports were placed at $1.6 billion; while by 1983 the balance of trade stood at $12.7 billion or the best of any industry. An aerospace firm, Boeing, has the highest exports to total sales ratio (43.3 per cent) of the top 50 US exporting companies in all industries.[6] Secondly, the Aerospace Industries Association estimated that the industry's investment in R & D equalled 23.7 per cent of its sales, a figure far larger than the electrical and electronics industry, the next largest investor with a value equivalent to 7.3 per cent of sales.[7] Thirdly, the industry's sales have been growing steadily, increasing by 11.5 per cent between 1982 and 1983 alone, and achieving an annual growth rate of 3.5 per cent throughout much of the 1970s. Such growth has translated into job creation with the industry employing more people in 1980 than it had done since the height of the Vietnam War eleven years previously.

Interestingly, little over half of the 1.21 million aerospace workers in 1981 were employed in airframe and aeroengine manufacture: the remainder were occupied in Tier II and Tier III operations on the one hand, and missiles and space vehicles manufacture on the other. Consequently, complete aircraft accounted for sales levels of about three times the magnitude of those attributed to missiles and space. A breakdown of US aerospace export sales for 1979 (Table 1.1) underscores the importance of aircraft production in American international trade relative to the contributions made by the other constituents of the aerospace sector. Moreover, that table indicates the pre-eminence of civil aircraft exports within the complete aircraft category. American dominance of world jetliner markets through the products of Boeing, McDonnell-Douglas(MD) and Lockheed is the major factor on this score. One estimate implied that of 259,640 workers directly employed in commercial aircraft manufacture, no less than 104,000 were working on export orders and, what is more, every 100 of those jobs was responsible for creating 163 in other manufacturing and services.[8] Only in recent years has the US emphasis on civil aircraft exports been challenged by concerted efforts to sell military aircraft, for, traditionally, the lion's share of combat machines has been earmarked for the US armed forces. Yet, after the mid-1970s, the US Government actively supported attempts by American aircraft firms to sell combat aircraft abroad in anticipation of sizeable benefits. It was suggested, for example, that if General Dynamics could supply, in the form of the F-16 , some 2,000 of the 'Free World's' requirement for 5,000 fighters, the USA would benefit to the tune of 900,000 jobs, $9 billion in balance-of-payments receipts, $6 billion in tax receipts, and would recover $470 million of its R & D expenditures.[9]

The importance of export sales from the aerospace sector has not been lost on the countries of the EEC; which together rival the Soviet bloc as the second concentration of global aerospace activity. In 1975 the EEC accounted for $8.25 billion of the Western World's $35.3 billion in comparison to the $24.04 billion contributed by the USA (Table 1.2). This 23 per cent share of the non-communist market was double the EEC penetration of the market of 1960: indication enough of the enhanced competitiveness of European

Table 1.1 : US Aerospace Exports 1979

Markets	Civil ($ million)	Military ($ million)
Transport aircraft	4,998	-
Light aircraft	650	-
Helicopter	207	-
Other	322	-
Combat aircraft	-	838
Total complete aircraft	6,177	838
Aeroengines	375	74
Aircraft and engine parts	3,220	492
Missiles and parts	-	571
Total	9,772	1,975

Source: Derived from _Flight International_, 7 February 1981.

aerospace. Indeed, European firms had acquired a one-third share of the world market for combat aircraft and helicopters along with a 32 per cent share of the market for civil light-turbine aeroplanes. However, they had scarcely dented the US hold on jetliner sales, accounting for only nine per cent of the market. Enjoined to make good the discrepancy, the EEC has devoted much collaborative effort to the Airbus family of jetliners. Initial success with the A300 and A310 airliners induced the Europeans to launch the A320 Airbus in 1984. Likely to cost over £2 billion, the UK Government was prepared to add £250 million to the £200 million-plus allocated to the project by BAe, while the French Government, for its part, was prepared to advance £430 million and the West German Government was forthcoming with £395 million.[10] Clearly, the virtual free-hand enjoyed by the Americans in jetliner markets for so long is now at an end.

In terms of individual EEC industries, the onset of the 1960s witnessed the eclipse of the UK by France in aerospace sales (Table 1.2). In 1961 French aerospace exports exceeded those of Britain for the first time: the result of sales of Mirage fighters, Caravelle jetliners, Alouette helicopters and Nord missiles. At that time, the 85,000 manpower of the French industry was comprised of 48,400 airframe workers, 16,400 aeroengine workers, and 20,200 in other lines.[11] Twenty years later, the French aerospace industry amounted to 150 firms employing 113,000 workers with export sales in excess of £3.3 billion. Composition of 1983 export sales was: complete aircraft (52.9 per cent), helicopters (7.2 per cent), aeroengines (18.1 per cent), missiles (3.3 per cent), space (2.7 per cent) and avionics and parts (15.8 per cent).[12] About 36 per cent of French aerospace exports derived from collaborative projects mostly with other EEC partners.[13] The largest single European aerospace manufacturer in terms of turnover (recording over FFr 13 billion in 1980), Aérospatiale, is a state-owned enterprise employing almost 40,000 which concentrates on airliner, helicopter and missile production. Conversely, the other major French airframe producer, Dassault, concentrates most of its efforts on fighters (the Mirage family), military jet trainers (Alpha Jet) and business jets (Falcon series); and used to be regarded as a classic example of the effectiveness of the private owner-designer model in aircraft manufacture.

Employing a larger workforce than the French (Table 1.3), the aerospace industry in the UK is dominated by the partially state-owned BAe (itself employing 77,500 in 1983). Organised into aircraft and missile divisions, BAe assigns particular aeroplane types to specific plants;namely, Warton(Preston) for Tornado MRCA and Jaguar fighter-bombers, Prestwick for Jetstream light turboprop airliners, Manchester for the BAe 748 turboprop transport and its ATP successor, Chester for BAe 125 bizjets and Airbus wings, Kingston for Harrier and Hawk military jets, and Hatfield for the BAe 146 airliner. The enterprise increased its sales by 24 per cent between 1981 and 1982 to record a figure of just over £2 billion. About 80 per cent of the firm's sales were destined for military customers. The only other UK airframe producers of importance are Shorts of Belfast, builders of small turboprop transports, Westland at Yeovil which concentrates entirely on helicopter manufacture, and PBN on the Isle of Wight, responsible for the Islander type of light transport.

The third EEC aerospace industry, that of West Germany, is substantially smaller than the industries in France and Britain (Table 1.3). In 1982 it employed about 76,000; of which 26,000 were working for the MBB enterprise. Gross sales in 1980 stood at $4.5 billion, of which no less than $1.6 billion was associated with the Tornado MRCA airframe programme

Table 1.2 : European and Western World Aerospace Sales, 1960 and 1975

Country	1960 ($billion)	% of West (rounded)	1975 ($billion)	% of West (rounded)
UK	1.43	7.8	3.55	10.1
France	0.48	2.6	3.61	10.2
West Germany	0.10	0.5	1.43	4.1
Netherlands	0.05	0.3	0.26	0.7
Belgium	0.01	0.0	0.10	0.3
Italy	0.07	0.4	0.59	1.7
EEC total[1]	2.02	11.0	8.25	23.4
Other European	0.05	0.3	0.62	1.8
USA	15.77	85.7	24.04	68.1
Canada	0.40	2.2	0.81	2.3
Japan	0.08	0.4	0.76	2.2
Other	0.10	0.5	0.80	2.3
Western World	18.40		35.30	

Note: 1. Less EEC intra-industry transactions
Source: Aviation Week & Space Technology, 6 June 1977, p.163.

Table 1.3 : European Aerospace Turnover and Employment

Country	Turnover[1] (ECU millions)	% Change 1970-78	Employment[2] ('000)
France	3482	63	103
UK	3211	45	215
West Germany	1284	-1	56
Italy	523	65	36
Total EEC	8802	41	421
USA	20661	-17	967

Notes: 1. European currency units for 1978 pegged to 1975 rates
2. 1978 Figures
Source: EEC, The European Aerospace Industry, Brussels 1980.

jointly conducted with the British and Italians, and a further $450 million stemmed from engine sales again largely deriving from the MRCA venture.[14] In fact, the West German aircraft effort was inordinately dependent upon international programmes with the Tornado (42.5 per cent share) and Airbus A300/A310 (37.5 per cent share) projects assuming greatest significance. During 1984-5 the industry will select a follow-on venture for the Tornado in order to keep itself occupied into the 1990s: the five-nation EFA combat aircraft has been touted for this purpose.[15] The second sizeable West German aircraft manufacturer, Dornier has produced a successful series of utility transports (models 28, 128 and 228).

Unlike the other EEC producers, Italy has clung to licence-production of foreign (mainly US) aircraft designs for the bulk of its aerospace activity. Agusta, for example, builds most of the Bell- Helicopter-Textron models at Cascina Costa and sells them to areas of the world (primarily the Middle East and Africa) in which the American licensor is somewhat unwelcome. While advantageous in so far as it reduces development costs, such practices require the Italian enterprise to import from the USA something in the order of 50 per cent of the value of each helicopter made.[16] As with Italian industry in general, the aerospace industry was heavily concentrated in the North of the country or around Rome. Since 1970, however, the two firms under state operation - Aeritalia and Agusta - have followed (at government instigation) a policy of expansion in the South. In no uncertain terms, the Italian Government has attempted to link the aerospace sector into its strategy for Southern regional development.

Other European aircraft industries of significance - both inside and outside of the EEC - include those of Sweden, Spain and Yugoslavia. The first is particularly noteworthy in light of Sweden's determination to maintain an independent defence-industrial base which includes a capacity to design and manufacture state-of-the-art combat aircraft. As a result, Saab-Scania has produced, since World War II, a series of fighter aircraft (types 29, 32, 35 and 37) equal to contemporary aircraft emanating from the great powers. Its technological expertise is currently being exercised in two directions: formulation of an MRCA to serve as Sweden's next-generation military aeroplane (known as the JAS 39 project) and co-production with Fairchild of the USA of a light turboprop airliner (the Saab-Fairchild 340). For these ends, major investments have been underway at the aerospace complex in Linkoping, including the erection of a new 270,000m^2 factory for airliner assembly and a carbon-fibre production facility for manufacturing the composite materials needed in the JAS programme.[17] The Netherlands, like Sweden, is keen on making its presence felt in the small airliner market. Its Fokker firm has built an enviable reputation in this field with the F-27 and F-28 models. Unable to internalise production of engines and parts, Fokker has relied on sub-contractors elsewhere in Europe; the F-28, for example, is about 60 per cent British supplied, receiving its engines from Rolls-Royce(R-R) and its wing sections from Shorts. Final assembly of the F-28 at Schiphol also requires delivery of fuselage sections, engine nacelles and empennage from MBB of West Germany.[18] The Spanish aircraft industry, in similar fashion to Sweden and the Netherlands, is centred on a single major enterprise; in this case CASA. This state enterprise acquires 'know-how' through offset agreements with foreign manufacturers which allows for part-manufacture and assembly in Spain of foreign military aircraft designs (e.g. MD F-18, Northrop F-5, Dassault Mirage, MBB BO105). It also undertakes a considerable amount of subcontract manufacture for foreign firms: its Getafe plant building horizontal stabilisers and passenger doors for the A300/A310 Airbus while similar fixtures are made for Boeing 727 and MD DC-9 and DC-10 aircraft. Its most recent venture, the CN-235 light transport, is a joint venture with Indonesia. In 1981 the firm enjoyed sales of £132 million of which £86 million was attributed to exports.[19] Yugoslavia also boasts a state aircraft enterprise - Soko - which again manages to produce its own designs despite major efforts devoted by the country to the procurement of foreign (Soviet in this instance) combat aircraft. Employing 3,000 at four factories (the largest of which are Mostar and Kraguj), Soko has produced the Galeb and Super Galeb trainer and Jastreb fighter equipped with British engines, wheels, ejection seats and avionics. It is currently co-operating with Romania in the production of an indigenous new-generation fighter.[20]

Other integral parts of the AIC aerospace sector are to be found in Canada, Japan and Australia. While producing its own aircraft designs in two state-owned firms, Canada depends on the US aircraft industry for much of its aerospace business, supplying to that country a host of parts and components ranging downwards from airliner wings. Australia, likewise, participates in US offset work, although to a much smaller extent than Canada. The policy of the

Australian Government is to obtain 30 per cent of the value of foreign aircraft acquisitions for its own aerospace industry. That industry, in turn, employs about 6,000 workers centred on three firms: state-owned Government Aircraft Factories, and privately-owned HDH and Commonwealth Aircraft Corporation. Only the first has an indigenous design in the STOL Nomad.[21] While only a little larger than the Canadian industry, Japanese aerospace displays much more ambition. Under the auspices of MITI, investment has been made available for several long-term projects aimed at turning Japan into a major player in aerospace. These include the YX modification of the 767 airliner with Boeing, the YXX 150-seat airliner, and the RJ500 fanjet in co-operation with R-R.[22] Furthermore, Japan has been much more adventurous in supporting large, domestically-designed aircraft programmes; no doubt a legacy of its pre-1945 Imperial stature. The Nihon Aeroplane Manufacturing Company - a combination of several firms brought together by MITI - not only engineered Japan's first turboprop airliner (the YS-11), but also produced one of the world's few military jet transport aircraft (the C-1).[23] By the early 1980s, 25,000 workers were employed in Japanese aerospace; engaged, in the main, in the aircraft divisions of the major conglomerates; namely: MHI (at Nagoya), Kawasaki (Gifu) and Fuji (Utsunomiya); with IHI (Tanashi) concentrating on aeroengine production. While largely occupied manufacturing US combat types under licence, these firms also produce aircraft to their own designs (e.g. Mitsubishi T-2/F-1/MU-2, Kawasaki XT-4, Fuji T-1/T-3). The most recent Japanese conglomerate to take an interest in aerospace, Mitsui, has agreed to produce the Bell 214ST helicopter in Japan with the aid of its US designer, Bell-Helicopter-Textron.[24]

The Communist Bloc

Rivalling the USA in the scale of its aerospace activities, the USSR is reputed to produce 1,800 aircraft per year.[25] The Soviet industry is overwhelmingly geared to defence production: even civil aviation coming under the rubric of the state's defence posture (with, for example, the state airline Aeroflot being commanded by an Air Force General and having its airliners earmarked as a reserve military air-portable service). American estimates suggest that the USSR manufactured 6,100 tactical warplanes between 1974 and 1982, double the US total, and completed a further 680 such aircraft in 1983-4.[26] The workforce employed to produce this effort is unknown, partly because of the secretive attitude of Soviet aerospace officials and partly because of the Soviet practice of undertaking diversified manufacturing in what are ostensibly aircraft plants. In order to maintain defence-production capability at a high level, military output has been linked with compatible civilian production (e.g. the manufacture of tanks and railway rolling stock in the same factory) with the result that special plant is not underused and workers skills are continually being honed.[27] Thus the Kiev factory formerly tasked with building An-24 transports also makes camping trailers, kitchenware and agricultural implements; the Kharkov plant responsible for Tu-134 jetliners also turns its attention to sporting goods and baby carriages; while the aeroengine factories at Zaporozhye and Perm produce marine and industrial engines as well.[28]

Given the overall direction of economic activity by the state, the Soviet aerospace sector differs fundamentally from its Western counterparts in separating design from production. The former is the bailiwick of various bureaux which specialise in particular aircraft classes - fighter, bomber, transport, helicopter - and respond to specifications handed down by military planners. The foremost airframe design bureaux are Tupolev, Antonov, Yakovlev, Ilyushin and MIG (Migoyan-Gurevich). Tupolev is renowned for its bomber and jet transport designs, Antonov for its transports, Ilyushin for its attack aircraft and the other two for their fighter aircraft. In addition, Mil is entrusted with helicopter design. Successful testing of the resultant designs leads to the allocation of the necessary production facilities by the Ministry of Aircraft Production. Operating about 40 Tier I plants, the Ministry delegates five of these for fighter production, nine for bombers and large transports (including airliners), ten for helicopters and light aircraft, and another ten for aeroengine production.[29] To all intents and purposes, the aircraft plants can be divided into a Western group and an Eastern group. The former occurs in the traditional industrial heartland of the USSR and, by and large, dates from Stalin's first and second Five-Year Plan initiatives (1928-32 and 1933-5 respectively). Located at Riga, Leningrad, Moscow, Taganrog, Rybinsk, Voronezh, Zaporozhye, Kharkov, Gorki, Saratov and Kazan; these facilities suffered extensive damage in World War II. Since rebuilt and enlarged, they continue as a vital component of the Soviet aerospace sector; Voronezh, for instance, formerly building the An-10 turboprop freighter and the less-than-successful Tu-144 SST whereas Saratov was reputed to produce one Yak-40 feederliner every second day.[30] Supplemented by the Eastern group as an emergency war measure, the plants beyond the Urals at Irkutsk, Semenovka, Tomsk, Novosibirsk, Sverdlovsk, Tashkent, Khabarovsk and Kuznetsk have assumed increasing importance in postwar years.[31] The process of geographic dispersion of the industry has not ceased; for factories have been established at Kuibischev, Tiflis, Ascha and other sites in the periphery of the USSR. A latecomer was the An-24 transport-aircraft factory at Ulan-Ude in southern Siberia created in the 1960s.[32]

Although mainly concerned to supply the aviation needs of Soviet and Warsaw Pact forces and airlines, the Soviet aircraft industry has emphasised exports to other countries in recent years. Undertaken both to acquire foreign currency earnings (especially from OPEC states) and bolster Soviet influence abroad, the sale of aircraft also alleviates the R & D and production costs burden shouldered by the USSR aerospace sector. Hard currency payments have been received from Iraq, Libya and Algeria in return for the best-selling Mig-21 fighter.[33] It has been estimated that 27 per cent of the Soviet Union's total output of combat aircraft was exported in the years 1967-73; 29 per cent during 1974-8, and a sharply increased 41 per cent for the 1977-80 period.[34] Soviet aircraft are comparatively cheap by virtue of their relative simplicity in contrast to most Western equipment and this has been a principal factor in their export success.

The aircraft industries in the Warsaw Pact states are virtual satellites of the Soviet aerospace sector. For the most part, they produce copies of aircraft designed in the USSR and their contributions to the aggregate Warsaw Pact armoury are quite substantial. The Czech Aero Trust, for instance, produced about three Mig-21 fighters each month and, at its peak during the Korean War, was capable of making three Mig-15s per day. Indeed, the East European aircraft industries are so integrated into the Soviet aerospace sector that they have been allowed to produce specific aircraft types not only for their own air requirements but in order to fulfil Soviet needs too. The Polish PZL works, for example, is authorised to manufacture general-aviation aircraft for the alliance and also utility helicopters such as the Mi-2 (Okecie and Mielec turning out a prodigious number of agricultural aircraft). The Czechs, in turn, employ much of their 28,000 strong aerospace workforce on the production of jet trainers for Pact air forces at Vodochody and Kunovice. The initial model, the L-29, had a production run of over 3,000 aircraft and was replaced on the production lines after 1974 by the L-39. Only the Romanian aircraft industry functions independently of Soviet directives and it has flourished as a consequence of joint ventures with Yugoslavia and Britain. While relatively small, the industry in Romania has managed to produce a derivative of the BAe 111 jetliner and a R-R Viper powered jet strike-fighter.

China is, of course, an autonomous member of the communist bloc and has gone its own way since 1960 in aerospace as in everything else. Nevertheless, its aircraft industry is still wedded to Soviet technology in terms of aeroplane design and production methods.[35] The Xian factory in Shensi Province, for example, manufactures modifications of the An-24 transport (called the Y-7) and the Tu-16 bomber (the H-6 in Chinese designation), while Hanzhong builds the An-12 tactical transport (as the Y-8). In a similar manner, the main Shenyang aerospace complex produces the F-6, a derivative of the Mig-19 fighter (also built at Tianjin); while Nanchang is tasked with producing an attack version of this aircraft known as the A-5.[36] All these types are powered by Soviet-designed Tumansky engines. It is only since the late 1970s that China has been able to break away from Soviet influence in its aircraft designs. In large measure, this new freedom arose out of agreements with Western aerospace firms for the transfer of technology. Aeroengine builder R-R was a prominent player in this process, allowing the Chinese to licence-build the Spey turbine at a specially-built plant at Hsian.[37] Other UK companies provided back-up facilities.[38] By 1980, China was able to fly its own jetliner, the Y-10, (looking remarkably like a Boeing 707) from the Shanghai aircraft factory equipped with US JT3D-7 engines and was intent on flying a new fighter - the Shenyang J-8 - powered by Spey turbofans. The industry had even been co-opted into the US airliner programme; providing simple machine parts for Boeing's 737 and 747 models and landing gears for MD's super 80.[39] The latter type is to be assembled in China by the Shanghai Aircraft Industrial Corporation to meet the needs of the country's airline. It will join another US type, the Bell 412 helicopter, in being assembled domestically (at Harbin in this instance). Chinese factories operate as self-sufficient entities, containing engine works, ejection seat plants and landing-gear assembly operations within the one complex. Such integrated production is necessary owing to the absence of Tier II and Tier III enterprises in the country: a state of affairs that China shares with other NICs.

The Newly-Industrialising Countries

The aircraft industry is promoted in NICs for two reasons: in order to further export-led manufacturing expansion in the first place, and to safeguard the supply of military hardware in the second. The former ploy is best exemplified by Brazil and Indonesia and, from the socialist camp, Romania. Those national industries are the subject of scrutiny elsewhere in this book (Chapter 8) and, therefore, will not be dwelt upon here. Most NICs, however, engage in aircraft manufacture for the second reason. Table 1.4 indicates the range of nations falling into this category. All of those countries persist in aircraft manufacture notwithstanding excessive costs and often inefficient production methods because national security concerns are paramount. Dependence on foreign suppliers carries with it an element of vulnerability to embargoes of spare parts. Israel, for example, opted to develop its own fighter aircraft after 1967 when France slapped a ban on the export of weapons to the Middle Eastern adversaries. The first effort of IAI at Lod Airport resulted in the Nesher in 1969; a virtual copy of the French Mirage. Subsequent marrying of a modified Mirage airframe and a US J79 engine resulted in the Kfir flying in 1974. Complementing the fighter programme was the Arava STOL transport (first flight in 1969) and the Westwind executive jet (developed from a US design). Currently, IAI is working on a new-generation fighter, the Lavi, with the aid of US funds, components and engines.[40] Under the wing of the Defence Ministry, IAI mostly produces for the military market (77 per cent of its output) and employs about 18,000 workers. It is supplemented by over one hundred parts and avionics firms and has a subsidiary - MBT Weapon Systems - devoted to the production of the locally-designed Gabriel missile.[41] South Africa, for comparable reasons, has attempted to become self-sufficient in warplane provision. Its Atlas Aircraft Company, a branch of the state Armaments Development and Production Corporation, has built Mirage fighters and Impala attack aircraft under licence from France and Italy respectively and has a workforce of about 3,500.

While not prone to embargoes to the same degree as Israel and South Africa, the largest Arab nation - Egypt - has attempted over the years to establish a warplanes industry for similar pressing national security reasons. In the 1950s inspiration for the

Table 1.4 : Aircraft Capability of NICs (Licence Production or Indigenous Design)

Country	Jet Fighter Production	Helicopter	Jet Trainers or Light Attack Aircraft
Turkey	licence		
Argentina	-	licence	indigenous
Brazil	joint design with Italy	licence	licence
Chile	-	-	licence
Peru	-	-	licence
Venezuela	-	licence	-
Nigeria	-	licence	-
South Africa	licence	licence	licence
Egypt	licence	licence	licence
Iran	-	licence	-
Israel	indigenous	licence	licence
India	indigenous	licence	indigenous
Indonesia	-	licence	-
North Korea	licence	-	-
South Korea	licence	licence	-
Pakistan	-	licence	-
Philippines	-	licence	-
Taiwan	licence	licence	indigenous

Source: Partly Derived from N.Ball and M.Leitenberg (eds). The Structure of the Defense Industry, Table 10.1, pp. 314-15.

Egyptian industry came from German and Austrian expatriate designers: the unsuccessful Ha-300 delta-winged fighter was the brainchild of Willi Messerschmitt while its turbojets were designed by Prof. Brandner. However, by the mid-1970s the aircraft plants at Helwan and Heliopolis were largely denuded of new construction.[42] It was only after the rapprochement with the West that the Egyptian industry was retooled; albeit to assemble aircraft and parts designed elsewhere. Starting with small assemblies for the Dassault Falcon 50 executive jet and Aérospatiale Puma and Gazelle helicopters, Helwan graduated to assembling the latter type as well as the

Franco-German Alpha Jet and is about to produce the Brazilian-designed Tucano turboprop trainer.[43] About 7,300 people are employed by the Arab Organisation for Industrialisation in airframe and aeroengine work at Helwan and this centre will begin to assemble the Mirage 2000 - the most complex of Dassault's family of fighters - by the end of 1986.[44]

The largest NIC aircraft industry is that of India. Under the auspices of state enterprise HAL, about 40,000 workers are devoted to meeting the country's huge military aviation needs. Most of this effort is, in conformity with other NICs, aimed at licence-production.[45] The sophisticated Anglo-French Jaguar fighter-bomber is, for example, produced at Bangalore along with its Adour engine. An associated avionics plant for the aircraft's navigational and attack systems has been established at Korwa in Uttar Pradesh.[46] To display even-handedness, as it were, the latest Soviet technology has been adopted in the form of licence-production of the Mig-21/27: the airframe emanating from Nasik, the engine from Koraput and the avionics from Balanagar. Military transports (initially BAe 748 and now Dornier 228) are the province of the Kanpur plant. Similar defence-oriented production is underway in Taiwan and South Korea. Established in 1969 at Taichung (with an engine factory at Kang Shan), the Aero Industry Development Centre is a spin-off of the Nationalist Chinese Air Force. In the succeeding years it produced American types under licence: the PL-1 trainer, the UH-1H helicopter and the F-5E fighter. Beginning in 1973 it also initiated indigenous projects: the T-CH-1 turboprop trainer followed by the XC-2 twin-turboprop transport. From 1980, Taiwan was persevering with the XAT-3 jet trainer assisted by the US Northrop Corporation.[47] South Korea, for its part, was assembling Northrop F-5 fighters at the Pusan factory of Korean Air Lines.[48] Other Asian nations undertaking aircraft construction include Singapore, Turkey, Iran, Pakistan, Thailand, the Philippines and, above all, Indonesia. The last is rather unusual for NICs in as much as the impetus for establishing an aircraft industry derives from civil rather than military objectives: indeed, aerospace is regarded as an integral part of Indonesia's national development programme (and as such, is subject to scrutiny in Chapter 8).

Latin America is the remaining venue for NICs with significant aerospace industries and its leading representative, by far, is Brazil. The Embraer company maintains initiatives in military and civil transport aircraft and co-operates with Italy in the development of the AM-X light ground-attack fighter. Brazil shares with Indonesia and Romania the central role accorded aerospace by the state in furthering national development and, like them, is reserved for detailed treatment later. Much more conventional in its military mould is the industry in Argentina. There, the military aircraft factory(FMA) at Cordoba concentrates on the locally-designed Pucara twin-turboprop ground-attack aircraft and the IA63 jet trainer: confining its civil involvement to the licence-production of US Cessna light aeroplanes and agricultural aircraft. Rivalry with Argentina renders it imperative for Chile to develop a military aerospace capability as well. Consequently, Indaer is building the Pillan primary trainer designed for it by the US Piper company and is also assembling the C-101 attack trainer under licence from CASA of Spain. Peru, likewise, professed an intention to manufacture light jet trainers/attack aircraft under licence, but in this case relying on Aermacchi (of Italy) for its MB.339. For that purpose, a $5 million complex at Collique, north of Lima, was commenced in the early 1980s, and was equipped with tools and machinery by Aermacchi worth a further $10 million. A modest 350 are employed in this enterprise which is currently stalled owing to the country's debt crisis.[49]

SUMMARY

The aerospace sector, to which the aircraft industry remains central, plays a leading role in the economies of the West, the communist bloc, and increasingly in the industrialisation strategies of NICs. Such a role derives, in the first place, from the fact that the sector can act as a major employer of manufacturing labour - in the USA it has traditionally vied with motor vehicles as the single largest source of manufacturing employment. Secondly, it is one of the few sectors in AICs which has continued to prosper as an export-earner. The USA, France, Britain, and now the USSR too, have all recognised the sector's importance in easing their balance of payments difficulties. Of course, the export aspect of aerospace serves as a useful supplement to the sector's production activity aimed at fulfilling domestic markets, and the whole issue of demand for aircraft is dealt with in Chapters 3 and 4. Before arriving at that juncture, however, it is necessary to outline the evolution of the industry - the subject of the next chapter - and in particular the inextricable connection between demand and technical change. Operating in tandem, those factors amount to a rationale for the emergence of aircraft enterprises and account for their subsequent expansion or contraction: the essence of Chapter 6.

The production patterns of the aircraft industry vary according to the source of demand: markets for civil aircraft (as explained in Chapter 3) behave in a markedly different manner from those regulating demand for warplanes (Chapter 4). In both instances, though, the state is a principal agent. What is more, the state also influences the location of aircraft plants (as elaborated upon in Chapter 5), provides the bulk of the R & D funds necessary to maintain the industry's technological progress (Chapter 6), and frequently offers an alternative form of business organisation to that available from private enterprise (Chapter 7). Finally, in recognising the development prospects of aerospace, the state often deliberately fosters it as an instrument of national and industrial expansion (Chapter 8). The remainder of this book examines the close interaction between aircraft enterprises, the state, and technological change under the broad rubric just outlined. A concluding chapter attempts to integrate the consequences of this interaction as it comes to bear on the world aircraft industry.

NOTES AND REFERENCES

1. AW & ST, 27 October 1980, p.59.
2. AW & ST,1 September 1980, p.83.
3. Ibid, p.284.
4. G. R. Simonson, 'Missile and Creative Destruction in the American Aircraft Industry,1956-61', Business History Review, 38 (1964), pp.302-314.
5. AW & ST, 26 December 1983, p.18.
6. *Fortune*, 6 August 1984, p.65.
7. AW & ST, 6 October 1980, p.18.
8. AW & ST, 30 August 1971, p.14.
9. AW & ST, 4 August 1975, p.7.
10. FI, 5 May 1984, p.1216.
11. FI, 15 March 1962, p.396.
12. FI, 7 April 1984, p.941.
13. FI, 5 December 1981, p.1686.
14. AW & ST, 19 October 1981, p.26.
15. FI, 19 May 1984, p.1327.
16. AW & ST, 1 February 1971, p.48.
17. AW & ST, 14 September 1981, p.141.
18. AW & ST, 27 April 1970, pp.99-100.

19. FI, 20 February 1982, p.416.
20. AW & ST, 2 June 1969, pp.207-212.
21. AW & ST, 23 November 1981, p.51. Note, all three firms are currently co-operating on the AAC (Australian Aircraft Consortium) trainer for the country's air force.
22. FI, 10 October 1981, p.1065.
23. Organised by MITI, Nihon was a joint venture of Mitsubishi, Kawasaki and Fuji, set up in 1959 and capitalised for $34 million. It produced 182 YS-11 airliners and was responsible for the design of the C-1 jet transports before liquidation in 1982.
24. AW & ST, 20 October 1980, p.33.
25. M. J. Armitage and R. A. Mason, _Air Power in the Nuclear Age_, (University of Illinois Press, Urbana, 1983), p.140.
26. Secretary of Defense Weinberger's figures quoted in FI, 12 February 1983, p.378.
27. F. M. Fabian, 'The Soviet Industrial Base' in L. D. Olvey, H. A. Leonard and B. E. Arlinghaus, _Industrial Capacity and Defense Planning_, (D. C. Heath, Lexington, 1983), pp.65-9.
28. AW & ST, 2 July 1973, p.28.
29. A. Boyd, _The Soviet Air Force since 1918_, (MacDonalds and Jane's, London, 1977), p.277.
30. AW & ST, 2 July 1973, p.7 and p.55.
31. Asher Lee, _The Soviet Air Force_, (Harper & Brothers, New York, 1950), p.84.
32. AW & ST, 9 March 1970, p.47.
33. David Holloway, 'The Soviet Union' in N. Ball and M. Leitenberg (eds.), _The Structure of the Defense Industry_, (St Martin's Press, New York, 1983), p.70.
34. Ibid, pp.70-1.
35. AW & ST, 11 May 1981, p.64.
36. AW & ST, 15 June 1981, p.63.
37. AW & ST, 19 January 1976, p.19.
38. To be specific: Lucas Aerospace (jet pipes,fuel control systems, pressure controllers etc.), Plessey Aerospace (gas turbine starters, engine pumps) and Dowty (afterburning fuel control systems). See AW & ST, 12 July 1976, p.16.
39. AW & ST, 22 June 1981, p.36.
40. AW & ST, 18 June 1984, p.15.
41. FI, 3 April 1975, pp.562-4.
42. FI, 13 March 1975, p.417.
43. AW & ST, 18 January 1982, p.61 and _Air Pictorial_, March 1984, p.84.
44. FI, 26 May 1984, p.1411.
45. India also has persevered with indigenous designs. Perhaps its most successful are the Kiran jet trainer and the Ajeet lightweight fighter (itself

a progressive development of the British Gnat aircraft).

46. FI, 18 December 1982, pp.1771-2.

47. Air Pictorial, May 1982, p.196.

48. AW & ST, 24 November 1980, p.27.

49. FI, 6 March 1982, p.530 and 2 October 1982, p.1028.

Chapter Two

EMERGENCE AND EVOLUTION

As a creature of technology, the aircraft industry is, in consequence, very sensitive to technical change. Its rapid evolution in this century has stemmed from recognition of the versatility of aircraft as weapons of war and vehicles for promoting rapid transportation of passengers and cargo. Yet, while the aircraft industry flourished as a result of those redeeming qualities, it transformed itself by way of continual technical progress and innovation into the medium capable of fulfilling the elevated views of its usefulness held by military and civilian organisations alike. In all likelihood, of course, the relationship between customer demand and technical progress is an interactive one; that is to say, innovation probably owes as much to customer stimulus as customer enthusiasm responds to technical performance. In other words, the evolution of the aircraft industry was rendered possible by a combination of technology-push innovations and demand-pull innovations. The former refers to innovations which influence subsequent activities: both in terms of the complexion of the industry and the conditions of the market. The latter, however, arises whenever the particular requirements of the market - the military or civil aviators - are met by new technology.[1]

The prime object of this chapter is to outline the evolution of the aircraft industry in light of the scope for expansion accorded it by technical developments on the one hand and the needs of its customers on the other. In reality, separation of technical change and market emergence is somewhat artificial and is only maintained initially to enable the salient steps in the industry's growth to be set down. For the latter part of the chapter, the interaction between technical change and markets is explicitly recognised and addressed from the point-of-view of a conceptual stance denoted as the 'wave-cycle' model. The position taken by the model, and adopted wholesale in this book, is that aircraft production is regulated, by and large, by the state and, correspondingly, owes little to orthodox market mechanisms. Before addressing such issues, however, it is necessary to briefly outline the sequence of technical developments experienced by the industry in the first place, and to elicit how the markets for aircraft evolved in the second.

EVOLUTIONARY HIGHLIGHTS

The story of the pioneering innovations in aeronautics has been told and retold elsewhere and need not concern us because it occupies an era prior to the emergence of a 'proper' aircraft industry.[2] The industry really came into its own during World War I when it blossomed to fulfil military needs. Hindered more than anything else by barriers in aeroengine design (e.g. most British designs in the beginning relied on the French Gnome seven-cylinder rotary engine), the industry was transformed in the space of four years from a crafts-oriented workshop operation into a manufacturing process geared to mass-production. With the exception of France, the monoplane was eschewed in favour of the biplane: a type of aircraft that was stronger, lighter and more manoeuvrable than its single-wing counterpart. The universal use of wood in airframe construction allowed for the infusion into the industry of a host of furniture makers either as sub-contractors or as full-fledged aircraft manufacturers. Such enterprises were adept at producing the wooden box-like structures coated with fabric, while automobile engineers were co-opted into manufacturing the rotary and radial aeroengines which had to be mated to the airframes. By 1918, a state-of-the-art fighter - the Fokker D.VII - was powered by a 160hp Mercedes six-cylinder water-cooled radial engine and weighed 670kg empty. Measuring 6.95m in length with a wingspan of 8.9m, this machine was capable of 189km/h maximum speed. By way of contrast, the world's first strategic bomber, the Handley Page V/1500, was powered by four 375hp R-R Eagle engines, weighed 7,352kg empty, was 18.89m long with a span of 38.4m, and was able to achieve 156km/h.[3]

There was little challenge in the 1920s to the supremacy of the biplane. However, the first aircraft to have a modern-style retractable undercarriage appeared as early as 1920 (the Dayton-Wright RB racer); although this innovation was slow in gaining acceptance. The principal change arose in respect to aircraft materials with wood steadily losing out to metal. In 1924 the UK Air Ministry, for example, ordered three experimental fighters; two of which had steel fuselages and wooden wings while the third was of all-steel construction.[4] By the end of the decade, the first all-metal transport (Boeing's Monomail) had materialised and was the precursor to a series of airliners in the early 1930s (Boeing 247, Lockheed 10, Douglas Commercial). Metal construction allied with the slim, liquid-cooled in-line engine was the epitome of aircraft design in the late 1920s.

The monoplane came into its own as the 1930s unfolded. Its acceptance entailed adoption of a host of associated novel features: retractable undercarriage, take-off and landing flaps, variable-pitch propeller and cockpit canopy. Representative of the all-metal, stressed-skin, low-wing monoplane was the Curtiss Hawk fighter of 1935. Equipped with a 1,050hp P & W Twin Wasp radial engine, the Hawk was capable of achieving 488km/h and weighed 2,060kg empty. Originating in the same year, the Douglas DC-3 airliner embodied most of the technical advances then extant.

> It had a robust structure of newly developed high-tensile aluminium alloy for long life and ease of maintenance; a fatigue-resistant multi-spar wing with split flaps... enabling the wing loading to be increased and resulting in a more efficient structure; two reliable supercharged air-cooled engines...; variable-pitch, feathering, three-blade, metal propellers with governors to keep them running at a constant, pre-set speed; and a retractable undercarriage with toe-operated hydraulic wheel blades.[5]

Nor was crew and passenger comfort neglected, for, the DC-3 boasted an autopilot and air-conditioning combined with noise-reduction. This impressive aircraft was able to carry two dozen passengers for up to 3,420km at a maximum speed of 370km/h.

World War II witnessed the ultimate development of the piston-engined monoplane and also ushered in jet-propulsion. Single-engined piston machines were developed in terms of toughness, speed, range and firepower. The P-51D Mustang, for example, had a combat range of 1,529km; the P-47D Thunderbolt was capable of carrying 1,134kg of bombs as well as packing eight 0.5in machine guns; whereas the Yak-9U could reach 700km/h, range up to 890km, and carry one 20mm cannon and two machine guns. The war also led to great strides in four-engined aircraft; perhaps best represented by the Boeing B-29. This strategic bomber had a tricycle undercarriage and pressurised cabin, and was able to carry 4,540kg of bombs for 5,230km. Developments in four-engined transports, the DC-4 and Lockheed Constellation in particular, set the standard for postwar commercial aviation. German and British jet-engine technology, formulated during the war, was instrumental in creating the best of the new generation fighter aircraft: represented by the US F-86 Sabre and the Soviet Mig-15. The former was the first to make use of German swept-wing technology and was, equally, the first production supersonic fighter. The latter, powered by a derivative of a R-R turbine, was so successful that about 8,000 were constructed in the USSR and extra sizeable runs emanated from Mielec (Poland), Vodochody (Prague, Czechoslovakia) and Shenyang (China). A comparison of the rapid progress in fighters and bombers after the war is discernible from Table 2.1.

It is evident, therein, that speed of aircraft climaxed in the early 1960s and that developments over the past twenty years have been less in terms of boosting speed and more in terms of enhancing the survivability of aircraft under combat conditions. One innovation flowing directly from this concern was the VTOL fighter (e.g. BAe Harrier) which dispensed with the need for the very long runways required by conventional high-performance aircraft. Advances in jet engine design by the early 1960s made possible the installation of sufficient power in an airframe to exceed the total weight and allow for vertical thrust. Another innovation was variable-geometry, or the ability to alter the configuration of the aircraft's wings to optimise missions of varying speed and altitude (e.g. the F-111, Mig-23, Panavia Tornado) and thereby produce a machine truly capable of multiple roles. Combat-aircraft developments were instrumental in fostering changes in materials too. The first aircraft built extensively of titanium was the North American F-100 fighter of 1953; whereas the same company's (albeit under different corporate guise) B-1 bomber was a pioneer in the use of composite materials in the early 1970s.

Since World War II two other important aeronautical breakthroughs have created the helicopter and the jetliner. The former had materialised during the war in experimental form (e.g. the Sikorsky R-4), but it was only through the Korean War that the helicopter's suitability for casualty evacuation and search and rescue was demonstrated. In 1955 the turboshaft engine was first used in a helicopter (the Alouette II) pointing the way towards designs with much

Table 2.1 : Post War Developments in Combat Aircraft

Year	Jet Fighters (maximum speed/range)	Bombers (maximum speed/range)
1944	Gloster Meteor (UK) (737 Km/h;2156Km)	
1948	North American F-86A(US) (1091 Km/h;745Km)	Boeing B-50A(US) (640Km/h;7886Km)
1950		Boeing B-47A(US) (980Km/h;5794Km)
1953	Hawker Hunter(UK) (1142Km/h;788Km)	
1955		Boeing B-52A(US) (1014Km/h;9978Km)
1956		Tu-20(USSR) (870Km/h;12,550Km)
1958	Su-7B(USSR) (1700Km/h;459Km)	
1960	SAAB-35 Draken(Sweden) (1487Km/h;636Km)	
1961	Dassault Mirage 111(France) (2349Km/h;1199Km)	
1962	McDonnell F-4(US) (2549Km/h;1056Km)	
1965		Tu-22(USSR) (1480Km/h;2252Km)
1968		F-111A(US) (2655Km/h;2413Km)
1971	Mig-23(USSR) (2445Km/h;1126Km)	
1974		Tu-26(USSR) (2655Km/h;11,496Km)
1975	MD F-15A(US) (2655Km/h;1930Km)	
1976		Panavia Tornado(European) (2574Km/h;1207Km)
1984		Rockwell B-1(US) (2124Km/h;9815Km)

Source: Compiled from information in C. Cook and J.Stevenson, The Atlas of Modern Warfare, (Weidenfeld and Nicolson, London 1978).

greater power-to-weight ratios than was forthcoming with the piston engine. Today, twin-turbine helicopters act as useful airlift vehicles not only for military tactical support but also in such civil operations as oilrig replenishment and intracity passenger transit. The jetliner, meanwhile, stemmed from experiments underway in the early 1950s in both the UK and USA (resulting in such first-generation machines as the DH Comet, Boeing 707 and Douglas DC-8). At one fell swoop, jet transports made trans-atlantic travel brief and comfortable and, subsequently, in the era of wide-bodied transports, made cheap long-haul travel much more widely available than hitherto.

Market Evolution

As intimated, the aircraft industry came into its own as a result of the demands of war. In World War I production figures were quite astounding for a nascent industry: Britain built 52,440 airframes, France 51,000, Germany 48,000; while Italy managed 6,488 in 1918 alone.[6] The USA and Russia were plagued by a variety of production difficulties: the former, given its late entry into the conflict, was deficient in aircraft design and had to rely inordinately upon licence-production of French and British machines. Nevertheless, it did make 13,111 machines between 6 April 1917 and 1 November 1919.[7] Russia was equally dependent on the Allies for assistance in aircraft production, although it was directed mainly at making up deficiencies in aeroengine capacity. The Tsarist state was only able to provide about 2,200 aircraft from its own resources in the years 1914-17.[8]

The cessation of hostilities cut the burgeoning industry in the bud and inaugurated a pattern of 'boom' and 'bust' which was to plague the aircraft industry hereafter. As elicited from Table 2.2, orders for British aircraft placed in the final year of war were slashed by half. To make matters worse, the brunt of the cancellations fell on machines newly entering production (e.g. the DH 10, Vimy, and the various late-model Sopwith designs).[9] The few types kept in production in the aftermath of war were ordered in minute batches. Orders for the Bristol F2B, for example, were placed in 1920, 1924, 1925 and 1926; but totalled only 379 aircraft in marked contrast to the 1,403 built in 1918-19 (not to mention the 1,747 cancelled at that time). Throughout the succeeding fifteen years new combat designs were ordered in penny-packet numbers and it was only with the rearmament schemes commencing in 1934 that production runs for military aircraft began to return to sizeable proportions. The DH Tiger Moth aptly illustrates the effect of rearmament. Conceived to fit a 1931 Air Ministry specification for a trainer, it was initially ordered in numbers of 35, 50, two and two;

but after the expansion schemes were effected, 30 civil machines were bought directly off the production line and fresh orders were placed for 50, 400, 300 and a further 400 prior to the start of World War II (which manifest itself through an immediate contract for 2,000 of these aircraft).

World War II was a replay of the pattern of the earlier war in terms of expansion of aircraft production: although now the totals were truly astronomical. The USSR made 137,271 aircraft between January 1941 and June 1945, the USA turned out about 300,000 machines (96,318 in 1944 alone), while the UK built in excess of 119,000 aircraft from 1940 to 1946 (29,220 of them in 1944). Germany was able, throughout 1944, to produce on average 2,811 aircraft each month. Production runs of tried-and-true designs were phenomenal: the Ilyushin Il-2 was built at a rate of 1,200 per month and total output exceeded 35,000 whereas the Messerschmitt Bf-109 was built in numbers exceeding 33,000. However, with the ending of hostilities orders were slashed across the board: the P-47 Thunderbolt, for example, had 10,154 units deleted after contracts for 15,683 had been completed.[10] Again, as with the earlier postwar episode, production contracts for new designs were largely abandoned and those for existing designs were sharply curtailed. Table 2.3 is eclectic in as much as it highlights a number of aircraft designs ordered into production in 1943 by the UK Government and traces the wartime output, end-of-war production termination, and postwar trickle of output for the types in question. Conforming to the standard strategic bomber format, the Lincoln was a progressive development of the Avro Lancaster and was ordered into large-scale production only to have the body of that programme dropped in 1945. The dribble of postwar output was merely to serve as replacements for attrition suffered by the peacetime air force. The Hornet case is comparable, although postwar naval requirements required a relatively significant production run. A new variant of the Spitfire/Seafire scarcely saw the light of day, however, with production plans being largely shelved: instead resources were redirected to producing new-technology jet fighters (Vampire and Meteor) which, consequently, escaped end-of-war cutbacks. Finally, the Brigand bomber also avoided cancellations but its overall production was very modest indeed compared to its immediate predecessor, the Beaufighter, of which almost 6,000 were built.

Limited production runs have been the order of the day for Western combat aircraft since World War

Table 2.2 : Impact of the Vanishing of Military Demand

Type	Number built	Number cancelled	%completed of total order
Airco DH4	251	0	100
DH6	100	0	100
DH9/9A	2163	1057	67
DH10/10A	237	454	34
AW[1] FK8	484	112	81
Avro 504K	2779	871	76
Bristol F2B	1403	1747	45
HP[2] O/400	139	130	52
V/1500	33	120	22
Martinsyde Buzzard	273	1286	18
Nieuport Nighthawk	41	109	27
RAF[3] FE2b	0	550	0
RE8	350	100	78
SE5A	1051	374	74
Sopwith Camel	1495	348	81
Snipe	647	2171	23
Salmander	124	1276	9
Dolphin	170	180	49
Cuckoo	0	50	0
Dragon	4	296	1
Vickers Vimy	199	899	18
Total	11,943	12,130	50

Notes: 1. AW = Armstrong Whitworth
2. HP = Handley Page
3. RAF= Royal Aircraft Factory

Source: Compiled from information in B. Robertson, British Military Aircraft Serials, (Patrick Stephens, Cambridge, 1979).

II. Unusual expansion arises only during hostilities or quasi-hostilities (chilly episodes in the Cold War). Thus, US aircraft production was greatly boosted during the Korean War following a period of quiescent military demand. Rae notes that two civil lightplane manufacturers - Beech and Cessna - had been engrossed in overhaul and the making of furniture and farm machinery in lieu of aircraft construction when the outbreak of war in 1950 immediately electrified their production divisions: Cessna, for

Table 2.3 : Transition From Wartime Production

Type	End-of-war completions	End-of-war cancellations	Postwar output
Lincoln 4-engine bomber	507	2220	21
Seafire(45-47) piston fighter	0	735	76
Hornet 2-engine fighter	35	495	209
Vampire(1-3) jet fighter	200	0	121
Meteor(4) jet fighter	100	0	316
Brigand 2-engine bomber	80	0	56

Source: Compiled from information in B. Robertson, British Military Aircraft Serials, (Patrick Stephens, Cambridge, 1979).

example, receiving a contract for 400 army liaison planes.[11] The brevity and general containment of such postwar 'emergencies' is evinced through the size of contracts: the USA building only 7,000 aircraft in 1952 at the height of the Korean War whereas it was forthcoming with 96,000 at the height of World War II. The British likewise have failed to come close to wartime production figures with the Falklands conflict, for instance, resulting in the purchase of 15 US F-4 fighters and orders for smaller numbers of Sea Harriers and helicopters as replacements for combat losses. All told, UK production of combat aircraft in 1983 scarcely mustered 100 machines.[12]

Commercial aviation, represented by the airlines, came to the fore after World War I. Its gestation period was long and difficult, however, partly because of the inadequacy of current aircraft and partly owing to the parlous economic conditions then prevailing which acted to impede market expansion. The first airline fares were so uncompetitive in comparison with other modes of transport that all UK airline companies had been forced out of business by 1921.[13] Inadequate equipment - mainly converted bombers - merely compounded the uncompetitiveness. They were not designed with either passenger comfort or fuel economy in mind, and, further, imposed high servicing costs upon their operators. Table 2.4 indicates the progress made in airliner development from the sorrowful machines of the 1920s through the tailor-made aircraft of the 1930s and after. It is no coincidence that many of the pioneering models issued from US factories while the Europeans persevered with 'conversions' of bomber types. The cross-fertilisation of airlines and aircraft manufacturers is one of the longstanding themes in the US aeronautical scene. It was only in the USA (aided by mail contracts) that routes were sufficiently plentiful and lengthy to warrant revenue-paying services and the incentive was therefore given to manufacturers to design suitable equipment. The innovating DC-3 has already been mentioned, but in the years following World War II US long-haul transports like the Constellation and DC-7 came to dominate the world's airlines. In spite of technical innovations on the part of the British (e.g. the Comet turbojet airliner and the Britannia turboprop transport), US aircraft maintained their dominance of world airline fleets (e.g. the classic Boeing 707) largely due to their catholic design characteristics geared to fulfil American market needs which, at one and the same time, constituted the lion's share of the world's commercial aviation market. As hinted in Chapter 1, it is only now that European manufacturers are in a position to challenge US firms in the wide-bodied airliner field.

The Wave-Cycle Model

It is abundantly clear that aircraft production is inordinately dependent on military demand - to the extent of something in the order of 60 per cent in the USA and UK - and consequently, is extremely sensitive to changes in such demand. That military demand is inconstant is equally apparent by virtue of the aforementioned crises in production following the two world wars. A cyclical schema has been promulgated by Higham to account for the responsiveness of aircraft output to the variability in military markets.[14] Formulated with the UK historical record in mind, the model seems germane for other countries as well. Fig. 2.1 attempts to summarise, in crude manner, the cyclical swings common to both national industries. Appended to the oscillations or 'waves' is the terminology coined by Higham and it is this, representing phases in military demand, which has general applicability for the aircraft industry. Hinging on the perceptions by policymakers and defence chiefs of the threats to national security, the wave-cycle posits a sequence of policy responses

Table 2.4 : Progression in Airliner Development

Year	Type	Passenger capacity	Cruising speed (Km/h)	Normal range (Km)
1922	DH34(UK)	8	168	400
1925	DH50(UK)	4	160	600
1928	Ford Tri-motor 4(US)	12	176	900
1933	Boeing 247(US)	10	303	803
1934	Lockheed Electra(US)	10	305	803
1935	Douglas DC-3(US)	21	305	1365
1938	Short Empire(UK)	17	257	964
1946	Lockheed Constellation(US)	51	498	3693
1949	Boeing 377(US)	70	482	4818
1952	DH Comet 1(UK)	40	803	2409
1953	Douglas DC-7A(US)	76	594	5781
1957	Bristol Britannia 300(UK)	120	562	7227
1958	Boeing 707-120(US)	132	947	4818
1964	Vickers VC-10(UK)	151	878	8078
1964	Boeing 727-100(US)	110	957	2570
1970	Boeing 747-100(US)	500	978	10650

Source: K. R. Sealy, The Geography of Air Transport, (Hutchinson, London, 1966), p.50 and A. Phillips, Technology and Market Structure,(D.C. Heath, Lexington, 1971), pp.140-4.

(reflected through military preparations) whereby the initial strategic balance is disrupted and replaced by various phases of disequilibria until a satisfactory balance is once more regained. Contracts and, allowing for a time lag, aircraft output are one manifestation of the received wisdom concerning international tension. Strategic balance translates into peacetime equilibrium in terms of aircraft procurement. In practice, that means limited budgets for new aircraft and steady-state air forces with orders issuing only to established manufacturers for replacement machines. Frequently, military business is confined to state enterprises (e.g. the Royal Aircraft Factory in Britain prior to 1914) or private contractors which compose the 'military-industrial complex' (as in the USA at the present time). The appearance of a perceived threat arouses enlarged military budgets and propels the aircraft industry into a phase of rearmamental instability. Not only are orders dramatically increased, but the industry is placed on a mass-production basis. In the initial stages, the established manufacturers are given the burden of meeting augmented production, but if expansion targets remain unfulfilled, other manufacturers are brought into the programme. The UK, for example, resorted to the motor vehicles industry in the late 1930s so as to overcome capacity bottlenecks prevalent in the mainstream aircraft industry. The phase of maximum output - wartime equilibrium - is only attained when the entire economy is put on a war footing. Priority is given to aeroplane manufacture and as many enterprises as possible are pressed into the production effort. A leading British example of an organisation cobbled together for such a purpose was London Aircraft Productions Ltd. In World War II it constructed 710 four-motor Halifax bombers; a reputable record for such an unlikely undertaking.

> London Transport acts as a co-ordinator for the group, each member of which was responsible for a particular section of production. Thus, Chrysler Motors was responsible for the rear fuselage, Park Royal Coachworks for the outer wings, Express Motor & Body Works for the intermediate wings and tail plane, and Duples' Bodies & Motors for the shell and components for the rear fuselage. London Transport itself undertook the manufacture of the centre section, the installation of the fittings and equipment for the front fuselage, the installation of the engine and the final erection and testing of the finished aircraft.[15]

Naturally, on account of the excessive cost, the production commensurate with wartime equilibrium was scaled down at the first opportunity; usually even before the official end of war.[16] The resultant demobilisational instability was characterised by widescale cancellation of contracts as the threat to national security had been eliminated. Enterprises unable to divert into civil lines are faced with the risk of bankruptcy as their military contracts dwindle away. A few - generally the long-standing contractors - are allowed to survive on the strength of a trickle of orders owing to the state's need to ensure a 'reserve defence capability'.

The form and intensity of those phases vary, of course, according to country and the meshing of military requirements with technical developments. With respect to the former, it is clear from Fig. 2.1 that US and UK phases are not entirely synchronised: rather, the British tended to enter rearmamental instability and wartime equilibrium sooner than the

Figure 2.1 : The Wave Cycle and Aircraft Production

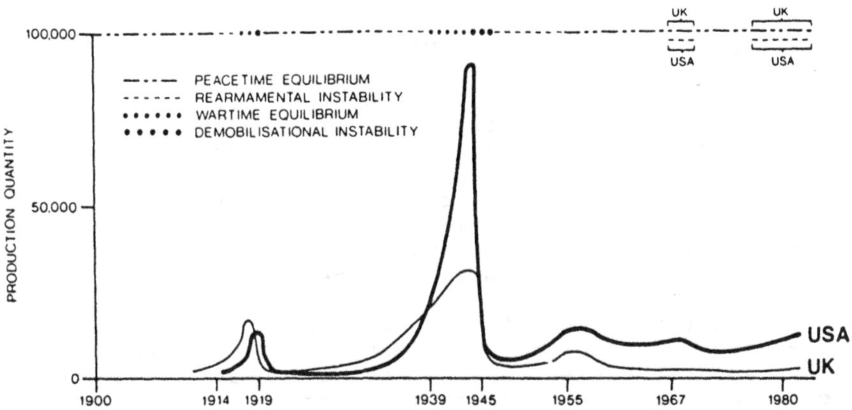

Americans. Moreover, US command of mass-production resources was far more telling than that of the British giving rise to much higher production peaks for the USA in the phase of maximum output in World War II. Further, different valuations given to minimum and necessary levels of peacetime forces result in different ideas of steady-state aircraft production: the UK post-1955 figure is considerably less than that of the USA with its notions of international responsibility while, US levels, in turn, have trailed behind those of the USSR in the 1970s. Arguably, the end of the 1970s witnessed a return to rearmamental instability on the part of both superpowers. Technical innovations also influence the phases. A comparison of the demobilisational instabilities following the two world wars evinces detailed differences. After the earlier episode, production was cut back to the bone because the technical development of aviation was sufficiently unconvincing as to throw its whole future into question as a genuine military arm. By way of contrast, the inception of jet-engine technology at the end of the second conflict meant that production of jet fighters was effected by the USA, UK and USSR despite cutbacks elsewhere in defence production. None the less, the phases are discernible in the patterns of aircraft production and act as useful indicators for relating activity levels in the industry to changes in the composition of military markets. What remains to be debated, however, is the impact of such cyclical swings on the individual enterprises constituting the industry.

THE EVOLUTION OF ENTERPRISES

The effects of the wave-cycle are perceptible for aircraft firms by way of two considerations: the form of expansion alternating with contraction as a common experience of such enterprises in the first place, and the means adopted by firms - in a word, diversification - in order to ameliorate the worst consequences of cyclical down-swings in the second. An obvious precursor to those considerations, though, is the entry of firms into the industry as a result of the direct stimulus afforded by the expansion phases. One need only look to UK evidence to find proof of the flood of new entries during World War I (Fearon cites an increase of firms involved in aircraft production from 771 in November 1917 to 1,529 in October 1918) and the example of the co-opted motor vehicles industry in World War II has already been mentioned.[17] The USA followed suit in that war, encouraging the giant automotive industry to engage in aircraft manufacture. General Motors entered the aircraft business through conversion of five of its existing vehicles plants to warplane output, whereas Ford's enthusiastic entry was manifested through the erection of a purpose-built bomber plant at Willow Run, Michigan, for the mass-production of B-24 Liberators.[18] New entries continue, for, Japanese military build-up in the 1980s has persuaded the Yamaha motorcycle firm to establish an aeroengine division in order to provide the prime movers for aerial target-drones.[19]

In reverting to the expansion-contraction theme, however, that issue can be addressed through the use of a disparate range of examples. Rising aircraft orders impel firms to initially expand their own production facilities and, subsequently, consider acquisition of other firms if the former policy is insufficient in meeting the enlarged demand. Facility expansion, in turn, can take two forms: the extension of existing premises and the erection of extra facilities on new sites. Since the late 1970s boosted US defence spending (partly in response to the Soviet invasion of Afghanistan) has triggered a phase approximating rearmamental instability and encouraged aerospace firms to undertake expansion.[20] Sikorsky Aircraft (a division of UTC), for instance, intended to invest $100 million in its Stratford and

Bridgeport, Connecticut, plants mainly as a result of the US Army choosing its UH-60A helicopter and the US Navy opting for the SH-60B.[21] Employment was planned to increase from 7,200 to 10,000 in the early 1980s; a figure approaching the peak 11,307 reached in 1957 as a consequence of Korean War-related orders. At the same time, Boeing wanted to expand its facilities in the Puget Sound area and take on a further 6,000-7,000 workers; although in this case soaring demand was attributed to the commercial aviation market. The launching of the models 757 and 767 airliners in the late 1970s had added 24,500 to the payroll in 1978-79.[22] In fact, Boeing was a beneficiary of enlarged defence spending too; and attempted to accommodate contracts for cruise missiles by establishing new plant sites. It announced, only 24 days after receiving the USAF contract, that it would build a $25 million factory at Kent, Washington. This facility would be replete with several NC machine centres, a chemical processing plant, and an autoclave required for bonding the missiles' wings.[23] MD was also a recipient of the cruise missile largesse; although in its instance new plant selection was spurned in favour of rehabilitating an existing components factory (Titusville, Florida) to the tune of $50 million and with the prospect of creating 600 new jobs.[24]

If rising demand continues to outstrip existing capacity and new facilities brought (or about to be brought) on stream, the enterprise may circumvent supply bottlenecks through a policy of acquisition. In this manner, it absorbs other firms with the requisite tools and plant that can easily be turned to fulfilling its own contract obligations. Again, a US example can be proffered to illustrate this situation: that is to say, the former Bell plant at Marietta, Georgia, which was reactivated by Lockheed during the Korean War in order to produce bombers and later, urgently-needed C-130 transports.[25] Most acquisitions in periods of rising demand, however, have occurred by virtue of the desire of firms to absorb those enterprises known to have bountiful defence contracts. It was in this light that Boeing acquired the Vertol Aircraft Corporation of Morton, Pennsylvania, in 1960 and thereby, entered the profitable military helicopter field.[26] In recent times, MD purchased Hughes helicopters of Culver City, California and Mesa, Arizona in order to profit from the US Army requirement for 515 Hughes Apache helicopters worth more than $7 billion.[27] From a slightly different viewpoint - that of a non-aerospace firm - aircraft manufacturers can appear as useful springboards to lucrative defence contracts. Accordingly, Rockwell-Standard (now RI) a major automotive components manufacturer, absorbed North American Aviation in 1967. This latter, a California aircraft firm, had sales in 1966 of over $2 billion and 95 per cent of its contracts stemmed from the US Government.[28] In fact, many entries into the aircraft industry were the actions of engineering companies (usually with considerable experience of defence production) wishing to diversify their armaments portfolios. Historically, the UK warship constructors Vickers and Armstrong Whitworth provide classic examples, and the details of their aircraft interests will be recounted below. However, this pattern was emulated by the Japanese with, for example, the shipbuilder Kawasaki Heavy Industries forming an aircraft division in 1918.

As to be expected, contraction during phases of demand downswings is translated into employee layoffs, plant closure and diversification into more promising lines of business. During the era of 'détente' in the mid 1970s, the American DoD estimated that excess capacity in the aircraft firms was equivalent to 20,000 underemployed workers maintained on 'make-work' defence contracts.[29] Withdrawal of such contracts led to significant layoffs: indeed, by 1976 aerospace employment stood at 903,000, barely 60 per cent of its 1968 figure of 1.5 million.[30] The rot had started with the rundown in Vietnam-related contracts. As Table 2.5 shows, most US aircraft producers reached peak employment during the 1967-69 period, and all had suffered sizeable cuts by the early 1970s. Particularly hard pressed was Boeing which had reduced its workforce to scarcely one third of the 1968 high. The company blamed the cutbacks on a depressed commercial aircraft market as well as its failure to obtain a USAF bomber contract and a US Navy missile project, not to mention the completion of the Saturn booster rocket programme. At all events, its layoffs were held culpable for a ten per cent unemployment rate in Washington State's King and Snohomish counties (the locations of the affected Seattle, Renton, Kent, Auburn and Everett plants), a drop in hotel business there of 25 per cent, a fall off in car sales of 35 per cent and real estate sales of 40 per cent, and, to cap it all, an overall loss in state income of $1.25 billion for 1970 alone.[31] Boeing attempted to stem further job losses by dispensing with sub-contractors as far as was practicable and 'internalising' production at its own plants. Thus, it curtailed subcontracts for Boeing 747 wing boxes and landing gear doors held by Goodyear's

Litchfield Park, Arizona, plant and had them made in its own premises.[32] Turnaround in the company's fortunes arose only when commercial aircraft markets revived later in the 1970s. Ironically, though, dampening of demand for airliners in the 1980s forced the firm to shed 5,000 workers in each of 1981 and 1982; and the only promising areas for job stability were associated with defence programmes.[33]

The recent experience of Boeing illustrates an important caveat; namely, that contraction can be effected by declines in civil aviation markets as well as those following from attenuated defence contracts. In France, Aérospatiale was especially hard hit in the mid 1970s when failure to garner orders for Concorde and A300B jetliners led to the possibility of 6,000 layoffs at Toulouse. The workforce had to be hastily shifted into military helicopter production or occupied in subcontract work for Dassault fighters acquired in desperation just to provide needed employment.[34] While patently technical breakthroughs, the two civil projects were not marketable in light of the prevailing depressed airliner markets. This enterprise continued in the doldrums for several years, closing its Chateauroux works, losing FFr 487 million in 1975 alone, and finding respite only in military programmes: the Transall transport and a 35 per cent share in the Mirage 2000.[35] Britain, likewise, did not escape the painful consequences of contraction, although most of its problems arose out of difficulties attributable to shrinking defence programmes. The cutback in warplane projects following the hiatus that arose after the Korean War and Suez episodes led to the closure of aircraft factories at Blackpool, Portsmouth, Christchurch and Gloucester. Twenty years later BAe was still confronted with problems deriving from defence cutbacks: in this instance it responded by closing its Bitteswell facility with the loss of 1,000 jobs.[36]

Frequently, the plight brought on by the erosion of demand compels the firms to contemplate merger or diversification either out of the aircraft business or into another part of it deemed less risky. A prominent example of merger was the United Aircraft and Transport Corporation. Formed originally in 1929 round the nucleus of the Boeing group (manufacturer and airline), it soon merged the interests of four other aircraft firms (Stearman, Sikorsky, Avion and Chance Vought), an aeroengine firm (P & W), two propeller manufacturers (consolidated as Hamilton Standard), and three air transport ventures. While conceived in an era of buoyancy, the combine weathered the impending depression better than most other US

Table 2.5 : Employment Cuts in the Aftermath of the Vietnam War

Company	Peak employment	Date	Employment in mid 1971
Beech	11,650	12/65	5,000
Bell	10,900	1969	8,000
Boeing	148,000	6/68	54,000
Cessna(Wichita)	9,500	8/68	4,600
Fairchild	13,000	6/68	7,500
GE Aircraft Group	29,000	12/69	25,000
General Dynamics(aircraft)	55,600	10/68	32,800
Grumman	36,025	12/67	25,500
Hughes Aircraft	32,107	7/67	27,437
Kaman	3,644	12/68	2,600
LTV(aerospace)	24,600	7/69	13,000
Lockheed Aircraft	99,700	9/69	71,500
MD	134,000	1967	92,854
North American Rockwell	104,000	1/65	37,500
Northrop	25,462	7/69	13,900
United Aircraft	81,600	1967	61,000

Source: Aviation Week and Space Technology, 12 July 1971, p.15.

aeronautical organisations and thus seemingly confirmed the effectiveness of merger during straitened times.[37] The option of using merger for diversifying into similar product lines that have more promising markets has been pursued in more recent years. McDonnell Aircraft of St. Louis absorbed Douglas Aircraft of Long Beach in 1967 (i.e. creating MD) owing to its desire to add a commercial-aircraft base to its defence interests which were jeopardised by the rundown of Vietnam involvement.[38] Similarly, the Raytheon Company and the Beech Aircraft Corporation agreed to merge in 1979 so that the former - preoccupied with missile production - could acquire the expertise of the latter in civil aircraft markets.[39] Outright purchases of smaller civil aircraft manufacturers by larger aerospace firms is represented by the cases of Fairchild Industries and Gulfstream American. The first bought Swearingen Aircraft of San Antonio in order to make good the evaporation of its defence business (for the A-10A strike aircraft) by substituting a product for the commuter and corporate aircraft market.[40] Gulfstream American, however, bought the general aviation division of RI, located at Bethany, Oklahoma, because it wished to consolidate its position in the commuter aircraft niche.[41]

Diversification outside of aerospace has proved popular when all aircraft markets seem particularly depressed. As previously hinted, such a state of affairs was perceived as being in effect in the early 1970s. Several firms reacted, at that point, through venturing into rail and rapid transit projects (e.g. LTV and the Dallas-Fort Worth Airport system along with Boeing-Vertol's manufacture of railcars for San Fransisco and the Massachussetts Bay authority). Indeed, Boeing entered the fields of computer services, housing, and hydrofoil boats. Perhaps its most unusual undertaking was the plan to convert 40,469 ha of Oregon desert into an agricultural community by means of irrigation.[42] Not to be outdone, LTV invested $10 million in a Colorado water-sports resort and considered investment in Hawaii tourism.[43] The scope for diversification, and the dependency of it upon the wave-cycle of demand, is immediately apparent from even a cursory examination of the Vickers experience.

Vickers as a Case Study

The firm of Vickers originated at Sheffield as a steel and heavy engineering company in the mid-nineteenth century. Its first flirtation with defence requirements occurred in the 1880s when it was encouraged by the UK Government to lay down gun-forging capacity.[44] By the turn of the century, it had become committed to defence production in a very serious way having acquired machine-gun plant and a shipyard specialising in warships. At the time of the Boer War the company functioned as an integrated armaments organisation producing armour plate (at Sheffield) for warships built at Barrow, which were armed from the firm's own gun foundries (at Sheffield and Barrow), ammunitioned from its own shops (Erith and Dartford) and equipped with its own brand of light artillery to boot (from Erith). To this impressive list of defence products (including light and heavy ordnance, battleships, submarines) was added an aircraft department at Erith in 1911. Massive orders for Vickers Gunbus aircraft in World War I were instrumental in founding aeroplane production lines at the existing Crayford works and a new site at Weybridge.[45] Moreover, the firm bolstered its aviation interests by acquiring the Tier II firms James Booth in 1915 (a manufacturer of duralumin used in airships made by Vickers) and S.E.Saunders in 1918 (producer of fuselage parts). Unlike its competitor (and, after 1927 partner through merger) Armstrong Whitworth, this defence contractor decided to persevere with aircraft on the vanishing of wartime contracts. Aircraft manufacture, after all, was characterised by high engineering standards and "its reliance upon scientific development, and its association with defence, was for Vickers a natural development which the production of consumer goods was not".[46] As suggested, diversification into civil products was less than successful.

In spite of severely curtailed orders from the RAF, Vickers secured its aviation position in the 1920s. In the first place, it bought the Ioco company of Glasgow - a producer of oilproofed silk for airships, and in the second, it acquired the Supermarine firm in order to diversify into seaplane manufacture. Rearmament in the second half of the 1930s had special meaning for Vickers when its Wellington and Spitfire designs were ordered into wholesale production. By 1939 the firm's aircraft business (valued at £8.3 million) outstripped its other defence interests (i.e. naval armament worth £7.1 million, land armament worth £5.1 million, and warship building worth £2.9 million).[47] During World War II it ran aircraft factories at Chester, Blackpool, Castle Bromwich and Swindon(South Marston) in addition to its main complex at Weybridge and the Supermarine Works at Eastleigh. In the postwar era the firm maintained its defence interests on a smaller scale (abandoning the Chester, Blackpool and Castle Bromwich sites), and tried to diversify into commercial aircraft production. Accordingly, from the defence viewpoint, it became a major player in the V-bomber programme of the 1950s, evolving the Valiant type. By the same token, the Supermarine division was tasked with producing carrier-borne combat aircraft culminating with the Scimitar fighter. Termination of these programmes left the firm bereft of combat aircraft production by 1960 (incidentally, leading to the closure of South Marston as an aircraft factory) and reliant, for the most part, on civil aircraft markets. The effects of peacetime equilibrium had strongly influenced the Vickers group, especially in so far as government policy appeared bound to reduce aircraft contracts even further. "In defence, the apparent implications of the Sandys White Paper in 1957 caused Vickers to conclude that, except possibly in naval shipbuilding, its role as a supplier of defence equipment must rapidly diminish".[48]

The evaporation of combat aircraft orders after the Korean War episode seemed to confirm Vickers' belief that diversification into civil aviation was the only long-term hope for its aerospace involvement. After all, it had produced the turboprop Viscount airliner which was a best-seller through the 1950s. However, the apparent success of civil projects was dispelled by the end of that decade. First of all, airliner development costs matched military aircraft programmes and were a constant drain on company resources given the long gestation period required before any sales revenues could be forthcoming. Secondly, markets for airliners turned out to be just as insubstantial as those for warplanes and, in practice, failed to provide the counter-cyclical property needed with the wide swings in defence procurement. After realising sizeable losses on the VC-10 jetliner project, Vickers chose to divest itself of direct involvement in the aircraft industry and merged its interests with those of English Electric into the British Aircraft Corporation(BAC) in 1960. Ironically, BAC made most of its profits from the much-maligned military and not from the civil programmes it inherited from Vickers (notably the BAC-111 or Viscount successor).[49] Equally paradoxical, Vickers reacquired an aviation interest in 1969 when the shipbuilding group purchased Slingsby Sailplanes; admittedly not for its place in the glider market but rather for its mastery of glass fibre technology which could be reapplied to submersibles.[50]

CONCLUSION

This chapter has stressed the simple proposition that technical development and market evolution of aircraft are woven together. It has been averred that while technical change - innovation - was instrumental in determining the marketability of aircraft as a product, it was also the case that markets served to mould the direction of development followed by the aircraft industry. Nowhere was market influence more paramount than in the instance of defence contracts. Indeed, the aircraft industry has become, to all intents and purposes, a hostage to the vicissitudes of military requirements. These requirements abide by cycles which bear little resemblance to orthodox business cycles: rather, they respond to the perceptions held by policymakers of the state of international tension. The resultant wave-cycle, quite bluntly, apportions its largesse to the aircraft industry precisely during the times of national insecurity - real or imagined. Alternate phases of stability or peacetime equilibrium are lean times for many enterprises in the industry and can only be overcome provided they garner a modicum of military business (either domestic or destined for exports) or are able to resort to the counter-cyclical expedient of diversifying into civil aircraft production or even out of aircraft altogether. Commenting on the efficacy of the wave-cycle model, Higham concedes that it varies for individual air forces and airlines but still allows for the making of general conclusions. Those conclusions point to the overriding importance of the state, both as regulator of military and commercial aviation markets, and ultimately, as a main force in the evolution of technical change. The first of these considerations, the scope of the market, is elaborated upon in the next chapter with reference to civil aircraft while Chapter 4 deals with it from the vantage point of military aircraft.

NOTES AND REFERENCES

1. See, for instance, E. Mansfield, The Economics of Technical Change (Longman, London, 1968) and J. Schmookler, Invention and Economic Growth, (Harvard University Press, Cambridge, Mass.).
2. Books on this topic are legion; a couple of examples will suffice here: H. Penrose, British Aviation: The Pioneer Years (Putnam, London, 1967) and C. H. Gibbs-Smith, The Aeroplane: An Historical Survey of its Origins and Development (London: HMSO 1960).
3. Information obtained from Bill Gunston, The Encyclopedia of the World's Combat Aircraft (Salamander Books, London, 1976).
4. P. Lewis, The British Fighter since 1912 (Putnam, London, 4th edition, 1979), pp.161-2.
5. FI, 3 July 1976, p.23.
6. R. Higham, Air Power: A Concise History (St. Martin's Press, New York, 1972), p.32.
7. W. G. Cunningham, The Aircraft Industry: A study in Industrial Location (Morrison, Los Angeles, 1951), p.202.
8. D. R. Jones, 'The Beginnings of Russian Air Power, 1907-1922' in R. Higham and J.W. Kipp (eds.), Soviet Aviation and Air Power: A Historical View, (Westview Press, Boulder, Colo., 1977), pp.15-33.
9. Cancellation of the entire FE 2b batch for 1918 was owing more to tardy deliveries of a state-factory product already obsolete than to the introduction of a new design.
10. R. Freeman, Thunderbolt: A Documentary History of the Republic P-47, (MacDonald and Jane's,

London, 1978), p.141.

11. J. B. Rae, Climb to Greatness: The American Aircraft Industry, 1920-1960, (MIT Press, Cambridge, Mass., 1968), p.197.

12. Editorial in Air Pictorial, April 1984, p.121. In fact, aircraft delivered in 1983 from British factories embraced 44 Tornadoes for the RAF from BAe Warton, three Sea Harriers (for the RN) and twelve Hawks (RAF) from BAe Kingston, and 64 helicopters to all three services from Westland at Yeovil: giving a total of 123 combat and training aircraft.

13. P. Fearon, 'The Formative Years of the British Aircraft Industry, 1913-1924', Business History Review, vol.43 (1969), pp.476-495.

14. R. Higham, 'Quantity vs. Quality: The Impact of Changing Demand on the British Aircraft Industry, 1900-1960', Business History Review, vol.42 (1968), pp.443-466.

15. The Economist, 9 December 1944, p.782.

16. The virtually unsustainable load imposed by maximum production is evident from a comparison of 1944 and 1945 production levels. The first year was peak output that was cut back even before the war ended. Figures for 1944 and 1945 are respectively: USA (96,318 and 47,714), Germany (39,800 and 8,000), USSR (30,000 and 25,000) and Japan (28,180 and 11,066). See E. Angelucci, The Rand McNally Encyclopedia of Military Aircraft 1914-1980, (Rand McNally, Chicago, 1980), p.361.

17. Fearon, 'The Formative Years', p.488.

18. Rae, Climb to Greatness, p.161.

19. AW & ST, 25 January 1982, p.15. Note, target-drones are small pilotless aircraft.

20. The shock of the Afghanistan invasion was immediately reflected in a stock prices spurt for US aerospace firms; Northrop jumping from a quotation of 40 to 49.5 virtually overnight, and most of the other companies faring almost as well. See AW & ST, 14 January 1980, p.21.

21. AW & ST, 3 April 1978, p.41.

22. AW & ST, 7 January 1980, p.25.

23. AW & ST, 12 May 1980, p.43.

24. AW & ST, 31 October 1983, p.26.

25. Rae, Climb to Greatness, p.199. The plant was actually owned by the US Government.

26. Ibid, p.203.

27. Air Pictorial, February 1984, p.44.

28. J. L. Atwood, North American Rockwell: Storehouse of High Technology, (Newcomen Society, New York, 1970), p.18.

29. AW & ST, 24 January 1977, p.11.

30. AW & ST, 3 November 1975, p.16.

31. AW & ST, 29 June 1970, pp.14-15.
32. AW & ST, 24 May 1971, p.20.
33. FI, 27 February 1982, p.475.
34. AW & ST, 7 October 1974, p.16.
35. FI, 3 July 1976, p.3.
36. FI, 27 March 1982, p.714.
37. J. B. Rae, *Climb to Greatness*, p.51. Note, anti-combine legislation was instrumental in breaking up this, and other comparable ventures, in the USA.
38. G. Adams, *The Politics of Defense Contracting: The Iron Triangle*, (Transaction Books, New Brunswick, 1982), p.342.
39. *Air Pictorial*, December 1979, p.460.
40. AW & ST, 8 November 1971, p.44.
41. FI, 26 February 1981, p.553. Note, the company is now styled Gulfstream Aerospace and is contemplating the sale of its Bethany plant and concentrating its activities on the Savannah, Georgia operation.
42. AW & ST, 29 November 1971, p.44.
43. AW & ST, 10 May 1971, p.66. It also had substantial steel interests.
44. C. Trebilcock, *The Vickers Brothers: Armaments and Enterprise, 1854-1914*, (Europa Publications, London, 1977), p.54.
45. J. D. Scott, *Vickers: A History*, (Weidenfeld & Nicolson, London, 1962), pp.117-18.
46. Ibid, p.151.
47. Ibid, p.264.
48. H. Evans, *Vickers: Against the Odds 1956-1977*, (Hodder and Stoughton, London, 1978), p.35.
49. Ibid, p.185.
50. Ibid, pp.157-8.

Chapter Three

MARKETS FOR CIVIL AIRCRAFT

Civil aviation is, to most aircraft manufacturers and states alike, an indivisible part of the larger concept of aerospace which is unavoidably influenced by defence considerations.[1] However, it does establish a distinct presence in so far as markets are concerned. Unlike the bulk of the industry whose production activity is tied to wave-cycles of military procurement, those aircraft enterprises pandering to civil aviation respond to conventional business cycles. While fluctuating in response to short-term rises and falls in economic well-being, markets for civil aircraft have followed a generally upward trend since World War II. Revenue-passenger miles for 'Free World' airlines increased, for example, from 75 billion in 1960 to 162 billion in 1965, 341 billion in 1970, and 501 billion in 1975. Correspondingly, cargo traffic witnessed a surge from 2,590 billion revenue-ton miles in 1960, through 5,874 and 11,105 billions in 1965 and 1970, to arrive at 16,553 billion in 1975. From the mid-1970s, however, the growth in demand for civil aircraft underwent a sharp downturn, partly in response to recession in AICs and debt-problems in NICs.[2] It was only in 1983-4 that orders for commercial aircraft began to significantly rise once more. Yet, the remainder of the 1980s offers lucrative possibilities for aircraft manufacturers capable of meeting the demands of the market, for, not only is the crucial North American airline sector picking up again, but many of the world's airlines are considering replacing second-generation jet transports with new-model airliners.

The purpose of this chapter is to review how this recent market environment has affected the activities of aircraft manufacturers. In particular, it traces the ways in which aircraft firms have responded to what was initially for a time in the 1970s a depressing market and what is now a more promising situation. Attempts at collaboration between firms in order to overcome problems of risk will be stressed, as indeed will be the participation of states who formulate strategies aimed at overcoming the general uncertainty of the civil aviation market. For obvious functional reasons, civil aviation is approached from two standpoints; namely, that of commercial aviation - in a word, the airline business - and that of general aviation. The latter embraces the markets for light aircraft and executive/business aircraft. In US parlance, general aviation covers aircraft used for "transporting company executives, salesmen, and other personnel for business purposes, air taxi services, crop dusting, surveying, advertising, photography, and recreational and instructional flying."[3] As shall be seen, the two branches of civil aviation affect aircraft companies differently but are united in underscoring the vital part played by the USA in regulating demand for non-military aircraft.

COMMERCIAL AVIATION

Commercial aviation is the province of the air carriers, or those organisations licensed to transport passengers or cargo on well-defined routes. The equipment that they use, airliners, varies widely in function and size. Some machines are capable of ready conversion from passenger to cargo configuration depending upon the immediate requirements of the carrier (e.g. Boeing 707 and DC-8). Others are limited to a specialised role: the Concorde as a vehicle for rapid delivery of businessmen across the Atlantic comes readily to mind. Much more mundane, but equally specialised in their own way, are the civil versions of the Lockheed Hercules and Short Belfast used for hauling heavy freight loads. What is more, most passenger airliners are geared to a specific market - long-haul or short-haul, high or low-density. Thus, the Boeing 707 is optimised for long-hauls and relatively low-density routes whereas the Boeing 727 is designed for intermediate-distance routes which are not unduly patronised. Conversely, in the high-density field, the Boeing 747 caters best for long hauls of up to 10,600km while the A300 Airbus is designed more with hauls of up to 1,600km in mind. It should be stressed, however, that manufacturers attempt to build a degree of flexibility into their aircraft, offering, for instance, sub-models optimised for varying combinations of route distance and load. The Boeing 707-120, for example, was designed to provide accommodation for as many as 181 passengers for a range of up to 6,800km, while the 707-320 has seating for up to 219 passengers and a range of 10,040km. Even airliners confined to a particular range category have optional load configurations. To give but two examples, the short-range Boeing 737 possesses seating for 115 passengers in its -100 form or seating for 130 passengers in its -200 form, while another short-range airliner, the BAe 111 comes with accommodation for 89 in the series 475 and 119 in the series 500. Notwithstanding such flexibility, it is possible to classify airliners by function and size, and Table 3.1 attempts to identify examples from among the set of aircraft in production in the early 1980s.

The light transports are really quite distinct from other airliners in that they are targeted at feederliner services or regional airlines, which is to say, the small carriers linking minor airports to the major centres of the trunkline carriers (in this respect they are analogous to railway branch lines). As a result, they need to be able to utilise short runways (hence the STOL capability of many of them) and be eminently economical (which accounts for turboprop or piston engines). Because large size is unnecessary, airliners of this ilk can be built by most aircraft manufacturers and, consequently, market success rests very much on price competitiveness. In the 20-passenger airliner category, the best price on offer in 1984 amounted to $1.6 million for both the Brazilian Embraer Bandeirante and the Canadian DHC-6. More expensive competitors were provided by West Germany's Dornier 228 ($1.9 million), Spain's CASA C-212 ($2.4 million), the Short 330 and 360 ($3.1 and $4.1 million) emanating from Belfast, and the joint Spanish-Indonesian CN-235 ($5 million).[4]

With larger airliners operating over trunkline routes, the advantages of propeller engines are lost. Table 3.2 displays the airliner direct operating costs prevailing in the 1960s for US domestic trunkline services (the last decade in which piston aircraft played a significant contribution). The superiority of large machines such as the DC-8 and Boeing 707 over smaller jetliners (e.g. Caravelle, Boeing 727, BAe 111 and DC-9), turboprops (e.g. Viscount, Electra and F-27), and piston-airliners (e.g. DC-6, DC-7, L-1049G) is readily apparent. Indeed, the classic piston-airliner - the DC-3 - had total operating costs more than double those applying to most jetliners: a state of affairs attributable to the age of the design imposing excessive maintenance costs on the one hand and labour-intensive crewing on

Table 3.1 : Commercial Aircraft Types

Category	Example	Normal Range (km)	Normal load (passengers)
Light utility transport	PBN Islander	1,400	10
Light STOL transport	DHC-6 Twin Otter	1,775	20
Short-range airliner	Boeing 737-200	3,815	130
Short-range large-capacity airliner	A300B Airbus	1,610	331
Short-range transport helicopter	Aérospatiale Puma	620	20
Short/medium-range airliner	MD DC-9/40	2,710	125
Medium-range airliner	Boeing 727-200	4,635	189
Medium-range freighter	Lockheed L-100 Hercules	3,425	- freight
Medium/long-range freighter	Il-76	5,000	- freight
Medium-long-range airliner	Tu-154	5,280	164
Medium/long-range large-capacity airliner	Lockheed L-1011 Tristar	7,189	400
Long-range freighter	An-22	5,000	- freight
Long-range airliner	Il-62	8,000	198
Long-range large-capacity airliner	Boeing 747-200	10,650	500

Source: Jane's Pocket Book of Commercial Transport Aircraft, (Collier Books, New York, 1980).

the other. The efficacy of large jetliners on trunk-lines both within and without the USA accounted for their widescale adoption by the world's major air-lines in the period of cheap energy prior to 1973. The so-called energy crisis of that year precipitated an instant reappraisal of the effectiveness of jet-liner operations. One US study remarks on the trans-formed situation.

> An increase of fuel price from ten cents a gal-lon to over a dollar caused the percentage of fuel cost to direct operating cost to rise to 50 per cent, driving the early pure jet DC-8s and

Table 3.2 : Airliner Direct Operating Costs for Trunkline Services (1966)

Aircraft	Flight personnel costs[1]	Fuel and oil	Direct Maintenance	Total including depreciation
Douglas DC-3	1.173	0.515	1.502	3.772
Douglas DC-6	0.658	0.542	0.500	2.125
Douglas DC-7	0.452	0.439	0.687	2.232
Douglas DC-8	0.190	0.377	0.242	1.151
MD DC-9	0.444	0.462	0.260	2.062
Lockheed L-1049G	0.585	0.540	0.389	1.883
Lockheed Electra	0.376	0.339	0.514	1.763
Vickers Viscount	0.577	0.437	0.587	2.194
Fokker F-27[2]	0.531	0.418	0.649	2.263
Sud Caravelle	0.500	0.588	0.462	2.559
BAe 111[3]	0.320	0.387	0.406	1.622
Boeing 707	0.214	0.401	0.264	1.318
Boeing 727	0.263	0.383	0.326	1.512

Notes: 1. costs throughout in cents per available seat mile
2. costs based on local service data only
3. then designated BAC-111

Source: Abstracted from R. Miller and D. Sawers, The Technical Development of Modern Aviation, (Routledge and Kegan Paul, London, 1968), pp.287-96.

even fan jet B-707 from regular service. The same increase in fuel price is rendering all but the most recent model DC-9s and high-density configured B-727s uneconomic at present fare levels.[5]

Figure 3.1 summarises the world fleet for the first-generation of four-engined jetliners as of 1977. That year is particularly appropriate because it represents a hiatus between the newly-demised era of cheap fuel and that of expensive fuel which compelled the airlines to adopt wide-bodied airliners offering a combination of fuel-efficient engines and scale economies in passenger capacity.[6] The aircraft in question conform to the long-range airliner category of Table 3.1. It is no coincidence that all four types displayed are US built - the products of Boeing (707 and 720), MD (DC-8) and GD (Convair 880/990) - by virtue of the pre-eminence of North

Figure 3.1 : The World Fleet of First Generation Jetliners in 1977

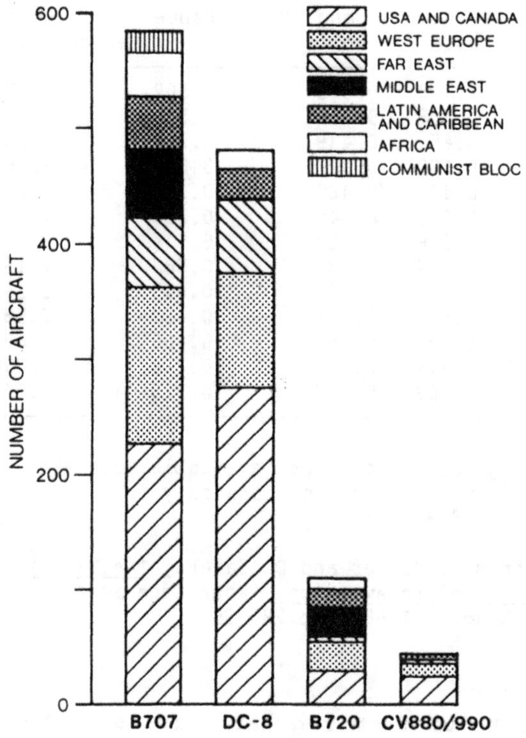

American markets. Fully 54 per cent of the four types considered were operating for North American airlines. In fact, as the majority of the world's large airlines (as measured in terms of aircraft fleets) originate in the USA, it is not surprising that they influence airliner manufacturing to the extent of stimulating a domestic industry to pander to their needs (Table 3.3).

The dominance of the North American market in the short and medium-range airliner markets is even more telling. The density of routes serving major cities of 500km to 1,000km apart accounts for the huge demand for Boeing 727 and DC-9 aircraft evinced by US carriers (Figure 3.2). Conversely, the failure of European-made aircraft such as the Caravelle and

Table 3.3 : Principal Airlines by Fleet Numbers, 1977

Rank[1]	Airline	Airliner total
1	United (US)	397
2	Trans World (US)	274
3	British Airways	183
4	Delta (US)	152
5	Eastern (US)	144
6	American (US)	139
7	Air France	136
8	Air Canada	119
9	Allegheny[2] (US)	107
10	Pan American (US)	104
11	Lufthansa	98
12	Braniff (US)	97
13	Iberia	86
14	All-Nippon	85
15	Western (US)	84
16	Japan Air Lines	77
17	Tarom/Romania	77
18	SAS	75
19	Alitalia	73
20	Northwest Orient (US)	68

Notes: 1. Excludes Aeroflot and Civil Aviation Administration of China
2. now US Air

Source: computed from G. G. Endres, World Airline Fleets 1977, (Airline Publications & Sales, London, 1977).

BAe 111 to make serious inroads into the North American market acted as a major constraint on their success since other regional markets (including Europe) were insufficiently developed to serve as substitutes. By the mid-1970s, the symbiotic relationship between US airlines and aircraft firms had given the latter such a commanding lead in world airliner markets that they appeared all set to monopolise the new-generation of wide-bodied transports as well. To that end, Boeing had sold 270 model 747s by 1977, MD had produced 244 DC-10s and Lockheed had built 151 Tristars. In sharp contrast, the European A300 Airbus had only recorded 34 sales and the Soviet Il-86 was scarcely out of the test hangar at Voronezh. So long as air travel remained determined by closeness

Figure 3.2 : Short and Medium-Range Jetliner Distribution in 1977

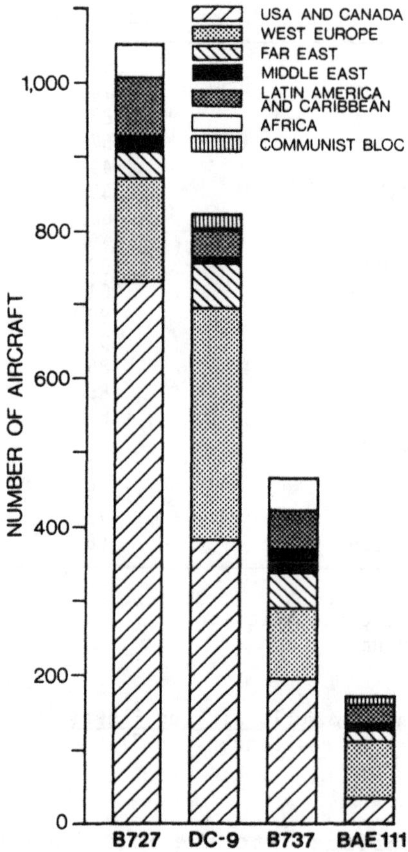

of cities containing a large proportion of affluent citizens, US airlines would have a market advantage over other national airlines and, to boot, would respond by providing competitive air services which would drum up yet further traffic growth.[7] In turn, competition among trunkline carriers required tailor-made equipment which effected the economies that the carriers wanted. The resultant aircraft, the products of Boeing, MD and Lockheed alluded to, were also suited to the requirements of non-US airlines. They were able to out-compete the products of other aircraft industries as a direct result of the favourable prices that occur as a concomitant of sizeable production runs. Table 3.4 makes abundantly clear the overriding fact that production runs of European airliners are far shorter than American ones. Table 3.5, for its part, brings out the price advantage usually enjoyed by US airliner producers. While the BAe 111 was very competitively priced in comparison to US short-range jetliners (Boeing 737 and DC-9) and the A300 Airbus undercut the prices of some US wide-bodied transports, the BAe 146, Fokker F-28 and A310 Airbus appeared unfavourably priced when compared to such American competitors as, respectively, the Boeing 737, DC-9 and Boeing 757. The prospect of more competitive prices for those European products hinges on longer production runs and the economies of scale that follow.

Impact on Commercial Aircraft Manufacturers

One immediate and obvious corollary of the recession in airliner markets in the 1970s was the parlous financial status of some aircraft enterprises. Lockheed, for instance, reputedly phased out its Tristar wide-body airliner owing to losses of almost $2.5 billion and the prospect of sales of only 24 aircraft a year from 1985-90 which would not make the venture profitable.[8] Indeed, an over dependence on airliner markets may spell doom for an aircraft firm as is evidenced from the collapse of Handley Page Ltd in 1970. This UK firm, based at Radlett north of London, was forced into receivership with debts of $18.4 million because of its emphasis on one product, the twin-turboprop Jetstream light airliner. The company had forsaken defence work (whose value dropped from $28 million in 1963 to only $7 million in 1968) to concentrate on development of the Jetstream. However, the scale of launch costs required was underestimated and, devoid of military programmes as stopgap measures, the firm foundered with the loss of 2,400 jobs.[9] Ironically, the Jetstream was resuscitated by BAe a decade later when market prospects appeared brighter.

It is precisely this burden of development or launch costs which appears problematical for aircraft firms. The gap between design and full-scale production must be covered by corporate reserves (or government launch aid) before revenues on airliner sales are forthcoming. An enterprise undertaking diverse projects may be better placed to cross-subsidise programmes occupying this vulnerable pre-revenue stage. Even these diversified enterprises, however, may find

Table 3.4 : Comparative Production Runs of Airliners: cumulative totals to 1976

Europe		USA	
Out of production		Out of production	
Sud Caravelle	278	MD DC-8	556
DH Comet	51	GD Convair 880/990	83
Vickers VC10	47		
Dassault Mercure	10		
In production		In production	
BAe 111	219	Boeing 727	1,195
HS Trident	117	Boeing 707/720	897
Fokker F-28	95	MD DC-9	802
Airbus A300B	23	Boeing 737	407
VFW 614	10	Boeing 747	283
Concorde	9	MD DC-10	240
		Lockheed Tristar	150
Total	859	Total	4,613

Source: <u>AW & ST</u>, 16 February 1976, p.22.

Table 3.5 : Airliner Price Comparisons ($'000 per seat), 1980

US Models		Other Models	
(twin jets)			
Boeing 737-200	92.3	BAe 111-500	84.1
Boeing 757	127.4	Airbus A300	114.8
Boeing 767	160.0	Airbus A310	160.0
MD DC-9 40/50	88.0	Fokker F-28 4000	126.5
MD Super 80	87.2		
(tri-jets)			
Boeing 727-200	89.9		
Lockheed L-1011/500	90.0		
MD DC-10 30/40	118.4		
(four-jets)			
Boeing 747-200	100.0	BAe 146-100	107.5

Source: various

summoning of the necessary resources a daunting task. BAe, for example, is obliged in 1984-5 to find development money amounting to £30.5 million for the BAe 146, £27.5 million for the ATP, £18 million for the BAe 125-800, and £15 million for the Airbus.[10] Boeing went so far as to put development costs of its 757 and 767 airliners at a staggering $4 billion.[11] Both of these firms have, accordingly, compensatory defence programmes (amounting to sales of $2.168 billion for Boeing in 1981). Yet, Aérospatiale was plagued throughout the 1970s by its commercial aviation projects in spite of vibrant warplane programmes. These did not prevent the enterprise from making overall losses in several years. The loss of $90 million in 1973, for instance, was ascribed to the Concorde, A300B Airbus ($36 million in cost overruns) and Corvette light jetliner ($20 million in losses).[12] All told, the Corvette was an unmitigated disaster, losing FFr 900 million by the time of its termination in 1977 and contributing "no less than 66 per cent of the total Aérospatiale deficit between 1972 and 1975."[13] Neither was the jetliner project of sister firm Dassault an admirable venture. Its twin-jet Mercure was cancelled after only ten had been produced in order to contain losses on a type which had failed to win orders. Dassault held culpable declining airline growth rates, dropping short-haul traffic, and price escalation as a result of dollar devaluation and problems with suppliers in Italy (Aeritalia), Canada (Canadair), Spain (CASA), Belgium (SABCA) and the USA (P & W).[14] Fokker-VFW's 40-passenger contemporary, the model 614 jetliner was also cancelled at this time: again, sales had not materialised and the enterprise could not support ongoing development costs. Production of the airliner terminated after only 16 had been built with the inevitable outcome of job losses at Spire (500) and Bremen (300).[15] Fortunately, defence contracts mitigated the worst effects of the ill-fated venture.

> The figures could have been higher were it not for a redistribution by the government to VFW of work on other West German defence programs, such as F-104 Starfighter overhaul and rework, and minesweeper production, and the start of production of 25 more C-160 Transall military transport aircraft for the French Air Force.[16]

In light of the heavy costs of development, not to mention the huge expense of failure, firms undertaking airliner projects attempt to alleviate the inherent risks by soliciting state aid with launch costs or through collaborative ventures with other firms. In some cases they do both, most notably the Concorde SST. Government assistance with airliner projects appears to be more readily granted when the firm in question is a state enterprise and this is nowhere more evident than in France. The French Ministry of Transport allocated $405 million for civil aviation in 1983, of which $139 million was destined for A300/310 Airbus development, $72.4 million for the new A320 and $31.8 million for the new ATR 42 turboprop airliner, while $116.5 million was destined for civil aeroengine development.[17] The whole line of Falcon bizjets and regional airliners was heavily incumbent on state launch aid. In return for Dassault agreeing to switch 55 per cent of airframe manufacture of the Falcon 50 to state-owned Aérospatiale, the government absorbed half of the costs of developing and producing the aircraft.[18] The updated version, the Falcon 900, which was due to go into production in 1986 was assisted to the extent of 30 per cent of its development costs by the French Government.[19] Such activity is not confined to France. In the UK, state-owned R-R received about $540 million in government aid during 1976-80, largely to support civil aeroengine R & D.[20]

Apart from the Concorde and Airbus projects (as much state programmes as collaborative ventures between firms), examples of firms combining their resources to build airliners have become commonplace in recent years.[21] The aforementioned ATR 42, to take but one example, is a joint Aérospatiale:Aeritalia venture with the French partner responsible for the aeroplane's wings, cockpit and final assembly (at Toulouse) and the Italian partner undertaking fuselage manufacture.[22] In a similar vein is the SF 340 commuter airliner currently being built by Saab at Linkoping and Fairchild at Farmingdale, New York. The Swedish partner is authorised to produce the aircraft's fuselage and fin, and in return for final assembly has found about two-thirds of the development costs. The US firm, meanwhile, provides the wings, engine nacelles and empennage, and the balance of the development costs.[23] In the more costly pure jet field, MD is seeking a partner to share the risks of developing a successor to the DC-9/super 80 series (i.e. the MD-80). After toying with a co-operative venture with Fokker (the MDF100), MD wants to establish a consortium comparable to the £2 billion joint venture put together by four West European governments in sponsorship of the A320 Airbus. Aiming at the market for short-range airliners (estimated at 862 aircraft by 1998), MD wishes to consolidate its success with the 150-seat MD-80; 167 of which were booked by American Airlines in a giant $3 billion transaction. Despite being hailed as the deal which put MD's commercial aviation division into a profitable position in 1984 for the first time in 15 years, still the company cannot afford to initiate major new airliner developments without contributions from other firms.[24]

The other major player in commercial aviation, Boeing, has attempted collaborative efforts, both officially and unofficially, since the beginning of the 1970s. Its earlier overtures were unofficial in the sense that the firm spread its risk load through the incorporation of many firms into its airliner projects as contractors and subcontractors. Thus, no less than 53 per cent of the model 757 is built outside of Boeing, whereas three Japanese companies are together responsible for 17 per cent of the model 767. In fact, a consortium of MHI, Kawasaki, Fuji, Shin Meiwa and Nippi has recently joined forces with Boeing to develop a 150-seat airliner for the 1990s. The YXX, as it is known, will continue the precedent set by the 767 but with the proviso that Boeing will allow the Japanese partner much greater scope in development of the machine (25 per cent share). Underpinning the Japanese participation is the direct encouragement (manifested through organisational and financial input) of the Japanese Government and this kind of indirect state involvement is prevalent in other aspects of the commercial aviation business.

Commercial Aviation Markets and State Influence

In one sense, governments can directly stimulate demand for airliners by compelling state airlines to buy the products of the national aircraft industry. It was in such a manner that BEA introduced the Vickers Viscount, BOAC shepherded into service the DH Comet, Air France the Sud Caravelle, and both of those latter, the Concorde SST. If the technical performance of the aircraft fall short of the state airlines requirements, governments may feel compelled to go a step further and subsidise the operations of the aircraft. The service records of Concorde with British Airways and Air France, and the Mercure with Air Inter (the French state-owned domestic airline) attest to this course of action. Nowadays, some NICs are following suit in obliging their own carriers to operate domestically-made transports and, furthermore, forbidding the import of comparable machines from the AICs. Indonesia, for one, announced in 1980 that it would prohibit the import of US aircraft which could perform similar functions to the locally-built C-212 turboprop airliner.[25] Brazil, for another, attempted to guarantee a domestic market for the Bandeirante light transport by excluding equivalent US aircraft.[26]

Even the world's single largest commercial aviation market is not free of import restrictions. American protectionism is manifested through the rubric of the 'Buy America Act'. Implemented originally in 1933, this act imposed penalties on US government agencies who preferred foreign equipment over domestic equivalents. In the 1970s, the US Coast Guard wished to adopt airliner-type aircraft for patrol purposes and VFW-Fokker, one of the contenders for the contract (proposing the ill-fated type 614), reckoned that the cost penalty imposed upon it for proffering a non-US built product would amount to six per cent of the total contract value or "as high as 12 per cent if a losing prime US competitor in the procurement was located in an area of heavy unemployment."[27] Eventually, much to the irritation of US firms, the contract was awarded to Dassault for its Falcon 20 but only after the French firm had established a US affiliate (Falcon Jet Corp) and the complaints of American aircraft manufacturers had been allayed. When the knocked-down aircraft was reassembled at Little Rock, Arkansas, and then furnished with US aeroengines and avionics, it was successfully claimed as being more than 50 per cent US built and, therefore, outside of the jurisdiction of the Buy America Act.[28] While on the subject of the US Coast Guard, it is interesting to record another instance of a foreign purchase being challenged by US competitors invoking that protectionist measure. In this case, Aérospatiale was able to demonstrate that even with a six per cent cost penalty, its successful SA-366 Dolphin helicopter was superior to the best American entrant in the competition and, what is more, in being assembled at Grand Prairie, Texas, fell within the 'domestic end product' definition.[29]

American firms have also used the argument of unfair competition as a result of state subsidies in attempting to block the import of foreign commercial aircraft into the US market. In 1978 Congress was asked to consider the proposition that both Eastern Airlines' $778 million order for Airbus aircraft and Pan American's $480 million order for R-R powered L-1011 Tristars was accredited to European subsidies to aerospace enterprises and the attendant 'unfair' financial concessions that they could, in turn, use to tempt orders out of US airlines. Congress, in due course, could arrive at no firm conclusions about the validity of the complaint.[30] A more recent instance, notable in that it represents the penetration of the US market by the product of an NIC aircraft industry, is that relating to the Embraer Bandeirante. This Brazilian turboprop light airliner, mentioned earlier, was so accused by the Fairchild aircraft enterprise. Claiming that the sales of its subsidiary Swearingen's comparable aeroplane, the Metro, was adversely affected by the entry of the Bandeirante, Fairchild filed a petition with the International Trade Commission (ITC). In particular, Fairchild (supported by Beech) felt that the subsidised financial package offered by the Brazilians sufficed to push the US market share held by the Bandeirante from seven per cent in 1978 to 35 per cent in 1981. A direct consequence of this penetration, it was averred, was the running of Swearingen's San Antonio plant at only 20 per cent capacity and with only 75 per cent of its workforce.[31] The rebuttal put forward by Embraer rested on two grounds: first, that its product was unpressurised, unlike the Metro, and therefore cheaper to produce (20 to 40 per cent less) and, moreover, catering for an essentially different clientele; secondly, that the eight per cent finance rates of Embraer, while half the commercial rates required for the Metro, were still within acceptable bounds when the "after-corporate-tax cash flow costs of the two aircraft were compared." These arguments were sufficiently compelling to induce the ITC to drop its investigation on the understanding that Fairchild was not "materially injured" by Embraer.[32]

The above case serves to highlight a major form of state support for commercial aviation; namely, by way of airliner financing. Special export credits arms of governments have intervened to underwrite airliner contracts at favourable rates. Indeed, the competition among countries to facilitate such contracts may become so intense that an element of rivalry develops between the various agencies. Nowhere is this more apparent than in the wide-body airliner field. The national export credit guarantee agencies of West Germany, the UK and France supported private banks in giving a $306 million ten-year loan at fixed rates to Singapore Airlines in order that the carrier could obtain an extra six A300 Airbuses: the loan covering 85 per cent of the contract cost.[33] Prior to 1981, the Europeans and Americans had bitterly vied with each other to offer preferable financial packages. It was alleged, for example, that the Europeans managed to sell nine A300s to Toa airlines of Japan in 1980 because the US Export-Import Bank could not match the financial package, forced as it was by the intransigence of Congress to operate with limited funds. Before an accord was reached in 1981 among the contending states to offer standard 12 per cent rates over ten years, the Export-Import Bank was forced to offer 9.25 per cent rates on export credits in comparison with the 7.5-9.0 per cent available from the Europeans. Airliners falling under the terms of the agreement include the US-built MD-80, DC-10, L-1011, Boeing 757 and 767 as well as the European-built Airbus.[34] However, the Americans do manage to reap benefits from European finance. The UK Export Credit Guarantee Department has been especially forthcoming in providing credits for US-made airliners fitted with R-R engines. The Lockheed L-1011 Tristar set the precedent: for example, a 100 per cent financial package to cover the $500 million cost for twelve aircraft persuaded Pan American World Airways to buy the Tristar rather than the DC-10 or Boeing 747.[35] Other loans arranged by British banks, but supported by the UK Government, facilitated Tristar sales to a host of airlines including TWA, Delta, Air Canada and Air Jamaica.[36] Since the demise of the Tristar, onus has shifted to the Boeing 757 as is testified by a recent sale of six of those aircraft to Air Florida.[37] It is worth recording too, that the UK Government indirectly subsidises airliner sales through its ownership of Shorts of Belfast. This enterprise recently established a line of credit with US banks (with the backing of the Export Credit Guarantee Department) in order to enable it to offer favourable financial terms in the competitive US commuter airline market.[38] The fact remains that government support of airliner contracts is indispensable: the 85 per cent financing of Alitalia's $1 billion order for 30 MD-80s by the Export-Import Bank in 1983 was, for example, instrumental in pulling off the largest civil export transaction in MD's history.[39]

GENERAL AVIATION

The general aviation market is, like that of commercial aviation, dominated by the USA. Demand for general aviation is rendered feasible by a combination of low airport costs, significant local population with substantial average incomes, a fair degree of industrialisation in the region and its corollary of airports replete with technically-proficient facilities: all factors abounding in the USA.[40] All told, the USA has more civil aircraft than the rest of the world combined, and all except a minuscule two per cent fall into the general aviation category.[41] Of the 124,237 light aircraft in use in the USA in 1969, no less than 49 per cent were single-engined machines seating four or more, 34 per cent were smaller single-engined aeroplanes, thirteen per cent were multi-engined aircraft and the remainder were, by and large, helicopters. The fastest growing category (by a factor of four since 1956) was the multi-engined which embodies business aircraft and those fulfilling air taxi duties. Two US light aircraft manufacturers loom over the market - Cessna and Piper - which together accounted for 73 per cent of all fixed-wing general aviation aircraft manufactured in the country.[42] They are supplemented by Beech, which tends to produce higher-value multi-engined types. A number of other enterprises have entered the lucrative business aircraft market, several of them being subsidiaries of non-US manufacturers.

As with commercial aviation, the general aviation market experienced a tumultuous decade in the 1970s. In 1971, US manufacturers produced 7,464 light aircraft; a drop on the average figures for the late 1960s, but still better than the production rate applying in the 1950s (Figure 3.3). Notably, however, it took the US market twenty years to return to the production level of 1947: a level reflecting the boom in flying stimulated by the flight students funded by the GI Bill.[43] The early 1970s was a period of recession for the industry with production levels reverting to 1960 standards. However, after 1973 demand skyrocketed, exceeding the late-1960s figures by 1977 and peaking in 1978 with almost 18,000 aircraft built. Yet the inherent precariousness of the market was demonstrated by the sharp reduction in output between 1979 and 1980; a reflection of declining economic well-being. Paradoxically, by 1983 the market situation had recovered with, for example, both Cessna and Beech recording record sales and net earnings ($370.6 million and $21.5 million respectively for the former firm with the equivalent figures for the latter being $204.6 million and $10 million: note, that in both cases defence sales were down).[44] Subsequently, however, sales have slackened.

Firms were forced to take measures to counter the effects of demand downturns in the early 1970s and again at the end of that decade. Cessna's response in 1971 was to close its Strother Field facility where the assembly, painting and delivering of its small Model 150 had been undertaken.[45] Another light plane manufacturer, Bellanca, was forced to suspend operations, and production of its Viking and Champion types could only be renewed after the US

Figure 3.3 : Production of US General Aviation Aircraft

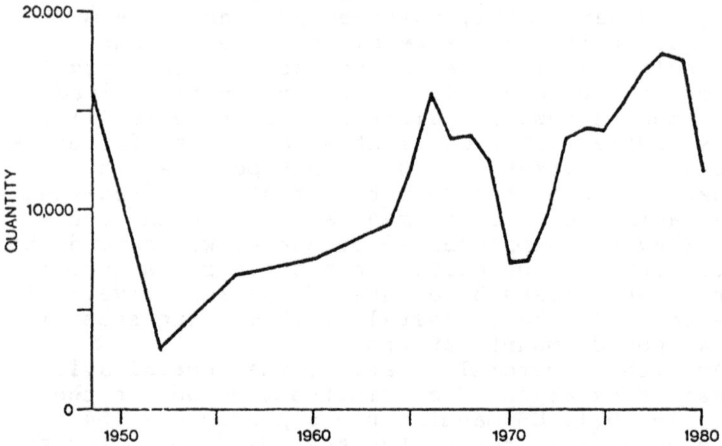

Government had agreed to underwrite the requisite loans.[46] Despite optimistic forecasts of a market for 3,600 business aircraft in the five years succeeding 1976, many firms were caught short in the recession at the onset of the 1980s after expanding capacity to meet this expected surge in demand. An extemporary solution was to extend vacation shutdowns of plants (practised by Cessna, Piper, and Gulfstream American's Bethany, Oklahoma plants). Alternatively, firms could redirect their business aircraft to military markets where they could be advertised as fulfilling the function of staff transports. To this end, Gulfstream sold three of its bizjets to the USAF as VIP transports, Cessna sold 15 Citation bizjets to the US Navy as navigation trainers, Gates Learjet leased 80 Lear 35As to the USAF as staff transports, as did Beech with the loan of 40 Super King Air machines. In the final analysis, firms could opt to slow the development of new projects: the poor showing in 1983-4 of general aviation turboprop aircraft had the effect of persuading Beech to delay production of its Lightning while prompting Gulfstream to delay delivery of its Commander 1200.[47]

In emulation of airliner producers, several manufacturers of bizjets have attempted to mitigate the risk factor by pooling their resources. These collaborative efforts have typically taken on an international flavour. One of the first occurred in 1973 when the US Atlantic Aviation Corporation redesigned the Jet Commander for IAI of Israel who then proceeded to make and market it as the Westwind (the latest model of which is called the Astra). Other projects have entailed manufacture in two countries. In 1975, for example, RI and Fuji jointly produced the Model 700 twin piston-engined business aircraft. Basically of Japanese design, Fuji was responsible for the manufacture of the primary structure and the subsequent shipping of fuselage, wings and tail to America where RI installed the US-made engines, undercarriage, avionics and interior fittings. Eight years later, a joint bizjet, the GP-180, was initiated by Gates Learjet and Piaggio. The US company would produce the forward airframe at Tucson, leaving the Italian firm to make the aft airframe, wings and tail at Finale Ligure.[48] A prime merit of such collaborative efforts on the part of non-US firms is the access to the US general aviation market gained by entering into partnership with American companies. Some non-US manufacturers attain the same end by setting up US subsidiaries. The French and Japanese have been particularly prominent in this respect. What is more, the state of Texas has been a principal beneficiary of their efforts.

French subsidiaries are centred on Grande Prairie, a suburb of Dallas. About 800 workers are employed, in the main, by the Aérospatiale Helicopter Corporation, but with a nucleus contributed by the Sfena Corporation and the Turboméca Engine Corporation. The first company was capitalised for $40 million by its parent and located at this site in 1980. Not only was it to support the sale of Dolphin helicopters to the Coast Guard (referred to earlier), but it was to reassemble and complete to customer specifications all Astar and Twin-star helicopters manufactured in knock-down condition by the parent company at Marignane. Sfena seemingly relocated to Grande Prairie 'by chance' because most of its business was concerned with supplying avionics to Bell-Helicopter-Textron and not Aérospatiale, but Turboméca intentionally placed its engine support and repair facility alongside its client Aérospatiale.[49] While Dassault also has an American associate to support its Falcon bizjet, it is MHI which has been the other major foreign aerospace presence in Texas. Adopting the mantle of Mitsubishi Aircraft International after 1970, MHI shipped its MU-2 aircraft to San Angelo beginning in 1966. The machine's fuselage and wings were shipped from Nagoya to Texas for installation of the engines, avionics and interiors. Final assembly at San Angelo allowed the Japanese parent to claim that 65 per cent of the firm's costs were spent in the USA.[50] MHI has switched its attention in recent years to the Diamond bizjet. As a point of fact, the boot is sometimes on the other foot with American firms establishing general aviation subsidiaries in foreign markets. Of special note is Reims Aviation in France, 49 per cent owned by Cessna, whose location enables the US company to circumvent French import taxes. The major assemblies of most Cessna models of light aircraft are manufactured in Wichita and delivered to Reims for final assembly.[51] Similarly, RI gained a privileged access to the Mexican market through its 30 per cent-owned Aeronautica Agricola Mexicana and to which it transferred production of its crop-dusting A-9 aircraft.[52]

CONCLUSION

While, in the aggregate, playing second fiddle to military aviation, the demand for civil aircraft is vitally important to many of the world's leading aerospace companies. Furthermore, as the main source of civil aviation demand resides in the USA, it is imperative that aircraft firms monitor cyclical trends in US economic well-being and draw up their aircraft projects on the understanding that only through making inroads into the US market are they likely to be forthcoming with a financially-successful product. In so far as the US commercial aviation market was concerned (and US carriers haul 38 per cent of the world's total passenger traffic), the recession of the late 1970s multiplied the attention given to obtaining competitively-priced airliners capable of efficient operation. In terms of the former consideration, airliner manufacturers and their government backers responded by formulating attractive financing arrangements and attempted to out-bid one another in wooing the airlines. Concerning the latter consideration, much was made of the various merits of company products. MD estimated, for example, that the maintenance costs in dollars per revenue flight hour were lower for its DC-9 (183) than those applying to the Boeing 727 (215) or 737 (225), while in the wide-body airliner market, its DC-10 recorded $532 as opposed to the $682 of the Boeing 747 and the $689 of the Lockheed Tristar. Boeing, for its part, makes much of the fuel efficiency of the 767 as reflected in lower direct operating costs than any of its competitors.[53]

The overriding fact emerging from the general aviation case is the sheer volume of production of light aircraft emanating from the USA. Certain firms, by dint of catering to this market, have emerged as specialist general aviation manufacturers. Firms such as Cessna, Piper and Beech have become, as a consequence of their commanding position in the US market, the dominant light aircraft manufacturers in the world by far. To all intents and purposes, the only possibilities for successful entry into the general aviation field by other firms is through product specialisation. In the last decade the most popular forms of product specialisation have occurred in the executive and commuter aircraft markets. Indeed, the pr fusion of bizjets on the market in the 1980s has been such as to lead to intense competition among manufacturers and, in several instances, to corporate failure. The issue of organisational survival in the face of market uncertainty is one which shall be addressed again in this book and not least in the next chapter where the whole question of corporate response to military aviation markets is reviewed.

NOTES AND REFERENCES

1. For example, the Rayner Report states "The evidence that we have had shows clearly the indivisibility of aerospace technology between civil and military applications". See Government Organisation for Defence Procurement and Civil Aerospace, (Cmnd. 4641, HMSO, London, 1971), p.48.

2. 'Dimensions of Airline Growth' (Boeing Commercial Airplane Company, Seattle, January 1977), pp.62-4. Note, that 1980 was for US scheduled airlines, the worst year for growth in annual traffic (-5 per cent) and only the third year since 1938 that the industry posted an operating loss. See N. K. Taneja, Airlines in Transition, (D. C. Heath, Lexington, Mass., 1981), p.6.

3. J. J. Warford, Public Policy toward General Aviation, (The Brookings Institution, Washington, DC, 1971), p.1.

4. FI, 21 April 1984, p.1081.

5. F. A. Spencer, 'A Reappraisal of Transport Aircraft Needs 1985-2000: Perceptions of Airline Management in a Changing Economic, Regulatory, and Technological Environment', NASA Langley Research Center, Hampton, Virginia, January 1982, p.111.

6. Interestingly, the usefulness of wide-bodied transports was fading by the end of the 1970s, in part owing to continued rises in fuel costs notwithstanding the fuel-efficient engines of these aircraft, partly owing to increased competition among carriers who had absorbed 370 wide-bodied aircraft in

the US alone, and also because of the declining traffic consequent upon the recession. Civil aircraft sales dropped in the early 1980s; in 1983, for example, they declined 4.7 per cent from the previous year. See AW & ST, 26 May 1980, p.26 and 26 December 1983, p.18.

7. For a review of airline traffic demand models, see N. K. Taneja, Airline Traffic Forecasting: A Regression Analysis Approach, (D. C. Heath, Lexington, Mass., 1978).

8. FI, 19 December 1981, p.1812.

9. AW & ST, 19 January 1970, p.79 and 9 March 1970, p.228.

10. FI, 28 April 1984, p.1171.

11. FI, 27 February 1982, p.475.

12. AW & ST, 8 July 1974, p.20.

13. FI, 9 July 1977, p.120.

14. AW & ST, 22 July 1974, p.34.

15. AW & ST, 2 January 1978, pp.29-30.

16. Ibid, p.30.

17. AW & ST, 4 October 1982, p.32. Interestingly, $4.73 million was set aside to subsidise the operations of the unsuccessful Mercure in airline operations.

18. FI, 18 September 1975, p.395 and 24 July 1976, p.213.

19. AW & ST, 4 June 1984, p.67.

20. AW & ST, 13 September 1982, p.96.

21. Concorde and Airbus programmes are reserved for Chapter 7.

22. AW & ST, 9 November 1981, p.36.

23. FI, 30 October 1982, pp.1274-5.

24. 'Firm seeks partners to develop airplane', Winnipeg Free Press, 27 August 1984. For the profitability of Douglas, see AW & ST, 18 March 1985, p.197.

25. AW & ST, 24 March 1980, p.11.

26. FI, 10 September 1977, p.733.

27. AW & ST, 19 January 1976, p.38.

28. AW & ST, 8 November 1976, p.19 and 10 January 1977, p.13.

29. AW & ST, 16 June 1980, p.29.

30. F. A. Spencer, 'A Reappraisal of Transport Aircraft Needs', pp.137-8.

31. AW & ST, 20 September 1982, p.115.

32. AW & ST, 27 September 1982, p.24.

33. AW & ST, 26 July 1982, p.34.

34. AW & ST, 15 September 1980, p.17 and 10 August 1981, p.25.

35. AW & ST, 10 April 1978, p.21.

36. AW & ST, 18 January 1971, p.20.

37. AW & ST, 16 November 1981, p.34.

38. AW & ST, 6 December 1982, p.43.

39. Air Pictorial, 45 (March 1983), p.82. Sometimes government support for airliner deals can appear quite bizarre: for instance, the agreement by R-R and Boeing to accept $1 billion-worth of oil in return for selling Saudi Arabia ten Boeing 747s. See AW & ST, 20 August 1984, p.28.

40. N. D. Baxter and E. P. Howrey, "The Determinants of General Aviation Activity: A Cross-Sectional Analysis" in G. P. Howard (ed.), Airport Economic Planning, (MIT Press, Cambridge, Mass., 1974), pp.177-90.

41. J. J. Warford, Public Policy, p.2.

42. Ibid, p.10.

43. Ibid, p.23.

44. AW & ST, 17 December 1983, p.52.

45. AW & ST, 25 January 1971, p.55. During the period from September 1969 to January 1971 Cessna's workforce dropped from 9,200 to 4,800.

46. FI, 24 April 1975, p.671.

47. See, AW & ST, 5 July 1982, p.25; 3 October 1983, p.43; and 21 May 1984, p.15.

48. Details are available in AW & ST, 1 March 1976, pp.62-3; 22 March 1976, pp.48-9; and 2 April 1984, pp.48-9.

49. AW & ST, 18 October 1982, pp.53-61

50. AW & ST, 5 March 1973, p.9; and 12 March 1973, p.53.

51. AW & ST, 28 May 1973, p.231.

52. AW & ST, 3 May 1971, p.25.

53. N. K. Taneja, Airlines in Transition, pp.191-8.

Chapter Four

MARKETS FOR MILITARY AIRCRAFT

As made evident in the preceding chapters, the aerospace industry and the state have historically maintained a mutually beneficial relationship.[1] In varying degrees, the state's sustained interest in the aircraft industry revolves around the strategic importance of the industry's output to national defence. The militarisation of aircraft evolved from humble beginnings and increased rapidly during World War I. Aerial warfare was not a novel idea, as balloons were utilised as observation platforms from the eighteenth century onwards, and the Austrians actually undertook a balloon bombing raid against Venice in 1849.[2] On 30 June 1910 Glenn Curtiss demonstrated that it was possible to drop weapons from an aircraft in flight, and on 20 August 1910 the first rifle was fired from an aeroplane.[3] Naval adaptations of aviation also emerged, with a Curtiss biplane flown off an American cruiser in November 1910, and in January 1911, another Curtiss biplane landed on a US armoured cruiser.[4] In general however, military aviation received a rather sceptical reception from the upper echelons of the military establishment. In 1910, for instance, Colonel J.E.B. Seely told a number of aviation pioneers that the UK Government, "does not consider that aeroplanes are of any possible use for war purposes".[5] Yet with the onset of war, the military uses of aircraft rapidly came to the forefront, and subsequent industry output paralleled the emerging demands of aerial combat.

Initially, aircraft were primarily utilised as observational platforms from which to conduct visual and, later, photographic reconnaissance missions, as typified by Geoffrey de Havilland's two seat BE2c biplane (produced at the Royal Aircraft Factory, Farnborough). Improved anti-aircraft fire stimulated improved aircraft performance. The need to clear the skies of intruding aircraft led to the development of armed aircraft. From modest beginnings with pilots taking potshots at each other with hand-held pistols to the 'Fokker scourge', the fighter aircraft evolved whereby forward fuselage mounted machine guns were synchronised to propeller rotations by the Fokker developed interrupter gear. At the same time, aircraft manoeuvrability increased, as did speed as 50-100 hp power plants were progressively replaced by 200-300 hp engines. As the war continued, aircraft were pressed into new roles and their capabilities were developed accordingly. Bombing missions, originally undertaken by adapted reconnaissance aircraft and the vulnerable Zeppelin airships, were subsequently carried out by specialised light bombers (e.g. the DH-4 of 1917 and DH-9A of 1918) and heavy bombers (e.g. the Handley Page 0/400, the German Gotha and Staaken R.VI). By the war's end, the Handley Page V/1500 bomber was capable of carrying 7,500 lbs of bombs at 79-90 mph over an action radius of 1,300 miles, a notable improvement over the 0/400 which flew at 60-80 mph with a bomb load of only 1,800 lbs.[6]

Notwithstanding the laudable technological achievements made during World War I (which, in any event, would soon be eclipsed), the most significant changes concerning aircraft production occurred in its institutional environment. First of all, aircraft had become indispensable to twentieth century warfare. Indeed the sanguine visions of creating a world of "next door neighbours" gave way to the lucid realities of airpower. As Orville Wright would exclaim, "when my brother and I built and flew the first man-carrying flying machine, we thought that we were introducing into the world an invention which would make further wars practically impossible"[7], only to concede, "What a dream it was; what a nightmare it has become."[8] By virtue of its historically vindicated contributions to national defence and given that the latter falls within the purview of state activity, the aircraft industry and the state laid down the foundations of what was to become the defence market. Such a relationship, however, was predicated on the existence of a fully-fledged aircraft industry. A second major institutional change, therefore, was the creation of an industry - the aircraft industry. In the USA, for example, whereas in 1914 there were sixteen firms listed by the Census Bureau as aircraft manufacturers with a combined output of 49 planes, by 1918 production reached a wartime peak of approximately 14,000 aircraft and employment totalled some 175,000 people.[9] In Britain, likewise, the exigencies of war had transformed aircraft production from relatively small-scale operations to true manufacturing enterprises capable of mass production. Finally, the war experience illustrated that successful military machines required a productive and co-ordinated industrial base. "Industrial production was as important, or more important, to military success as tactics or strategy. Relating its supply and procurement apparatus to a mobilised economy had to be part of the military mission in modern times."[10] In capitalist economies, the mobilisation effort presented particular problems in so far as production remained outside of state authority. The institutional integration of suppliers (e.g. aircraft producers) and the state became imperative. The cessation of hostilities in 1918 eliminated the immediate need for a stable integration between industry and the military - with severe consequences for the aircraft industry. However, the relationship forged between defence suppliers and the state during the war would evolve, albeit in a restricted form, throughout the interwar years.[11]

A scant 21 years later hostilities would again erupt and the aircraft industry would again mobilise to meet the demands of war. As was the case in World War I, aircraft were an important element of conflict; if anything, more vital than in the earlier conflict. Aircraft capabilities progressed rapidly. At the outset of war, the twin-engine medium bomber (e.g. Bristol Beaufort) was capable of carrying a bomb load of 1,000-1,500 lbs over a range of up to 1,000 miles at speeds averaging 200 mph; by the end of the war, the B-25 Mitchell could carry 2,000 lbs of bombs over a 500 mile radius, but at speeds in excess of 300 mph. Four-engine heavy bombers replaced the medium bombers, and the four 1,280 hp R-R Merlin-engined Avro Lancaster night bomber could carry a bomb load of 12,750 lbs for a 1,200 mile radius at 160 mph.[12]

Coupled with a changing technical environment, the institutional relationship between the aircraft industry and the military shifted from a depression-subsidy perspective to one of war-time mobilisation. This was manifested in the USA through a number of legislative actions including the approval of negotiated (as opposed to competitive) contracts with a single contractor (in 1939) and the right to exclude firms deemed unqualified (by the government) to produce aircraft in quantity from the bidding process (in 1942).[13] Despite the strengthened structural relationships forged between industry and the state, the termination of the war again proved extremely disruptive. However, in contrast to the post World

War I period, the US aircraft industry would assume an unprecedented position in the nation's defence. In the words of the Finletter Commission,

> Our military security must be based on air power ... A strong aircraft industry is an essential element in the nation's air power. Our air establishment would be useless unless backed by a manufacturing industry skillful in technological application, efficient in production, capable of rapid expansion, and strong in basic financial structure.[14]

Moreover, the ascendency of air power in the nation's defence entailed significant implications for industry-state relations, or more correctly, extended into peacetime that which had evolved and matured during wartime,

> Whether we like it or not, the health of the aircraft industry, for the next few years, at least, is dependent largely upon financial support from Government in the form of orders for military aircraft.[15]

MILITARY AIRCRAFT TYPES

In general, the Tier I output of the aerospace industry targeted for the defence market may be divided into two broad categories: piloted aircraft and non-piloted aircraft and/or products. The latter category encompasses aeroengines, rockets, launch vehicles, spacecraft, remotely piloted vehicles (RPV), surveilance and target acquisition drones, and a variety of missiles. While the above constitute an important part of the industry's defence output, the emphasis of this chapter is on the second category, piloted aircraft. There are two basic airframe configurations - fixed wing and rotary wing - manufactured for the defence market but, among these configurations, there are a myriad of aircraft types. In 1978, for example, there were 125 types of helicopters in production and more than 341 types of fixed-wing aircraft in production.[16] The various types of aircraft are classified on the basis of the nature of the mission they are expected to perform.

Two general types of fixed-wing aircraft may be identified; namely, combat aircraft and non-combat aircraft. The former are designed to use their own armament for the destruction of enemy forces. In so doing, they are expected to perform a number of specific missions, and corresponding to these primary missions are a variety of aircraft types of varying capabilities. Attack aircraft are designed for attacking surface targets of a tactical nature, as in the case of interdiction and close air support missions. Fighter aircraft are designed to intercept and destroy other aircraft. Bomber aircraft are designed with the primary purpose of carrying and releasing bombs over designated strategic targets. In practice, individual aircraft may fulfil a number of mission requirements. Thus, fighter-bombers are able to intercept and destroy other aircraft, and at the same time are able to carry air-to-surface weapons for ground attack and interdiction requirements (e.g. the GD F-111). Similarily, the Panavia Tornado was designed to meet the multiple mission requirements of the UK, Italy, and West Germany. In addition, combat aircraft are differentiated on the basis of the service roles they play; hence, fighter aircraft are designed to meet the particular needs of the air force (e.g. the MD F-15) and the navy (e.g. the Grumman F-14). With respect to non-combat fixed wing aircraft, a number of different types are also available. Transports are designed to carry ten or more passengers or equivalent cargo and are distinguished from utility aircraft on the basis of maximum take-off weights in excess of 12,500 lbs (5,670 kg.).[17] There is a great variety of transport aircraft, extending from the DHC UV-18A (the military version of the Twin Otter) with a gross weight of 12,500 lbs, to the giant Lockheed C-5A Galaxy with a gross weight of 837,000 lbs. Utility aircraft are generally used to carry small payloads. In addition to transport roles, they perform "odd-jobs" and are occasionally equipped with mission interfaces, for example, photographic reconnaissance equipment. Other military non-combat aircraft include reconnaissance, observation, early-warning, electronic warfare aircraft, and trainers. In some instances, these military aircraft simply utilise commercial airframes suitably re-equipped for military roles, as is the case with the Boeing E-4A/B early warning aircraft which use a Boeing 747 airframe.

Rotary-wing aircraft - helicopters - are similarily differentiated on the basis of mission requirements, having functions such as combat, observation, utility and transport. Specific combat versions include attack (e.g. Hughes AH-64A Apache), anti-tank (e.g. Agusta A129 Mangusta) and anti-submarine warfare (e.g. Sikorsky SH-60B Seahawk). In a similar fashion to fixed-wing aircraft, helicopters frequently combine multiple mission capabilities, and tend to be marketed to meet the needs of the individual services. In sum, the composition of defence output of the aircraft industry is generally determined by the mission requirements laid out by the military. The myriad of aircraft types destined for the defence market, therefore, may be differentiated on the basis of these requirements. What is more, there tends to be a number of potential aircraft with varying capabilities designed for specific missions. Outside of transport and utility roles, aircraft serve as platforms in a weapons system which also consists of weapons (e.g. guns, missiles and bombs) and a means of command and communication.[18]

THE DEMAND FOR MILITARY AIRCRAFT

As a part of conventional military hardware, the demand for military aircraft is dependent on the size of the defence budget. The factors determining the size of the defence budget, and thus the demand for military aircraft, are manifold and complex. Concerning the budget process, former US Secretary of Defense Robert McNamara noted, "(P)olicy decisions must sooner or later be expressed in the form of budget decisions on where to spend and how much".[19] Fundamentally, the size of the defence budget is contingent upon 'national security' considerations, which are inextricably bound up with questions concerning national sovereignty and real or perceived threats to the nation-state. Real and/or perceived threats to national security emanate potentially from both external and internal sources. It follows that the relative size of defence expenditure will generally show a positive relationship with the 'size' of the perceived threats confronting the stability and sovereignty of the state. Moreover, the perception and definition of national security will vary with the political economy and the geopolitical position of various countries. In addition to 'security' and 'nationalistic' factors, the size of the defence budget will also be affected by internal political and organisation pressures (e.g. between the military establishment and civilian groups), the potential development role attributed to defence expenditure, and the fiscal capacity of the state.[20]

Broadly speaking, therefore, the potential market for military aircraft is determined by the size of national defence budgets of the world's countries. In aggregate, this is indicated by world military expenditure and is presented in Table 4.1. In 1983, it amounted to nearly $637 billion at 1980 prices (or

Table 4.1: World Military Expenditure
(in millions of $ at 1980 prices and exchange rates)

Region Year	1973[1]	1974	1975	1976	1977	1978	1979	1980	1981	1982	1983
USA	145237	143656	139277	137126	137126	137938	138796	143981	153334	167673	186544
NATO Total	239988	241262	238859	233236	240340	244975	248151	256278	267118	233826	307171[3]
USSR[2]	118800	120700	122600	124200	126100	123000	129600	131500	133700	135500	137600
WTO Total[2]	128156	130866	133542	135618	137835	140073	141828	143900	146250	148635	151130
Other Europe	12025	12903	13423	14047	14029	14232	14979	15470	15348	15291	15338[3]
Middle East	19672	23431	35076	33670	37256	37017	33893	40695	45990	52350	50000[2]
South Asia	4745	4569	5006	5681	5497	5739	6220	6460	6395	7620	7865
Far East (excl. China)[2]	16730	17970	19930	21750	23220	25630	26610	27600	23790	31100	32950
China[2]	30700	35000	36300	37600	36200	40500	52700	42600	36300	37700	35800
Oceania	4802	3976	3845	3331	3848	3913	4029	4270	4488	4623	4868
Africa (excl. Egypt)	7763	9439	11416	12618	12971	13198	13526[3]	13555[3]	13590[2]	13800[2]	14100[2]
Central America	1242	1351	1502	1700	2173	2312	2468	2484	2625	2815	2825[3]
South America	7959	7998	8911	9444	10170	9980	9941	10230	10584	15745[2]	14745[3]
World Total	473732	493865	508310	514195	523539	537569	559345	563542	577978	613500	636790

Notes: 1. SIPRI Yearbook 1983
2. Estimates with a high degree of uncertainty
3. Uncertain Data.

Source: SIPRI, Yearbook 1984.

between $750-800 billion at current prices), an increase of $23 billion over the 1982 level. Over the period 1972-82, the average real growth rate of world military expenditure was 2.9 per cent.[21] Within this period, the volume increase has accelerated from an average of 2.4 per cent per year between 1975-79, to 3.3 per cent for the 1979-83 period. Geographically, military expenditure is highly variable. In terms of magnitude, the two major power blocs, NATO and the Warsaw Pact, account for about 70 per cent of total world military expenditure. The Soviet Union is overwhelmingly the major source of military expenditure within the Warsaw Pact, accounting for approximately 91 per cent of total outlays. Similarly, NATO expenditure is dominated by the USA which, in 1982, accounted for about 60 per cent of total NATO defence outlays. Overall, NATO military expenditures have experienced a dramatic increase in recent years, rising from a 3.3 per cent real growth rate in 1979-80 to an 8.2 per cent growth rate in 1982-83. In the main, this increase is spurred by the massive rearmament drive in the USA, as indicated by the US growth rate of military expenditure increasing from 3.7 per cent in 1979 to 11.3 per cent in 1982-83.[22] Table 4.2 provides a breakdown of NATO country defence expenditures (and includes France) over the period 1974-83. As can be seen, the USA is obviously the major defence market among these nations, followed by the UK, West Germany, France and Italy.

Military expenditure has also been increasing in areas outside of the two power blocs. During the 1972-83 period, for instance, the average real growth rate of Less Developed Country(LDC) military expenditure exceeded the global average and amounted to five per cent annually. As a result, LDCs increased their share of global military spending by 4.9 per cent from 18.4 per cent to 23.3 per cent.[23] To meet this increasing demand for military hardware, the share of world arms imports attributable to LDCs has increased from 71.5 per cent to 81.9 per cent over the 1972-82 period, or at an average annual real growth rate of 7.1 per cent.[24] The Middle East constitutes the largest arms market among Third World countries, with nearly $46 billion (at 1980 prices) spent on defence in 1981, and an average annual real growth rate of 11.4 per cent between 1972-82.[25] Over this period, imports grew at an average annual (real) rate of 11.5 per cent and accounted for 41.9 per cent of total world arms imports. Among the Middle Eastern countries, the largest military markets are Saudi Arabia, Iran, Israel, Iraq, Syria and Egypt. In addition to the Middle East, other LDC areas

Table 4.2: NATO Military Expenditure
(in millions of $ at 1980 prices and exchange rates)

Country	1974	1975	1976	1977	1978	1979	1980	1981	1982	1983	1
North America											
Canada	4128	4070	4341	4622	4792	4550	4703	4735	5254	5426	3
USA	143656	139277	311712	137126	137938	138796	143981	153884	167673	186544	100
Europe											62
Belgium	3028	3299	3473	3562	3798	3882	3958	3995	3862	3723	2
Denmark	1417	1539	1518	1525	1584	1593	1618	1636	1683	...	1
France	20788	21709	22635	23916	25384	25962	26425	27066	27623	28042	15
West Germany	25335	25219	25044	24952	26007	26355	26692	27114	26759	27355	15
Greece	1781	2288	2508	2658	2715	2630	2276	2693	2746	2748	1
Italy	8304	7728	7687	8257	8608	9154	9578	9781	10463	10892	6
Luxembourg	36.1	38.4	41.1	40.3	43.8	45.1	52.5	54.3	54.8	55.9	neg.
Netherlands	4572	4306	4746	5237	5106	5413	5269	5325	5306	5330	3
Norway	1331	1444	1479	1507	1612	1651	1669	1686	1752	1780	1
Portugal	1572	1083	846	779	788	800	868	864	865	873	.5
Turkey	1793	2870	3295	3173	2906	2578	2442	3015	3296	3214	2
UK	23522	23490	23910	22916	23694	24744	26749	25221	26439	29443	16

Note : 1. Indicator of the relative size of military spending 1983 figures U.S.A. = 100

Source: SIPRI, Yearbook 1984.

experiencing military expenditure growth rates equal to, or in excess of, the average for all LDCs are Africa as a whole (eight per cent) and Latin America (five per cent). Finally, the fastest growth in military expenditures since 1972 has occurred in OPEC member countries, with the average real growth rate per year (1972-82) reaching 13.3 per cent, and the organisation's share of world arms expenditure tripling from 2.4 per cent to 7.5 per cent.

An obvious limitation associated with using aggregate military expenditure as an estimate for demand for warplanes is that military expenditure (the defence budget) consists of a number of spending categories. In particular, military expenditure generally includes, among other things, outlays on military personnel (e.g. pay and various allowances), civilian pay, infrastructure(e.g. construction), operations and maintenance, general equipment and supplies. The relevant component of the defence budget in terms of aircraft demand is that portion allocated for procurement of major equipment and armaments, and more specifically that portion directed towards procuring complete aircraft. In the case of LDCs and in the absence of detailed data, a general estimate may be formulated based on the premiss that most warplanes are produced outside of the Third World. Thus, LDCs must import most major military aircraft. Growth of arms imports by LDC area roughly indicates the potential growth in demand for military aircraft and is presented in Table 4.3. Table 4.4, meanwhile, provides an indication of the numbers of military aircraft (by type) delivered to LDC areas over the successive periods covered in Table 4.3. For AICs, the share of total military expenditure devoted to procurement of major military equipment in 1983 (or 1983-84) ranges from 14.9 per cent in the case of Belgium to 46.9 per cent in the case of France. However, the largest market for military aircraft is the USA. Although its procurement component of the defence budget was significantly less than that of France, the size of the defence budget is far greater than that of France. As elicited from Table 4.5, there has been a general tendency for the procurement aspect of military expenditures to increase since the mid-1970s. In all ten of the countries listed, the procurement portion of the defence budget has increased in 1983 relative to 1974. Of particular significance has been the general increase in US procurement allocations, which have risen to 26.1 per cent in 1983 (1983/84) from a low of 17.4 per cent in 1976 (1976/77). In 1984, procurement outlays amounted to nearly $62 billion, or roughly 27 per cent of total national defence budget outlays, while procurement budget authority came to $86 billion or 32 per cent of total defence budget authority.[26] In fiscal year 1971, 50.8 per cent of total US military procurement was allocated towards the purchase of aircraft and missiles and the corresponding figure for fiscal year 1975 was 52.4 per cent.[27] For fiscal year 1985, aircraft procurement is scheduled to reach $41 billion (in current dollars) or 42.3 per cent of total procurement, added to which is a further $10.1 billion for missile procurement.[28] In general, then, the demand for military aircraft basically parallels the size of the defence budget, and more particularly that part of military expenditure directed towards procurement of aircraft. Current increases in military expenditures and a greater emphasis on procurement of military hardware have had a positive impact on the demand for military aircraft. As evident from the figures, the single largest market for military aircraft is the USA.

The importance of the defence market to the aircraft industry is readily demonstrated from consideration of the dependence of its major producers on defence production. For example, the European aerospace companies Aérospatiale , Dassault-Breguet and MBB depend on defence demand to the extent that 50, 94, and 60 per cent respectively, of their turnover is attributable to defence sales.[29] The major US and UK aerospace firms are similarly dependent on the defence market. Given such dependence, the historical pattern of military demand has significant implications for the aircraft industry. As outlined at the beginning of this section, the demand for military aircraft is a function of military expenditure (the defence budget). Size of the defence budget is, in turn, a function of the real or, what effectively amounts to the same thing, perceived threat confronting the nation-state - as determined by national leaders and the military establishment. The size of the defence budget, therefore, is subject to drastic changes depending on the state of international tension. Consequently, military-industrial production is similarily subject to volatile oscillations, which are reflected in shifts to or from relative tranquility and war. Based on the British experience, though applicable generally, Higham has conceptualised the volatility of defence production (and in particular the aircraft industry) by way of a 'wave-cycle model'.[30] As outlined in Chapter 2, that model indicates that the magnitude and composition of output in the aircraft industry is dependent on the state of international relations, and the perceptions of these by

Table 4.3 : Arms Imports

	Level (millions of 1981 $) and Share (in %) 1972	1982	Average Real Growth Rate (1972-1982)
World	20189 (100)	34424 (100)	6.1
LDCs	14431 (7.15)	28190 (100)	7.1
Africa	952 (4.7)	5144 (14.9)	8.9
East Asia	7605 (37.7)	3366 (9.8)	-5.4
Latin America	758 (3.8)	2631 (7.6)	13.9
Middle East	3880 (19.2)	14421 (41.9)	11.5
Oceania	213 (1.1)	179 (0.5)	6.3
South Asia	719 (3.6)	1730 (5.0)	9.0

Source: Derived from United States, ACDA, World Military Expenditures and Arms Transfers, 1972-82, April 1984.

Table 4.4 : Number of Aircraft Delivered between 1973-77 and 1978-82 to LDCs from Major Suppliers[1]

Aircraft Type	Cumulative 1973-77	Cumulative 1978-82
Combat Aircraft		
Supersonic	3181	3505
Subsonic	1248	565
Helicopters	2562	2435
Other Aircraft[2]	1640	1665

Notes: 1. Major suppliers included are: The Soviet Union (and other Warsaw Pact countries), United States and other NATO countries, France, and China.
2. Other aircraft include reconnaissance aircraft, trainers, transports and utility aircraft.

Source: compiled from United States, ACDA, World Military Expenditures and Arms Transfers; selected years.

Table 4.5: Expenditure for major purchases of military equipment as a share of total military expenditure, fiscal years 1974-83

Country	1974 or 1974/75	1975 or 1975/76	1976 or 1976/77	1977 or 1977/78	1978 or 1978/79	1979 or 1979/80	1980 or 1980/81	1981 or 1981/82	1982 or 1982/83	1983 or 1984/84
Belgium	8.8[1]	9.0	11.0	11.9	13.9	13.1	14.4	14.0	13.6	14.9
Canada	5.9	6.3	8.0	8.5	10.0	13.8	15.4	15.9	17.4	18.8
Denmark	19.3	19.0	19.4	21.8	16.4	16.3	18.1	17.5	16.8	17.3
France	44.7	42.6	41.1	39.2	40.2	43.0	44.5	46.0	47.8	46.9
West Germany	11.9	11.8	13.2	12.5	13.0	13.7	14.8	17.3	17.3	17.6
Italy	15.2	13.9	13.1	15.3	16.2	15.1	17.5	17.3	13.2	18.5
Netherlands	13.2	15.7	15.5	21.0	18.3	20.2	18.0	18.8	20.4	22.0
Norway	11.6	11.6	11.4	14.2	18.3	19.5	19.3	19.0	19.5	18.3
UK	17.2	19.3	20.6	22.0	23.0	23.2	25.2	26.5	25.4	28.2
USA	18.1	17.5	17.4	17.5	20.0	19.5	20.3	21.3	23.9	26.1

Note: 1. Figures are percentages.

Source: SIPRI, Yearbook, 1984.

the national elite.

The wave-cycle model identifies four general phases relating political tension and aircraft production. Peacetime equilibrium is characterised by relative calm and stability in the political sphere, while aircraft manufacturers must grapple with limited military demand for aircraft because of economic and political constraints on defence budgets. At the same time, new-generation aircraft development is limited, reflecting not only smaller defence budgets, but also the absence of an identifiable threat for which a new aircraft may be designed to counter. Upon perception of an identifiable and impending threat, the state and the aircraft industry enter a period of rearmamental instability. For its part, the state initiates the mobilisation of the economy, as manifest through rapidly expanding defence outlays and the creation of mobilisation agencies. In the USA, for example, military outlays increased from $1.2 billion in 1939 (and 13.2 per cent of federal budget outlays) to $23.6 billion (or 68.3 per cent of total federal budget outlays) in 1942.[31] Concomitantly, aircraft production capacity expanded, with factory floor space rising to a wartime peak of 16.26 million m^2 up from a scant 1.21 million m^2 in 1939 and employment increased from 76,000 to 1.7 million. Aircraft sales followed suit, increasing from $244 million in 1939 to $8.2 billion in 1944. The mobilisation period may also bring about a qualitative change in production techniques.

> In Britain, the industry started off early in the twentieth century as a foundling which was taken in by amateur gentlemen as an avocation ... as war loomed on the horizon about 1911 or 1912 the industry began to find itself moving from haphazard hobby full of hope to honest (mass production) manufacturing.[32]

Of course, such rapid expansion of industrial capacity confronts a myriad of supply constraints. To overcome these, the state may establish its own production facilities and/or convert potential factory space of other industrial sectors to wartime production, as was the case in Britain and the USA with the conversion of automobile plants to aircraft production. In terms of the composition of output, aircraft production becomes almost entirely defence oriented. Moreover, the variety of aircraft types is rationalised in order to facilitate mass production. Whereas between 1934 and 1942 the RAF had a total inventory of 75 designs (including those on order in the USA), only eight of these were produced in quantities in excess of five thousand.[33] When the entire economy is fully mobilised, a period of wartime equilibrium exists. During this period, capacity utilisation is maximised, and the composition of aircraft output is governed by strategic priorities and operational requirements as well as by supply constraints. When the perceived threat has diminished, the state and the aircraft industry are faced with a period of demobilisational instability. From the latter's perspective, military demand for aircraft production falls off rapidly and the industry is confronted with serious questions of resource adjustment in preparing for a return to peacetime equilibrium. Again, with respect to the US aircraft industry, sales, production (in terms of millions of airframe pounds per year), and employment dropped from $8.2 billion, 1.1 billion, and 1.7 million during the peak war period in 1944 to $711 million, 24 million, and 221,000 respectively in 1946.[34] Fully half of the sixteen leading aircraft companies identified by the President's Air Policy Commission (i.e. the Finletter Commission) did not show a profit in 1947.[35] Over this period of demobilisational instability, defence outlays declined from a figure of $79.9 billion in 1944 to $13.8 billion in 1947.[36] In terms of the composition of output, the cessation of hostilities shifts the onus of production increasingly towards civil products, although at least a minimum defence capability (surge capability) is maintained as a part of the nation's defence. Yet, as an integral component of national defence, the cyclical nature of the demand presents particular problems to defence planners. The need to maintain a surge capability for periods of emergency must therefore be institutionalised in the defence budget. It is this consideration which tempers the contemporary defence market, and it will be addressed shortly.

THE SUPPLIERS

The design, development and production of major aircraft and aeroengines (and missiles) is undertaken by a number of large corporations commonly denoted as prime contractors. Table 4.6 presents a general overview of the composition of output and size of the major aircraft producers in the USA and Western Europe. As can be seen, most major aerospace firms are engaged in production of a number of aircraft types, with the larger corporations generally producing more types than the smaller firms. Equally evident, is the fact that the major US aerospace companies are substantially larger than their European counterparts. The ownership characteristics also vary between the American and European suppliers. As regards the former, all the major aerospace defence contractors are privately-owned corporations. In the European case, however, there is a marked propensity towards state ownership, with virtually all the major aerospace contractors having substantial state involvement. Recently, though, the UK Government has announced its intention to divest itself of BAe. Political inclinations notwithstanding, the UK Government has pledged to maintain a 'special share' of BAe to ensure at least a watchful eye on the company's future.

Another feature of the American aerospace corporation is its tendency to specialise in particular weapons types for the particular services. Thus, for example, Boeing, GD and RI are bomber enterprises for the USAF. Grumman, LTV and, more recently, MD make fighters for the Navy, while GD and MD have displayed an affinity for manufacturing USAF fighters. In fact, the 'dividing up' of airframe manufacturers dates back to at least 1940. At that time, the military services allocated 'qualified bidder' firms amongst themselves and began augmenting the production capacities of the specific firms within their respective supplier stables. Thus, the Navy maintained jurisdiction over Brewster, Chance Vought, Consolidated, Grumman, Spartan and part of Douglas, while the Army scooped up Beech, Bell, Boeing, Cessna, Curtiss, Fairchild, Lockheed, Martin, North American, Ryan, Stearman, Stinson, Vultee and also part of Douglas.[37]

The foregoing sections have briefly outlined the demand for military aircraft and presented the major aerospace corporations catering to the defence market. The following section will describe the workings of the defence market. Based on the predominance of US aerospace corporations in the defence market, and given that the single largest market for military aircraft is the United States, the focus of the following section will be on the USA.

THE DEFENCE MARKET: THE MILITARY-INDUSTRIAL COMPLEX

In a narrow sense, the MIC and the defence market are synonymous. From a strategic perspective, the volatile nature of the demand for aircraft has significant implications, given the importance of aircraft to national defence. In contrast to the period fol-

Table 4.6 : The Military Aircraft Enterprises

	Attack	Fighter	Bombers	Transports	Utility	Training	Reconnaissance	Observation	Early waiving	Electronic warfare	Patrol and Anti-Submarine	Helicopters	Missiles	Turnover
USA														
Boeing			x	x		x			x				x	$11.1[1]
GD		x	x	x						x			x	$ 7.1[1]
MD	x[a]	x		x			x						x	$ 8.1[1]
RI			x			x		x					x	$ 8.1[1]
Lockheed				x			x				x		x	$ 6.5[1]
Grumman	x	x						x	x	x				$ 2.2[4]
Northrop	x	x				x	x							$ 2.5[4]
UTC												x		$14.7[1]
Hughes												x	x	
Bell												x		
Fairchild	x					x								$ 1.1[4]
France														
Aérospatiale	x[b]			x		x						x	x	3331[2]
Dassault-Breguet	x[c]	x	x			x					x			1967[2]
Germany														
Dornier	b				x									662[2]
MBB						x						x		2391[2]
UK														
BAe	x[a,c]	x	x	x		x	x		x				x	3663[2]
Westland												x		506[2]
Sweden														
SAAB-Scania	x	x				x	x						x	13426[3]
Other Europe														
Fokker				x							x			516[2]
Aeritalia						x								612[2]
Macchi	x					x								
Agusta												x		503[2]

Notes: 1. Source Fortune 30 April 1984 p. 44 (in 1983 $ billions).
2. AW & ST, 12 March 1984 p. 74. Figures are 1982 million European Currency Units. In 1982 1 ECU was equivalent to $0.98.
3. In Ball and Leitenberg (eds.), The Structure of the Defense Industry, 1983, p. 152. Figure is for 1979 and in million Skr.
4. Fortune 2 May 1983, p. 238 in 1982 sales in billions of $.

lowing World War I, the USA emerged from World War II with a distinct geopolitical vision, that is to say, Pax Americana. As a part of its military role in world affairs, the United States required a strong aircraft industry. Yet, disarmamental instability left the industry in a shambles. In recognition of the industry's dependence on military demand, and consistent with the nation's global objectives, the Finletter Commission outlined the principles of what would be coined the MIC.[38] Specifically, the Commission argued,

> In a freely competitive economy the number of companies manufacturing a particular product levels off at a point determined by the ordinary laws of economics. In the case of the aircraft industry, however, it would be dangerous to rely only on the operation of these laws. The demand factor fluctuates so violently from peace to war. If a reasonable degree of expansibility is to be maintained for periods of emergency, it is necessary to exercise some industry wide control in the interests of national security. It may even be desirable to keep a few marginal manufacturers in business who might be forced out if the normal laws of supply and demand were allowed to operate...[39]

Moreover, in order to facilitate design, development and production continuity, "each company should, at any given time, have at least one type in production, one in development, and one in the design-study stage".[40]

Structure

Defence production is characterised by a highly concentrated market structure. On the demand side, the government is the sole purchaser of defence output (although export sales are also a source of demand) and thus is a monopsonist. While the Department of Defense (DoD) is formally the single buyer, in reality, it consists of a number of different factions. To be specific, the various services - the Army, Navy, Marines, and the Air Force - each have particular requirements and compete with each other for defence dollars and, in so doing, influence defence demand. Similarily, within the individual services themselves, there are a variety of different factions with competing objectives and visions, which also influence the nature of demand.[41] On the supply side, there are a handful of large corporations, the prime contractors, which form a monopolistic/oligopolistic structure. The structural framework of the defence market, therefore, is typified by a monopsonistic - monopolistic/oligopolistic setting.

Defence demand is realised through the allocation of prime contracts for major weapons systems. Not surprisingly, given the market structure, the allocation of these awards tends to be concentrated in the hands of the major defence contractors. Historically, the top 100 defence contractors have generally received about 60 per cent of the US military prime contract awards since World War II. In fact, between June 1940 and fiscal year 1965, the top 50 prime contractors received from 56.3 per cent to 66.9 per cent of the total major awards.[42] The historical legacy has remained intact to this day. In fiscal year 1983, the top 100 defence contractors received $89.6 billion (or 69.9 per cent) out of total military prime contracts valued at $128.2 billion.[43] In the same year, the top ten defence contractors, nine of which were major aerospace corporations, received prime contracts worth roughly $44 billion or 34.4 per cent of the total major awards.[44] Further, the tendency for particular defence contractors to specialise in the production of specific weapons systems obviously results in high concentration ratios in those product areas. The evolution of the industrial structure for selected aircraft types is depicted in Table 4.7 and illustrates the extent of market concentration. Thus, in fiscal year 1967, for example, the top four firms received 97 per cent of the major contract awards for fighter and attack aircraft. Meanwhile, the top eight firms received virtually all the main contract awards for most military aircraft.[45] Judging from Table 4.7, it is reasonable to suppose that the concentration ratios have increased since 1967. It should be mentioned, moreover, that not only are defence contracts concentrated among the top defence contractors, but these firms are also among the largest corporations in the United States. Fully 75 per cent of the top 100 defence contractors were among the top Fortune 500 list of firms, and 29 out of the Fortune top 50 were major defence firms in 1968.[46] In 1983, nine out of the top ten defence contractors were all among the Fortune top 60.[47] In general, then, the major military prime contracts are concentrated in the hands of few large corporations, many of which are major aircraft (and aeroengine) producers.

The obverse of concentrated defence contract allocations is a marked dependence on defence sales by the recipient firms, especially aerospace companies. This acute dependence on defence production is vividly illustrated in Table 4.8 for selected US aerospace firms. In the cases of GD, MD, Lockheed, Grumman and Northrop, dependence is especially pronounced over the period covered, with defence sales accounting for well over half of the firms' turnover. Boeing, though somewhat less dependent than the other firms, none the less, relies on defence contracts for its survival. RI is also heavily dependent on defence sales in the first and last period. The smaller portion of its turnover directed towards the DoD during the 1970s is offset by the fact that RI

Table 4.7: Competing Firms in the American Aircraft Industry, 1960-76

	1960		1968		1976	
Fighter and attack planes	Lockheed Convair Douglas McDonnell Vought	Republic Northrop Grumman Rockwell (L.A.) Rockwell	Douglas McDonnell Vought Republic GD (Forth Worth)	Northrop Grumman RI (L.A.) RI (Columbus)	MD Vought Fairchild	GD (Fort Worth) Northrop Grumman
Bombers	Boeing GD (Fort Worth) Rockwell	Lockheed Douglas	Boeing GD (Fort Worth) Rockwell		Boeing RI	
Military transports	Boeing Lockheed Douglas	Fairchild Grumman Convair	Boeing Lockheed Douglas		Boeing Lockheed MD	
Commercial transports	Boeing Douglas Lockheed	Fairchild Convair	Boeing Douglas Lockheed		Boeing MD Lockheed	
Helicopters	Boeing Lockheed Bell Sikorsky Hughes	Kaman Hiller Gyrodyne Cessna	Boeing Lockheed Bell Sikorsky	Hughes Kaman Hiller	Boeing Bell Hughes[1] Sikorsky	

Note: 1. Hughes Helicopters has been acquired by MD. See AW & ST, 2 January 1984, p. 22.

Source: Gansler, 1980.

received NASA contracts in excess of $500 million in six out of the ten years covered.[48] Consequently, the structure of the defence market in the USA is best described as a highly 'imperfect' entity characterised by a monopsonist - monopolist/oligopolist framework. The historical evolution of this structure has given rise to a unique set of market conditions, and it is to these that we now turn.

Defence Contracting

The crux of the defence market is the relationship between the defence contractors and the state. Ostensibly, in the United States, this relationship is expected to be at arm's length, given that the defence contractors are private corporations and outside of direct state authority. However, in their role as 'guardians' of national security, and as 'national' assets (albeit privately owned), the defence contractors do not expect to be compelled to do business at a loss and, furthermore, rely upon government support to maintain capacity and ensure at least minimal profit levels. To facilitate these ends, the institutional milieu in which defence contracting occurs resembles an 'Iron Triangle',

> A political relationship that brings together three key participants in a clearly delineated area of policy-making; the Federal bureaucracy, the key committees and members of Congress, and the private interest.[49]

In the context of defence contracting, the relevant participants are the DoD, the House and Senate Armed Services Committees and Defense Appropriations Subcommittee, and the members of Congress whose districts contain defence firms; and the firms and various participants in the defence industry. The outcome of these affinities is a "community of shared assumptions" which blurs the distinctions between public and private interest.[50] As a result, industry may appropriate aspects of state authority, and in the case of defence, the defence contractors play a role in defining national security and its requirements.

The institutionalised interdependence between the state and the defence firms stands in sharp contrast to the usual customer-producer relationship extant in the civilian economy. As such, and in contradistinction to that posited in conventional theory, the defence market exhibits a variety of special features. In the first place, only a select few

Table 4.8 : Dependence on Defence Production of Selected US Aerospace Firms (DoD Contracts: Amount and % Total Sales)

Firm	1961-1967[1]		1970-1979[2]		Fiscal 1983[3]	
	$m	%	$m	%	$m	%
GD	8824	67	17901	74	6818	95
MD	7681	75	18461	56	6143	76
Boeing	7183	54	12039	29	4423	40
Lockheed	10619	88	17473	56	4006	62
RI	6265	57	8322[5]	20	4545	56
UTC	5311	57	13734	33	3867	26
GE	7066	19			4518	17
Grumman	2492	67	10773	90	2298[4]	
Northrop	1434	61	6175	58	847[4]	
Raytheon	2324	55			2728	46
LTV	1744	70			1343[4]	

Notes: 1. Source: Carroll W. Purcell, ed., The Military-Industrial-Complex, 1972, Appendix 5.
2. Derived from Gordon Adams, The Politics of Defense Contracting (Transaction Books, New Brunswick, 1981). The figures do not include NASA contracts.
3. Fortune, 30 April 1984.
4. AW & ST, 23 April 1984.
5. RI receives significant NASA contracts although these are not included here.

firms are actually eligible to bid on defence contracts. The DoD has a highly complex set of procurement regulations with literally thousands of pages of text outlining the manner in which defence contracting is to be undertaken. Conforming to these regulations requires special accounting procedures as well as specific quality-control and production procedures. In this fashion, the DoD (the purchaser) is able to impinge upon the internal decision-making of the firm. As a consequence, traditional supplier decisions such as whether a particular component is to be produced in-house or subcontracted may in fact be made by the defence department. In view of this highly regulated environment (a somewhat unique environment in that the regulator and the buyer are the same), firms simply submitting a lowest bid on a particular project need not be awarded the contract. In addition to cost considerations, defence contractors must be 'responsible', that is, the contractor must demonstrate its capability to perform successfully in the defence environment - a task which presupposes defence experience and a reasonably large resource base.[51] That a large resource basis is required is due to the high cost, in terms of technical expertise and time, of preparing contract proposals. The proposal of LTV submitted to the Navy for a new aeroplane consisted of 194 bound volumes totalling some 82,000 pages (and yet the company failed to win the contract).[52] The above example points to another aspect of the defence market which has grave implications for defence firms and generally differentiates this market from civilian ones. Specifically, competition among defence contractors for a particular proposal usually involves an 'all or nothing' situation. While civilian firms compete and advertise to capture relative market shares, there is no comparable situation for military prime contract awards: rather, the DoD mostly selects a single supplier to produce the entire requirement.[53] Firms, therefore, are required to allocate substantial resources for developing new products (i.e. major aircraft and weapons systems) embodying extensive technological sophistication (and thus significant R & D efforts) and present these proposals in a highly structured way, yet without any assurance of a possible market. The complexity of the process presents a unique environment of uncertainty in the defence market. Thus, in contrast to the civilian economy,

> (T)he weapons acquisition process is characterised by a unique set of uncertainties which differentiates it from other economic activity. To be sure, uncertainty is a pervasive feature of all economic activity, and most of all the uncertainties in weapons acquisition have their commercial counterparts. But there is uniqueness in both the magnitude and the diverse sources of uncertainty in weapons acquisition.[54]

Indeed, not only is there an inherent technological uncertainty, but a myriad of political and bureaucratic pressures ultimately colour the acquisition process.[55]

Figure 4.1 indicates that the lion's share of defence contracts is awarded on a non-competitive basis. Approximately 90 per cent of total dollars allocated to defence contractors is done on the basis of negotiation, and the remaining 10 per cent is allocated on an open format. Ostensibly, the DoD is pledged to make use of competitive bidding in the awarding of defence contracts. Notwithstanding this

Figure 4.1 : Trends in the Awarding of Department of Defense Contracts

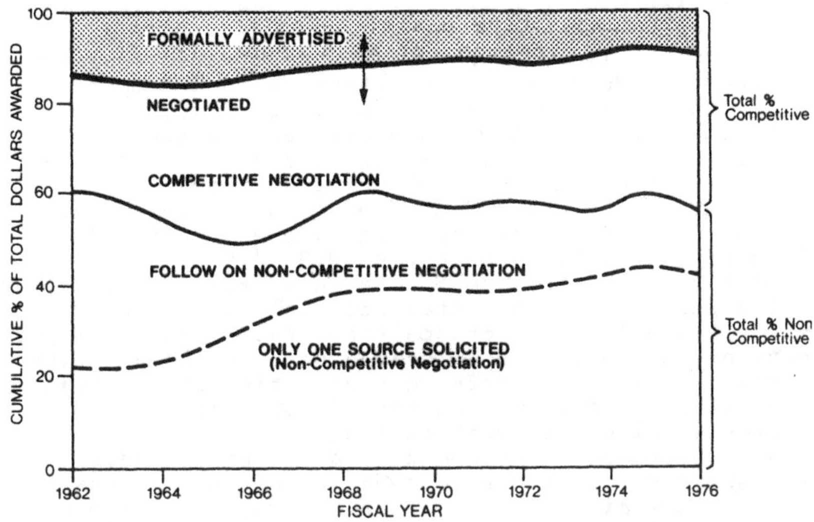

commitment, most defence contracts are awarded under 'exceptions' to competitive bidding requirements. Among these exceptions are: public exigency, experimental, developmental, or research work, specialised capital investment, critical schedules, prior investments, and national security and/or industrial mobilisation considerations.[56] The last consideration is generally held as sacrosanct. Yet even detractors of the existing procurement patterns recognise the need for some flexibility on this account as the recent US Senate proposals to increase competitive bidding on defence contracts duly attests. But two exceptions to the proposed Bill, which is designed to increase competition in the award of defence contracts, are made explicit. In the first place, it may be necessary to award the contract to a single source in order "to maintain an essential industrial capacity, achieve industrial mobilisation or establish or maintain an essential research capability". Secondly, exception is justified when, "disclosure of the agency's needs to more than one source will compromise the national security."[57] However, the institutionalised interdependence of the defence contractors and the state (the Iron Triangle) acts to make the determination of "essential" and "national security" extremely problematic - in so far as the individuals making these decisions belong to a "community of shared assumptions".

In fact, most contracts are awarded on an exclusively non-competitive basis, owing to either a single-source solicitation, or as a negotiated follow-on contract. Moreover, the extent of non-competitive contracting displays a positive relationship with the size of the defence contract in question. A DoD report revealed, for example, that in fiscal year 1972, contracts in the $100,000 realm had 57.9-59.6 per cent of the dollars awarded on a non-competitive basis, while the corresponding figure for the $1 million to $10 million range was 60.8-68.9 per cent. Significantly, those contracts in excess of $10 million (39.2 per cent of the total dollars), which encompass virtually all major aerospace contracts, had 76.8 per cent of the contracts allocated on a non-competitive basis.[58] Obviously, defence contracting is a special kind of business. The extent of non-competitive awards is also a product of the stage of the contracting process. Frequently, a number of major aerospace corporations compete in the initial phases of a future aircraft programme. Thus, for example, LTV (V-1100), Northrop (P-530, P-610), GD (GD-401), Boeing (Boeing-618) and Lockheed (X-27) all responded to the USAF Systems Command Aeronautical Systems Division (ASD) request for proposals for a lightweight fighter. Of these, the ASD recommended the selection of the GD and one of the Northrop designs as the competing prototype developments, and awarded $37.9 million and $39 million respectively for this purpose. Subsequently, the two firms went all out to win the contract with the eventual winner being the GD-401 (restyled the YF-16 and later, the F-16).

At the point when a particular prototype (contractor) is selected for full-scale engineering and production, the market structure is significantly altered. Although only two competitors may be vying for a single contract, competition may be extremely intense, so much so that, "competition in the limiting case of only two rivals may be just as effective from a behavioural standpoint as competition among a few firms."[59] However, once a contractor is selected, the government is 'locked in' to a single source of supply for the duration of the project. The market structure is, therefore, radically transformed into a monopsony-monopoly situation. Much of the government's previous bargaining leverage is lost owing to the highly specialised nature of capital investment associated with major aircraft production. In preparing for the renewed B-1B programme, for instance,

RI invested $150 million for production machinery and an additional $150 million for facility construction, including an $83 million final assembly plant at Palmdale, California.[60]

In the circumstances, the firms are able to pass the burden of cost-overruns and technical problems on to the purchaser, the DoD. The all or nothing nature of defence contracting coupled with the transformation of the market structure upon the award of a major contract induces firms to 'buy-in'. This entails a firm submitting a low initial bid for a particular project, then, assuming its proposal is technically acceptable, renegotiating the terms of the contract once selected as a prime contractor. A successful buy-in can guarantee the firm a stable production rate for many years. Notably, however, the genesis of most production contracts rests in antecedent R & D contracts. It is in this light that Boeing, Lockheed and MD reportedly employed some 6,000 specialists to formulate their proposals for the C-5A programme.[61] Successful competition for these contracts is essential, since "a contractor that gets a project to the prototype stage often has a procurement package that is almost unstoppable."[62] Attesting to the strength of the momentum is the case of the B-1 bomber. In 1977, after $6.1 billion had been spent and four prototypes nearly completed, President Carter suddenly cancelled the project, denouncing it at one point as "wasteful".[63] A project of the magnitude of the B-1 is not easily quashed, however, and it was subsequently re-established by the Reagan administration with a cost estimate of over $20 billion.

A salient characteristic of the defence market for aircraft is that the contract terms rest primarily on the grounds of technical criteria at the virtual expense of cost-competitive (price) criteria. This technological imperative promotes, "rapid technical change, in which every component part of successive weapons systems is pursued up to and beyond the state of the art."[64] Underpinning this technological imperative is substantial state underwriting of aerospace R & D expenditure, as evidenced in Table 4.9. Clearly, throughout the 1970s the technological dynamic of the industry was driven by the liberal provision of R & D monies to the main aerospace defence contractors. In virtually all instances, US Government sponsored R & D exceeded that undertaken by the firms themselves. The fiscal year 1983 figures on DoD prime RDT & E contract awards (those with a net value over $25,000) further vindicates the technological predominance of major aerospace defence contractors. Of the top ten award recipients, nine are major aerospace corporations with contracts valued at greater than $7.3 billion.[65] As was the case with the distribution of prime military production awards, prime military RDT & E contracts are concentrated among the top defence contractors which tend to be aerospace corporations. This positive relationship lends credence to the importance of antecedent R & D to future production contracts. The concentration of R & D contracts in the hands of the major contractors, therefore, reinforces the concentration of defence production.

The dimensions of technological change in the aircraft industry, including the defence segment of the business, are discussed in Chapters 2 and 6, and thus will only be considered here from the perspective of defence contracting. Technological competition in the aerospace defence market emphasises the progressive improvement of a particular set of performance characteristics.[66] Coined "baroque" by Kaldor, this technological dynamic is characterised by trend improvements and the multiplication of roles, and results in aircraft which can fly at greater speed with greater and more effective payloads. By virtue of the historic relationship between the military and the defence contractors, the pattern of technological change is 'conservative' in that neither the prime aerospace defence contractors nor the generals are prepared to develop revolutionary weapons systems which would undermine their own institutional basis. (Noteworthy in this respect is the ongoing saga of the relative merits of long-range manned bombers in an era of ICBMs). This technological change is motivated by a number of factors. From the perspective of the prime contractors, it is the desire to capture major defence contracts which are awarded, by and large, on technical grounds. From the DoD perspective, there is the imperative to stay ahead of the enemy. In terms of the latter, the DoD defines a 'mission' for which a major aircraft may be developed. The determination of this 'mission' is based in varying degrees on the perceived threat confronting the nation's security. In the absence of detailed information concerning the enemy's capabilities, the DoD is forced to formulate threat scenarios, which may or may not be realistic. The problem in ascertaining what constitutes a plausible threat and what does not is that the relevant information may be sensitive and thus not divulged. While it is expected that the military defines the mission requirement and awards R & D monies to potential suppliers to design and develop an appropriate

Table 4.9: Dependence of US Aerospace Firms on State Sponsored R & D

Firm	Total Sponsored by US Government, 1970-79 ($ million)[1]	Total Company-Sponsored 1970-79 ($ million)[1]	Fiscal 1983 DoD Prime RDT & E Awards ($ million) and Rank[2]	
Boeing	5622.8	1884.1[3]	1703.5	1
GD	3614.4	207.8[3]	643.5	7
Grumman	2306.0	3119.0	131.8	28
Lockheed	4982.8	473.6		9,22[7]
MD	6571.4	1634.3	647.3	5
Northrop	821.7	229.3[4]	245.5	16
RI	6884.4	638.9[5]	1171.7	2
UTC	2252.8	2781.1[6]	339.4	10

Notes:
1. Derived from Gordon Adams, The Politics of Defense Contracting, 1981.
2. AW & ST, 18 June 1984 p. 85.
3. For the period 1973-79.
4. For the period 1971, 1973-79
5. For the period 1973-79
6. For the period 1972-79
7. Lockheed Missiles and Space Co. ranked number 9, while Lockheed Corp. ranked number 22. Their respective awards were $509.2 million and $194.4 million.

weapons system, the institutional interrelationship between the military and industry has bridged the gap between the two stages. In effect, defence contractors have internalised the process, since defining a mission often presages the definition of a new weapons system. A Raytheon (a major aerospace defence contractor) representative aptly reveals this state of affairs.

> The day is past when the military requirement for a major weapons system is set up by the military and passed on to industry to build the hardware. Today, it is more likely that the military requirement is the result of joint participation of military and industrial personnel, and it is not unusual for industry's contribution to be a key factor. Indeed, there are highly placed military men who sincerely feel that industry currently is setting the pace in the research and development of new weapons systems.[67]

Two levels of technological evolution may be discerned. On the one hand, there is the successive improvement of a particular aircraft type as indicated by varying marks (e.g. F-16A, F-16C). On the other hand, there is a compelling force driving weapons systems to the fringe-of-the-art. Hence, the USAF's advanced tactical fighter programme, the replacement of the F-15 air superiority fighter, is expected to incorporate the most advanced technology, including the use of very-high-speed-integrated-direct technology, to integrate avionics systems and advanced composite materials.[68] Similarily, the US Army's current LHX helicopter programme advocates technological advances in rotor design, composite structures, flight control systems, drag reduction, propulsion, mission equipment and cockpit automation and integration.[69] Equally indicative of contemporary technological change in aircraft is the multiplicity of mission requirements and increasing reliance on avionics systems. In terms of the latter, whereas about ten per cent of the engineering effort on the Army/Bell AH-1 (one of the helicopters to be replaced by the LXH) was devoted to avionics, the corresponding figure for the LHX is expected to be around 50 per cent.[70] With respect to the former, the LHX is being designed to replace eight existing types of helicopters utilised in light utility, scout and attack roles. An industry spokesman captured the essence of the technological imperative of the LHX in these words: "We are working at the cutting edge of technology across the board ... there is not one area in which we're not challenging our technical capabilities."[71]

The technological imperative built into the defence market does have a number of serious side effects. Most obvious has been the rapid escalation of programme costs. The LHX, for example, will be the most expensive helicopter programme ever undertaken by the Army, with development costs pegged at $3 billion and procurement costs at more than $30 billion.[72] The projected cost of the LHX is, in fact, a logical outcome of the general trend pervading all major aircraft developments. As technical complexity has increased so too has costs. A caveat is in order, however, in that it is difficult to draw a strict comparison between say the Supermarine Spitfire of 1936 (cost of about $300,000) and the Panavia Tornado of the later 1970s (cost of around $10 million) since in many respects they are qualitatively different products. The fact remains, though, that cost escalation is universal.[73] The origins of cost increases are manifold. In part, unit costs may increase due to continued improvements in aircraft capabilities. The Navy's decision to equip its F/A-18s with forward looking infrared and laser spot trackers is estimated to add approximately $2 million to the aircraft's $24.1 million (in 1982) price tag.[74] On the other hand and perhaps more importantly, there are costs associated with working at the technological frontier and attempting to integrate multiple systems into a single aircraft as is blatantly evident in the massive cost overruns of the Lockheed C-5 and GD F-111 programmes. The B-1 programme, moreover, had a cost escalation of 18 per cent over seven years which, in view of the sheer scale of the venture, amounted to $3 billion dollars. In the case of the Panavia Tornado, the decision to increase engine thrust resulted in a ten-fold increase in development cost over the original estimates.[75] In most major aerospace programmes, in fact, there is a constant revision of technical criteria and specifications which escalate development costs, and which necessitate constant contract negotiations (and frequently result in cost-plus type contracts). Many defence development contracts have these cost-growth clauses imputed at the outset. Fairchild's recent contract for the USAF next generation trainer provides an example. The contract award to Fairchild is a 'fixed-price' contract for $104 million for the design, development, fabrication, test and delivery of prototype aircraft. Its terms allow the service to absorb 85 per cent of cost increases during the programme up to a maximum of 125 per cent cost growth, beyond which Fairchild is wholly responsible. Total costs for the trainer programme are estimated at $3 billion. In addition to the cost growth problems arising from technical complexity, programme stretch-outs also result in cost overruns. In the case of the A-10 attack aircraft, the primary cause of cost growth was attributable to programme slippage, which resulted in cost increases of 17 per cent.[76] Slippage in this case was largely ascribable to a reduction in production rate of from 20 to 14 machines per month. To offset the problem of cost growth, be it of technical origin or programme management, the DoD has increasingly instituted multiyear funding contracts, as opposed to the historical use of annual allocations, to allow contractors to order long-lead-time requirements and realise economies of scale, quantity purchase benefits and greater production continuity. The savings may, in fact, be quite substantial. At the micro level, Grumman estimated that multiyear contract savings on the purchase of power unit nose landings for a combat aircraft amounted to 41 per cent (or about $5 million). At the macro-level, programme saving can be significant. In the above case, the multiyear procurement award was expected to allow the Navy to procure 39 E-2Cs for the price of 35. In reference to smaller countries, the acceleration of production costs has compelled them to enter into international joint ventures in order to share the burden of development and production outlays over longer production runs. Given the importance of technology to contemporary defence aircraft, and given the political aversion to technological dependence in key strategic industries, European nations have banded together to attempt to increase production runs and spread development costs, as is evident in the current European military helicopter programmes: EH-101 (Italy-UK), PAH-2 (France-West Germany); and NH-90 (Italy, West Germany, the Netherlands, France and perhaps the UK). As an indication of the relative disparity in production runs, the LHX's development cost of $3 billion is expected to be spread over programme procurement of some 5,000-6,000 aircraft, whereas the PAH-2 procurement has been tentatively set at 400 aircraft.

The Kurth Follow-On Imperative: The Strategic-Political Interface

Conforming to the Finletter Commission's assessed need to maintain a "reasonable degree of expansibility" for periods of emergency, the awarding of prime military aircraft contracts in the recent period has conformed to a follow-on imperative.[77] Major aircraft manufacturers require relatively constant design, development, and production activity in order to keep vital design and production teams together. From a strategic perspective, it is argued that at least a minimum surge capability is required for national security. Simply, surge capability is the ability to rapidly expand production in periods when threats to national security loom large. The precarious nature of defence demand, as encapsulated in the wave-cycle model, requires some institutionalised basis by which a degree of stability may be afforded to the aircraft industry while, at the same time, vouchsafing national security. As we have stressed, the state's principal means for accomplishing this task is through the allocation of prime military contract awards. As a matter of course, all DoD requests for funding for particular programmes must be approved by Congress. Defence spending on major prime contract awards to large aerospace corporations possesses an important feature not lost on astute Congressmen. In contrast to the diffuse nature of many social welfare expenditures (e.g. unemployment benefits or health services), major defence awards are a very visible and positive form of government expenditure. For example, the $20.5 billion B-1B programme is expected to generate 4,700 jobs at a newly constructed Palmdale, California, facility (costing $83 million) and utilise 5,300 subcontractors including a $1.5 billion award to LTV Corporation.[78] By the same token, failure to win such awards, or cancellation of them, has a negative impact on the communities hosting the firms in question (recall Table 2.5). The cancellation of the original B-1, for example, was expected to result in over 10,000 layoffs at RI alone, never mind the thousands of subcontractors dependent on the programme.[79] The pervasiveness of political influence on defence expenditures has been systematically studied by R. J. Johnston.[80] In particular, Johnston has attempted to ascertain whether states represented on the relevant committees and subcommittees will receive a greater per capita allocation of defence dollars, under its various spending categories, than the states not represented on those committees. By comparing the mean per capita expenditure per state Johnston discovered that, in terms of prime military supply and R & D contracts, there is evidence of substantial pork-barrel activity in the House and Senate Armed Services Committees. Thus he concludes, "The main contracting sectors, apparently are the major areas of pork-barrel politics within the defence budget ... (and) the main pork-barreling for these contracts appears to take place in the House Armed Services Committees and its Subcommittees".[81] Indeed, at the end of a long career as chairman of one of those committees, Mendall Rivers (Democrat-South Carolina) wryly noted that the rationale underpinning the location of a Lockheed plant in his state reduced to: "I asked them to put a li'l old plant here."[82] Given that for every billion dollars of defence purchases an estimated 35,000 jobs are created, and that ten states (including the important electoral college states of California, Texas, and New York) receive in the order of 65 per cent of the total prime military contract awards, political influence on the contracting process is inevitable.[83]

The twin concerns of maintaining a strategic surge capability and a politically acceptable level of development and production activity conflate in the follow-on system. Table 4.10 indicates the allocation of selected prime military contract awards for a number of the large aerospace firms over the period fiscal years 1981 to 1985. As is evident, all the major aerospace firms have been kept relatively active with a number of major programmes. In all years covered, with the exception of RI in 1981, each main aerospace corporation has received major contracts amounting to at least $500 million, with most receiving in excess of a billion dollars since 1982. It is fairly obvious then, that a concerted effort is being made to ensure relatively high activity levels in those firms. A problem occurs when scheduled production (and/or development) runs are nearing their completion. It is at this stage that the follow-on imperative becomes operational. The follow-on system basically parallels the broad tenets laid down by the Finletter Commission's report to the President. In order to counter the inherent instability of government policy and the business cycle, state procurement policies have evolved in such a manner that successive weapons systems 'follow' each other on the production line. Specifically, as one production line begins to phase out manufacture of a particular aircraft (or missile) type, a government contract is soon awarded to ensure that the factory remains continuously active. As argued earlier, R & D contracts are vital antecedents to production contracts, and thus are also amenable to the basic precepts of the system. The follow-on system, therefore, was responsible for the revitalising of Boeing throughout the postwar period with successive defence orders for the B-50, C-97, KC-97, B-47, B-52 and KC-135 underpinning the firm's success well into the 1960s.[84] In the

Table 4.10 : Selected Prime Contract Awards to Major Aerospace Corporations

(dollar values in brackets - in millions)

	Fiscal 1985[2]	Fiscal 1984	Fiscal 1983	Fiscal 1982	Fiscal 1981
Boeing[3]	KC-135 (986) B-52G/H(229) CH-47 (498)	KC-135 (552) B-52G/H(149) CH-47 (358)	KC-135 (496) B-52G/H(389) E-3A (217) CH-47 (236)	KC-135 (271) B-52G/H(389) E-3A (310.3) CH-47 (310)	KC-135 (119) B-52G/H(459) E-3A (335)
GD	F-16 (2,655)	F-16 (2,655)	F-16 (2,334)	F-16 (2,330)	F-16 (1,995)
RI	B-1B (8,220)	B-1B (6,360)	B-1B (4,737)	B-1B (2,093)	
Lockheed	C-5B (2,238) TR-1/U-2(365) P-3C (522)	C-5B (1,367) TR-1/U-2(218) P-3C (312)	C-5B (803) TR-1/U-2(195) C-5A (196) P-3C (318)	C-5 (270) C-5 (202) TR-1 (153) P-3C (461)	C-5 (178.5) TR-1 (125.3) P-3C (348)
MD[4]	F-15 (4,228) KC-10A (718) F/A-18 (2,818) AV-8B (1,010)	F-15 (1,655) KC-10A (811) F/A-18 (2,527) AV-8B (1,015)	KC-10 (919) F-18 (2598) AV-8B (1,033)	F-15 (1207) KC-10A (360) F/A-18 (2623) AV-8B (896)	KC-10A (327) F-15 (1101) F/A-18 (2054) AV-8B (331)
Grumman	F-14 (1001) EA-6B (440) E-2C (404) A-6E (276)	F-14 (1021) EA-6B (527) E-2C (371) A-6E (244)	F-14 (1,140) EA-6B (345.1) E-2C (346) A-6E (249)	F-14 (1,206) E-2C (285) EA-6B (288) A-6E (295)	F-14 (925) E-2C (261) A-6E (252) EA-6B (228)

Notes: 1. The figures were derived from AW & ST annual reports on the DoD aerospace budget. The programme dollar amounts awarded for the various fiscal years was assumed to be the figures reported in AW & ST as the previous year's award. For example, the fiscal 1984 figure was taken from the fiscal 1985 issue, which lists the administration's current request, and the previous year's figure.
2. Administration's fiscal 1985 request, subject to change.
3. The Boeing B-52G/H, and Boeing B-52H programme.
4. The F/A-18 programme also involves Northrop, and the AV-8B programme involves BAe.

Source: Compiled from AW & ST various issues.

later 1960s and early 1970s, Boeing was again in a precarious position, facing reduced demand in both civil and defence markets. Company employment plunged from a peak Vietnam War level of 148,000 to 54,000 by mid-1971.[85] The firm's fortunes took a turn for the better, however, with the receipt of E-3 and E-4 aircraft procurement awards from the DoD.[86] Similarily, Boeing's Vertol Division lost two successive major helicopter awards and was subsequently awarded a CH-47 upgrading contract. Kurth went so far as to examine the allocation of prime contracts throughout the 1960 to 1972 period. The follow-on model appears relevant in no less than eleven out of twelve major contracts during the period examined.[87] The selection of the GD F-111 against military advice was occasioned by that firm's Convair division recording losses of some $400 million. The awarding of this contract to the firm literally saved it from impending bankruptcy.[88] Evidently, the follow-on system is alive and well in the 1980s, for, phase out of the A-10 attack aircraft at Fairchild's Farmingdale, New York, plant was prompty co-ordinated with the planned phase in of the USAF next generation trainer (T-46A) with a scheduled production run of 650 aircraft. Choice of Fairchild for the trainer rested partly on the grounds "that Fairchild's A-10 production is winding down in 1985, and the (trainer) production will fit in after that date."[89] To ease the transition, the DoD awarded Fairchild $29 million for termination costs.[90] Other comparable machinations concern the apportioning of work between Lockheed and MD on transports (C-5 and C-17 respectively; the latter of which is now projected to go into full-scale production at the Long Beach plant) and MD and Northrop on tactical fighters (F-18).[91] The foregoing evidently indicates that technological superiority and the supposed 'all or nothing' nature of defence contracts must at least be tempered by inevitable political influence.

In addition to formal budget allocations by the DoD, contractors can rely on Congress to provide minimal funding to help tide over their fortunes. Thus, the state may prolong production contracts or provide R & D monies through the use of 'add-ons'. Specifically, these are subsidiary allocations, not necessarily requested by the military, but added as supplementary contracts following political lobbying. LTV's A-7D aircraft procurement programme underwent several contract extentions. For example, LTV received a $115 million contract to supply 24 A-7D aircraft to the National Guard (despite the DoD not requesting funds) as a direct result of Congress overriding President Ford's decision to withdraw funds from the programme.[92] Similarily, Congress authorised $53.9 million for the procurement of eleven AH-1S helicopters despite the Reagan administration's decision not to procure the aircraft. The Congressional action came at a time when Bell, the AH-1S manufacturer, was undergoing extensive layoffs at its Fort Worth facility.[93]

The interplay of strategic interest and political sensitivity is also apparent where questions of foreign sources of supply are concerned. From a strategic perspective, there is a general preference to buy defence items from domestic suppliers since the advent of hostilities may place the nation in a precarious position if supplies are somehow truncated. From a political perspective, defence dollars are visible evidence of government activity, and thus are a means to influence votes. Imports remove this tangible source of political jockeying. Furthermore, defence contracts can be disbursed in the name of job creation. In light of the above, it is not surprising that a number of restrictions are invoked to secure the domestic market for indigenous producers. The most obvious of these is the 'Buy America Act' (noted in Chapter 3) which provides domestic producers with a six per cent cushion against foreign competition. In fact, domestic producers may at times enjoy as much as a 12 per cent cushion if they happen to be located in areas experiencing high unemployment.[94] More importantly, the 'specialty metals clause' of the Defense Appropriations Bill effectively closes the US defence market to foreign firms because nearly all arms components include some specialty metals.[95] To give an example, the replacement for the CT-39 (Rockwell Sabreliner) in the USAF had to be assembled in the United States and use an airframe produced in the USA.[96] Similarily, in a sudden turn of events, the UK Martin-Baker ejection seat selected (following a competition) for the F/A-18 was subsequently rejected by a Congressional edict, and replaced by an American produced seat. Political sensitivity to foreign sourcing of defence equipment is no less pervasive elsewhere, as the current UK trainer competition makes manifest. The UK Ministry of Defence reinstated the Hunting Firecracker into the RAF trainer competition (after it had been eliminated) because of political upheaval over the decision to drop the only British designed aircraft in the competition.[97] Clearly, whether for questions of national security or expediency, the expenditure of large sums of public funds is a highly politicised affair and nowhere is this more evident than in the procurement of military aircraft.

NOTES AND REFERENCES

1. Chapter 7 will develop more fully a number of contemporary themes dealing with state-industry relationships.

2. Charles H. Gibbs-Smith, Aviation: An Historical Survey From its Origins to the End of World War II, (Science Museum, HMSO, London, 1970), p.179.

3. David Mondey (ed.), The Complete Illustrated Encyclopedia of the World's Aircraft, (A & W Publishers Inc., New York, 1973), p.19.

4. Ibid, p.19.

5. Peter Fearon, 'The Formative Years of the British Aircraft Industry, 1912-1924', Business History Review, Vol. 43 (1969), p.479.

6. Gibbs-Smith, Aviation, p.176.

7. Ibid, p.225.

8. Cited in Jane's 1984-85, p.67.

9. John B. Rae, Climb to Greatness: The American Aircraft Industry, 1920-1960, (MIT Press, Cambridge, Massachusetts, 1968).

10. Paul A. C. Koistinen, 'The "Industrial-Military Complex" in Historical Perspective: World War I', Business History Review, Vol. 4, (1967), p.389.

11. See Paul A. C. Koistinen, 'The "Industrial-Military Complex" in Historical Perspective: The Inter War Years', Journal of American History, Vol. 56, (1969-70), pp.819-839 and Randolph P. Kucera, The Aerospace Industry and the Military: Structural and Political Relationships, (Sage Publications, Beverly Hills, California, 1974).

12. Gibbs-Smith, Aviation, pp.203-216.

13. Randolph P. Kucera, The Aerospace Industry and the Military, p.24.

14. Finletter Commission, 'Survival in the Air Age' in Carroll W. Purcell (ed.), The Military-Industrial Complex, (Harper & Row, New York, 1972) cited on p.179, 182.

15. Ibid, p.183.

16. SIPRI Yearbook 1979, Table 2:3, p.66.

17. Bill Gunston, Jane's Aerospace Dictionary, (Jane's, London, 1980). The actual cut-off point is subject to variation. For example, AW & ST classifies the Beech RU-21J as a utility aircraft even though its gross weight is 15,000 lb. (AW & ST, 12 March 1984, p.136).

18. See Mary Kaldor, The Baroque Arsenal, (Hill and Wang, New York, 1981), Chapter I.

19. Cited in Arnold Kanter, Defense Politics: A Budgetary Perspective, (University of Chicago Press, Chicago, 1975), p.5.

20. For an elaboration of some of the factors affecting the size of military expenditure see David K. Whynes, The Economics of Third World Military Expenditure, (University of Texas Press, Austin, 1979), Chapter 2.

21. United States, Arms Control and Disarmament Agency (ACDA), World Military Expenditures and Arms Transfers 1972-82, April, 1984, p.3.

22. SIPRI, Yearbook 1984.

23. United States, ACDA, p.1.
24. Ibid, Table A, p.3.
25. Ibid, p.7.
26. AW & ST, 11 February, 1985, p.17.
27. Helena Tuomi and Raimo Vayrynen, Transnational Corporations, Armaments and Development, (St. Martin's Press, New York, 1982), p.20.
28. AW & ST, 5 November 1984. The missile procurement figure does not include Navy missiles. All figures used are those approved by the Appropriation Conference.
29. Figures are taken from Nicole Ball and Milton Leitenberg (eds.), The Structure of the Defense Industry, An International Survey, (St. Martin's Press, New York, 1983). Note, the figures refer to 1977.
30. Robin Higham, 'Quantity vs. Quality: The Impact of Changing Demand on the British Aircraft Industry, 1900-1960', Business History Review, Vol. 42, (1968), pp.443-466.
31. Carroll W. Purcell (ed.), The Military-Industrial Complex, Appendix 9.
32. Robin Higham, 'Quantity vs. Quality', p.445.
33. Ibid, p.453.
34. Finletter Commission, 'Survival in the Air Age', p.188.
35. John B. Rae, Climb to Greatness, p.190.
36. Carroll W. Purcell, ed., The Military-Industrial Complex, Appendix 9. Graphically, Figure 2.1 attempts to summarise the process.
37. Randolph P. Kucera, The Aerospace Industry, p.24. It will be recalled that the USAF, as a separate service, was not created until 1947.
38. The expression, the MIC, was first used by President Eisenhower in his farewell address.
39. Finletter Commission, 'Survival in the Air Age', in Carroll W. Purcell (ed.), The Military-Industrial-Complex, (1972), pp.184-185.
40. Ibid, p.195.
41. For an intriguing account of the internal divisions within the DoD and the USAF in the context of the F-16 project, see Ingemar Dorfer, Arms Deal: The Selling of the F-16, (Praeger, New York, 1983).
42. Carroll W. Purcell (ed.), The Military-Industrial-Complex, 1972, Appendix 10. During the period described in the text, the figures are not strictly comparable due to reporting changes and methodological changes. None the less, the thrust of the argument remains valid.
43. AW & ST, 23 April 1984, p.166.
44. Ibid, p.166. The extent of market concentration in the USA is by no means unique. In Italy

for example, the top 10 companies account for 42.5 per cent of total Italian defence sales. Sergio A. Rossi, 'Italy' in Nicole Ball and Milton Leitenberg (ed.), The Structure of the Defense Industry, p.221.

45. Jacques S. Gansler, The Defense Industry, (MIT Press, Cambridge Massachusetts, 1980), p.42.

46. Gavin Kennedy, Defence Economics, (Duckworth, London, 1983), p.156.

47. Fortune, 30 April 1984, p.44. The ninth ranked defence contractor, The Howard Hughes Medical Institute, did not have a Fortune ranking listed.

48. Gordon Adams, The Politics of Defense Contracting: The Iron Triangle, (Transaction Books, New Brunswick, USA, 1981), p.394.

49. Ibid, p.24.

50. Adams argues that these shared assumptions are fostered through a "revolving door" of personnel transfers between industry and government. In fact, between 1981 and 1983 some 2,000 Pentagon employees left for jobs with defence contractors. The extent of the flow has caused some alarm, prompting congressional members to move towards passing legislation to impede the flow. Fortune, 18 March 1985, p.139-140.

51. J. F. Gorgol, The Military-Industrial Firm: A Practical Theory and Model, (Praeger, New York, 1972).

52. Jacques S. Gansler, The Defense Industry, 1982, p.296.

53. Recently, the USAF has split the procurement of aeroengines for the F-15 and F-16 between P & W (F100-220) and GE (F110). In fiscal year 1985, GE received 75 per cent of the procurement award and is scheduled to capture 54 per cent in fiscal year 1986. The split contract is intended to increase competition and ensure the maintenance of a fighter engine industrial base. AW & ST, 14 January 1985, p.16.

54. Merton J. Peck and Frederic M. Scherer, The Weapons Acquisition Process: An Economic Analysis, (Harvard University Press, Cambridge, Mass., 1962), p.17.

55. See for example, Gordon Adams, The Politics of Defense Contracting, and Michael R. Gordon, 'Are Military Contractors Part of the Problem or Part of the Solution?' in Lee D. Olvey et al. (eds.), Industrial Capacity and Defense Planning, (D.C. Heath and Company, Lexington, Mass., 1982), pp.93-102.

56. Jacques S. Gansler, The Defense Industry, p.75 and Gordon Adams, Politics of Defense Contracting, p.21.

57. AW & ST, 30 January 1984, pp.22-23.

58. Jacques S. Gansler, The Defense Industry, p.297, footnote 26.

59. F. M. Scherer, *The Weapons Acquisition Process: Economic Incentives*, (Harvard University Press, Cambridge, Mass., 1964), p.48.
60. AW & ST, 1 August 1983, p.34.
61. Gordon Adams, *The Politics of Defense Contracting*, p.96.
62. Michael R. Gordon, 'Are Military Contractors Part of the Problem or Part of the Solution?', p.95.
63. AW & ST, 4 July 1977, p.14-16, and 1 August 1983, p. 34.
64. Mary Kaldor, *The Baroque Arsenal*, p.18.
65. AW & ST, 18 June 1984, p.85.
66. Mary Kaldor, *The Baroque Arsenal*, p.20.
67. Gordon Adams, *The Politics of Defense Contracting*, p.98.
68. AW & ST, 19 November 1984, p.46.
69. AW & ST, 14 January 1985. Special issue on advanced helicopter technology.
70. Ibid, p.43.
71. Ibid, pp.41 and 43.
72. AW & ST, 3 September 1984, p.46.
73. For the evolution of combat aircraft costs, see Mary Kaldor, 'Technical Change in the Defence Industry', in Keith Pavitt (ed.), *Technical Innovation and British Economic Performance*, (Macmillan, London, 1980), pp.100-121.
74. AW & ST, 6 September 1982, p.14.
75. AW & ST, 20 December 1982, p.24.
76. AW & ST, 12 July 1982, p.18.
77. James R. Kurth, 'The Political-Economy of Weapons Procurement: The Follow-on Imperative', *American Economic Review Papers and Proceedings*, Vol. 62, (1972), pp.304-311.
78. AW & ST, 1 August 1983, pp.34, 52, 59.
79. AW & ST, 4 July 1977, p.14.
80. R. J. Johnston, 'Congressional Committees and the Inter-State Distribution of Military Spending', *Geoforum*, Vol. 10, (1979), pp.151-162.
81. Ibid, p.158.
82. Cited in Robert W. DeGrasse Jr., 'Military Spending and Jobs', *Challenge*, Vol. 26, (1983), pp.4-15.
83. The jobs created figure is from AW & ST, 11 February 1985, p.19, while the state expenditure is from DeGrasse, p.8.
84. J. B. Rae, *Climb to Greatness*.
85. AW & ST, 12 July 1971, p.15.
86. Gordon Adams, *The Politics of Defence Contracting*, p.231.
87. James R. Kurth, 'The Political-Economy of Weapons Procurement'.
88. I. F. Stone, 'Nixon and the Arms Race', in

Carroll W. Purcell (ed.), The Military Industrial Complex, 1972, pp.221-235.

89. AW & ST, 12 July 1982, p.18.

90. AW & ST, 23 August 1982, p.16.

91. See, for example, issues of AW & ST for 25 January 1982, p.19; 12 March 1982, p.47; and 9 August 1982, p. 68.

92. AW & ST, 12 May 1975, p.17.

93. AW & ST, 11 October 1982, p.23.

94. AW & ST, 15 December 1980, p.19.

95. AW & ST, 17 January 1983, p.16.

96. AW & ST, 20 June 1983, p.27.

97. AW & ST, 21 January 1985, p.25. In the event, the Brazilian Tucano was selected by the RAF, albeit built under licence by Shorts of Belfast.

Chapter Five

SUPPLY FACTORS AND INDUSTRIAL LOCATION

In his seminal work on the location of the US aircraft industry, Cunningham asserts that certain unique qualities associated with its geographic distribution; namely, "the absence of response to the traditional factors of location" combined with "its strategic and vulnerable nature", make for a subject of inquiry which is, at one and the same time, divorced from the standard precepts of economic geography while being of vital importance for the national economy and polity.[1] In essence, Cunningham is making the point - brought out in the last chapter - that as a creature of the state, the aircraft industry's location is determined for the most part by the whim of governments. It is all very well to aver that aircraft enterprises, as manufacturing operations, locate at given sites because of locational considerations (unique to the industry or otherwise), but the simple fact that the enterprises are likely to depend on government orders for their survival (and 'cost-plus' contracts to boot) means that the marginal efficiencies involved in selecting optimal plant locations are totally overwhelmed by the need for the enterprises to convince the state of the technical attributes of their own designs. As we have intimated, this central truth of the technological-imperative overrides the kind of marginalist economic thinking which pervades location theory.

While demand considerations constitute the crucial factors for aircraft enterprises, they do not manifest themselves in ways that present a readily identifiable spatial focus. In other words, demand does not reside in a geographical market centre: rather, it is to be found in the aspatial polity which, while occupying a spatially-determinable capital, sets procurement goals that mean delivering of the aircraft product to bases and installations throughout the state and even beyond to garrison forces overseas. The evidence for aircraft firms gravitating to the national capital in order to be more accessible to policymakers is very scanty indeed. Cunningham's example of the Glenn L. Martin Company's decision to move from Cleveland to Baltimore in 1929 and thereby ensuring, among other things, "proximity to the military markets in Washington" is perhaps an exception to the rule that the 'Iron Triangle' does not need a geographic market centre.[2]

None of this is to say that supply factors are unimportant to the aircraft industry: in fact, quite the reverse applies. Because labour costs at airframe plants can equal the costs of materials, they are of vital interest to all aircraft manufacturers. And, more to the point, because labour is spatially uneven in its quantity and quality, it forces firms to contemplate a geographical dimension in the formulation of plans to establish plants. In view of the predominance of the wage bill in production costs, this factor tends to outweigh any other supply factor as a locational consideration. Owing to the industry's requirement for such scarce labour, the tendency is for it to gravitate to major agglomeration centres containing well-established trades and engineering structures or, alternatively, to evolve on 'green-field' sites where the local environment is conducive to the maintenance of a pool of skilled workers. In both instances, establishment of aircraft plants has been triggered, to a large extent, by the existence of local entrepreneurs (a supply of human capital, as it were) well versed in expertise which subsequently became germane to this particular industry. The question of entrepreneurial talent introduces the notion of the effects of locational inertia, which is to say, the outcome whereby many aircraft firms were located in the centres in which their founders 'cut their teeth' in associated industries. Of special note were men who had previously worked in automotive engineering, coach-building and boat-building (recall the similarities between wooden craft, be they coaches, powerboats or primitive aircraft fuselages) and frequently, they set up their aircraft operations in the vicinity of those formative industries. This kind of 'seed-bed' development has been recognised in the locational literature.[3] So long as the firm is small, underfunded and technologically immature, it will have precarious prospects, and the entrepreneur will best serve his interests through 'hedging his bets' and remaining in close contact with his previous employer.

Historically, the locational inertia in the

formation of the aircraft industry was especially telling when such associated industries decided to diversify into aircraft manufacture and created aeronautical divisions of their own. Almost invariably, these aircraft departments were lodged in existing premises belonging to the organisation or, very much the same thing, in plant extensions of those premises. Understandably, as an arm of the MIC, aircraft manufacture was taken up by firms already prominent in defence production. Vertically-integrated arms producers such as Vickers instituted aircraft manufacture at existing sites: the Crayford machine-gun shops for aeroplanes and the Barrow shipbuilding complex for airships.[4] Other UK defence contractors established warplane factories on sites as geographically proximate as possible to existing works. Thus, naval shipbuilders William Beardmore, Harland & Wolff and J. S. White all sought factory space as close as possible to their shipyards at Dalmuir, Belfast and Cowes respectively. The Royal Navy even went one step further, actually using the slips of Malta Dockyard to build Felixstowe F3 flying boats in 1918.

The fact remains, therefore, that with the exception of labour and the amalgam of entrepreneurship and inertia encapsulated in the term agglomeration, supply factors coming to bear on the aircraft industry are not especially pertinent to locational analysis. As Cunningham stresses, the aircraft industry is a consumer of semi-manufactured materials and has "no reason for becoming material-oriented".[5] Not only are the materials fabricated in the airframe plant of high value in relation to weight - and therefore dismissive of transport costs - but the plethora of components and parts which go into the finished aircraft derive from a vast number of enterprises spread throughout the spatial economy. The dispersed nature of the supplier firms, and their very number, deny a geographical focus or 'locational pull' to the airframe plant in its assembly operations. This is why the industry has never been overly concerned about minimising the distance of its interindustry linkages.[6]

Given this context of demand pre-eminence in the first place, and a supply concern which is not primarily spatial in the second, the object of the present chapter is to provide an overview of the factors of production applicable to the aircraft industry and, then, to extract those elements of the supply-side that are genuine locational factors. To this end, a brief discussion of the construction materials used by the industry is followed by an outline of the role played by labour in the production process. At that juncture, the locational aspect is made explicit. A number of factors which conspire to create an aircraft-plant site are enunciated and the chapter concludes with a review of the attempts made by governments to steer aircraft plants to particular locations; in a word, regional policy.

INDUSTRIAL CHARACTERISTICS

The aircraft industry is, first and foremost, a high value-added sector demonstrating high levels of productivity. One indication of this situation is the fact that in 1970, for instance, each American aerospace worker produced an average $26,000 of sales, while his French counterpart produced $13,750, his West German co-worker turned out $13,200 and the British worker was responsible for sales worth $11,350.[7] More modern comparative output figures have been expressed in European Currency Units, a better standard of comparison for the non-US aircraft industries.[8] For example, 1978 figures suggest that, at 33,667 units, the turnover value per employee of French workers was higher than the productivity of aerospace workers in West Germany (22,787), the USA (21,366), the UK (14,941) and Italy (14,473).[9] By the beginning of the 1980s, French supremacy in the productivity stakes was confirmed with a sales-to-employment ratio of 75,000 units; a marked improvement on the 52,000 figure for the USA or the 46,000 of Japan, the 45,000 of West Germany and the 32,000 of the UK.[10] It virtually goes without saying, of course, that such national indices of productivity are only composites of the performances of individual enterprises. French labour efficiency, for example, was underpinned by an astounding 117,000 units per man for Dassault and a very respectable 65,000 units for Aérospatiale. The most productive US firms were Boeing, P & W, MD and Lockheed (with 64, 55, 53 and 52 thousand units respectively); but they failed to equal the two leading French enterprises. In fact, only two other firms approached the American level of 'best-performance' firms; namely, Kawasaki (62,000) and MBB (50,000). Major organisations of the likes of GD (40,000), BAe (31,000), R-R (36,000), GE (42,000), and MHI (42,000) appeared to perform only moderately well in the productivity ratings.[11]

As with any other manufacturing industry, the performance of the aerospace sector, whether considered on a national or corporate basis, is affected by the scale and timing of production. By the former is meant the economies of scale phenomenon. Sizeable production runs averaged over relatively fixed overheads are conducive to enhanced productivity figures. Conversely, limited production runs averaged over the same commitment to overheads is tantamount to low productivity and, indeed, accounts for the relatively poorer performance of European industries and firms (with the aforementioned exception of the French) when compared to those of the USA. But even the Americans are not immune to the cost escalation (and productivity drop) which follows from production cutbacks. GD, for instance, estimated that a slowdown in production of F-16 fighters from fifteen to ten aircraft per month was sufficient to add $3 billion to the contract cost notwithstanding the fact that procurement totals remained intact.[12] Timing comes to bear on productivity in terms of 'learning curves', that is to say, workers acquire greater expertise with experience as a project unwinds. MBB aptly illustrates this point when it notes that the first A300 Airbus manufactured by its Hamburg plant required 340,000 man-hours of work in contrast to the 78,000 man-hours entailed in the construction of the 87th copy, and the 56,000 man-hours anticipated for individual airliners when the production run exceeds three hundred.[13] In part, this marked improvement in productivity is attributable to enhanced experience, but it is also due to technological progress, especially the greater use of computers (CAD/CAM) and the further application of composite materials. The first example of technical change, incidentally, was also lauded by Boeing. That company thought the application of CAD/CAM in wing construction was directly responsible for the Boeing 767 production costs materialising at 50 per cent less than expected.[14] The application of composites, meanwhile, is addressed in the next sub-section.

Materials

Primary materials, as such, play little part in the manufacturing activities of airframe plants: instead metal 'skins' and forgings have traditionally been supplied by one or two specialist forges which cater for the entire materials needs of a national aircraft industry. These secondary products - steel alloys, aluminium sheet and castings, and magnesium castings - are high in value and low in relative transport costs. One organisation, Interforge of France, supplies most of the European demand for large forgings. With a 67,000 tonne hydraulic press, Interforge possesses the largest press outside the USSR which has two 75,000 tonne presses. American needs are met, in the main, by two USAF-owned presses operated by Wyman-Gordon and Alcoa.[15] In recent years, however, the use of materials in aircraft construction has dramatically changed. Technological developments have centred around the application of titanium on the one hand, and composites on the other.

The advantage of titanium is its strength, being twice as strong as aluminium. Offsetting that advantage, though, is the fact that it is 60 per cent heavier than aluminium. It was first used in the 1950s in military aviation where weight drawbacks were less important than in civil aviation (excessive weight in the latter tended to curtail payload and thus affected the costs:revenue ratio). Commencing with the airframe of the North American F-100, titanium was also used in the airframes of Boeing's B-52 and MD's F-4; and not least, in P & W's J57 engine. While high-performance aircraft of recent years have used more titanium (e.g. the Lockheed SR-71 'spy plane' is almost entirely made of the metal), the largest single market has been that of aeroengines. The B-1 supersonic bomber makes extensive use of the material both in its airframe (125,000 lbs of mill products) and its engines (17,600 lbs). The B-1's structure is 21 per cent titanium, while the F-14 is 24.4 per cent and the F-15 is 26 per cent.[16] As a result of programmes such as these, American titanium producers have undertaken major expansions: American Cyanamid adding 10,000 tons of capacity, Oregon Metallurgical extending sponge plant by 50 per cent and ingot capacity to 16 million lbs, TIMET investing $50 million, and RMI increasing ingot capacity by 20 per cent. Even UK producer IMI Titanium (the only UK producer and the world's third ranking) was establishing a Denver office to serve the American market.[17] Expansion plans were equally apparent in Japan. A subsidiary of MHI was aiming to produce 500 tonnes of titanium monthly to supplement the 30,000 tonnes already produced annually in Japan (in contrast to the US figure of 22,000 tonnes and the USSR level of 35,000 tonnes).[18]

In spite of this expansion, however, titanium contributes a mere four per cent of the materials used in the average aircraft in comparison to the 82 per cent contribution of aluminium and the 13 per cent of steel (the residual one per cent being made up of fibreglass). Yet by 1985, a typical subsonic 'new-generation' aeroplane may be constituted mostly from composite materials: that is, a whopping 65 per cent of the aircraft composed of composites and only 17 per cent of it made of aluminium, 15 per cent of steel and three per cent of titanium.[19] The advantages of composites are generally summed up as half the weight and twice the strength of aluminium. They have been used since the 1960s in the form of bolt-on parts (e.g. control surfaces) which could easily be removed and replaced, but only in the 1980s have they emerged as primary structural components of airframes. The revolutionary Learfan 2100, the subject of detailed scrutiny in the regional policy section of this chapter, was designed around graphite-reinforced epoxy wings, empennage and fuselage. In the military arena, the Anglo-American AV-8B has an airframe which is 26 per cent composite by weight. Strides are also being made in helicopter manufacture. Already, there are viable composite rotor blades and the acceptance of transmissions, drive shafts, rotor hubs and control components of the same material is imminent. A helicopter made largely of composite materials (i.e. 85 per cent) is regarded as the next major breakthrough in rotorcraft technology.

Composites come in many varieties: carbon epoxies, graphite, fibreglass, carbon fibre reinforced plastics (CFRP), boron fibre reinforced plastics (BFRP) and glass reinforced plastics (GRP) are perhaps the more prominent. They all suffice to give weight and fuel savings; for example, they offer a weight saving of 25 per cent over the previously used materials when built into Boeing's 757 and 767 airliners. Translated into operating costs, that can mean savings of 22,000 gallons of fuel per year in the case of the Boeing 757. Initially, research focused on asbestos composites in the UK and glass fibres in the USA, but later attention switched to carbon fibres in the former and boron fibres in the latter. Carbon (i.e. CFRP) enjoys widespread availability and is cheap to produce, but boron (i.e. BFRP) is twice the strength of carbon. However, it is expensive ($180 per lb) compared to carbon ($90 per lb) and even titanium ($150 per lb), and therefore finds a market mainly in warplane production (e.g. the Grumman F-14 and MD F-15) where costs tend to play second fiddle to technical criteria.[20] MD is, accordingly, embracing composite technology with gusto, investing $100 million in composite manufacturing facilities at St. Louis and Long Beach in order to annually process 400,000 lbs of composite materials for its AV-8B and F-18 programmes.[21]

Components and Parts

The new composite materials were introduced into aircraft construction by way of bolt-on parts and only later adopted as primary structural materials. In so doing, the process highlights the fundamental role played by components and parts in the aircraft industry. Furthermore, these components and parts come from a wide-ranging assortment of industries, firms and locations. An input-output study of processing sector inputs for Boeing of Washington, for example, arrived at the following order of industries supplying that firm: other aerospace ($750.3 million in 1967), electrical equipment ($316.5 million), business services and trade ($58.6 million), light fabricated metals ($39.7 million), aluminium ($29.1 million), finished plastics ($28.1 million) and printing and publishing ($27.2 million).[22] Interestingly, only $164.3 million of this total of $1.37 billion in processing sector inputs originated in the local region: the remainder was obtained from outside Washington state. Of the regional purchases, the main stimulus was given to the aluminium industry, followed by purchases from other aerospace firms. Yet, in light of the predominance of extra-regional linkages, the principal suppliers of Boeing were found to reside in two concentrations: Hartford, Connecticut, and southern California. The first was important because it housed P & W; the main source of Boeing's aeroengines. The second figured prominently presumably because many aerospace firms are located there.[23]

In fact, most modern aircraft programmes draw on a host of components suppliers that are located virtually randomly in relation to the site of airframe assembly. Four examples are selected for the purposes of explication. As an example of an aircraft using nationally-made inputs for all but a minor aspect of construction, the PZL organisation set up to produce the An-28 is considered. This Soviet-designed twin-turboprop airliner is a successor to the An-24 and PZL has been assigned authority to manufacture all Warsaw Pact requirements for it. Final assembly at Mielec is a culmination of manufacture undertaken elsewhere in Poland (Figure 5.1). The fuselage is built in Lublin, the licence-built Glushenkov TVD-10B engines derive from Rzeszow, hydraulics are produced at Wroclaw, control surfaces and landing gear are made at Krosno, while Warsaw is responsible for aircraft equipment.[24] By current standards, the An-28 programme entails few supplier linkages: a much more extensive network of linkages is evident from the TSR-2 programme. This aircraft, a product of BAC, was brought to the production stage in the mid-1960s but was then cancelled on the grounds of cost escalation. Table 5.1 highlights the array of suppliers as the aircraft was poised for production. Apart from airframe assembly at Preston and aeroengine construction at Bristol, the vast majority of contractors hailed from the London area, especially the suburban new towns. The same general pattern emerges for subcontractors, although the linkages to the London area are leavened by those to primary-metals suppliers in the West Midlands and in Sheffield. On the whole, however, the TSR-2 case illustrates the fact that the airframe plant may be located at a site eccentric in relation to the geographic centre of gravity of the components and parts suppliers.

Supplier linkages can extend to a continental or indeed, international scale as is evident from our next two examples, both the products of Boeing, namely: the civil 757 programme and the military NATO/AWACS venture. The first, graphically represented in Figure 5.2, requires inputs from suppliers in 15 states as well as the home state of Washington where the airliner is assembled. What is more, Boeing also calls upon the services of suppliers in Australia, Canada, Japan, Spain and the UK. As a point of fact, about 53 per cent of the 757 derives from sources outside of Boeing, including most of the fuselage. Body sections of the airframe originate in Maryland by courtesy of Fairchild-Republic, Oklahoma as a product of RI (Tulsa) and Texas, through the efforts of LTV. The engines are either obtained - as with earlier Boeing aircraft - from P & W in Connecticut or from R-R, which commands the energies of a number of factories in Britain. While retaining prime responsibility for the wing, Boeing still calls on Tennessee's Avco for wing centre sections, New York's Schweitzer for wing tips, and Australia's HDH for wing inspar ribs.[25] When all the avionics and instruments suppliers are added to these airframe structural suppliers, the spatial extent of linkages from Puget Sound is truly pervasive.

The NATO/AWACS venture involved Boeing in the manufacture of a batch of E-3A 'surveillance' aircraft which were jointly funded by the NATO members (excluding Britain which opted for its own AWACS variant of the Nimrod) and stationed at Geilenkircken in West Germany. Ultimately, a derivative of the Boeing 707, the E-3A differs in being stuffed with sophisticated electronic monitoring equipment. Consequently, a large part of the project cost revolves around supply of avionics and other systems. To complicate the supplier situation further, the international nature of the project demands a production work-sharing scheme which placates the individual members of NATO. The outcome is the industrial collaboration programme summarised in Table 5.2. That table pinpoints the

Figure 5.1 : Production Linkages for An-28

suppliers drawn upon because of the political complexion of the venture: in other words, contractors outside the USA who are involved because it is a NATO effort. The prime contractor, of course, remains Boeing, and much of the avionics as well as the aeroengines are American sourced.[26]

A final point worth making with respect to the extent of spatial linkages is that, more often than not, factories providing parts for aircraft assembled by a particular company are also participants in the same business organisation. In other words, a firm may utilise its own far-flung facilities to provide much of the mass of inputs required in aircraft assembly. The PZL example is a case in point, but the practice extends beyond state-monopoly aircraft enterprises. A dramatic example in the American context is that offered by RI, the prime contractor for the USAF's new strategic bomber, the B-1B. Fulfilment of the contract for 100 aircraft by the late 1980s will require workforces of 22,000 at the company's plants: 8,500 at El Segundo (California), 4,000 at Palmdale (California), 7,500 at Columbus (Ohio) and 2,000 at Tulsa (Arizona).[27] Final assembly in California notwithstanding, major components and

TABLE 5.1 Contractors and Subcontractors of TSR-2

Contractor	Location	Subcontractor	Location
BAC	Weybridge*	Elliott Bros	Borehamwood*
	Preston		Sydenham
Bristol Siddeley Engines	Bristol	S. Smith	Basingstoke*
	Leavesdon*	Decca	Heysham
Plessey	Titchfield	STC	London*
Ferranti	Edinburgh	Dowty	Cheltenham
	Manchester		Coventry
EMI	Hayes*	Martin Baker	Denham*
AEI	Coventry	Plessey	Ilford*
Mullard Electronics	Crawley*	HS Dynamics	Hatfield*
S.Smith & Sons	Barkingside*	Aviation Tool	Hounslow*
Cossor	Harlow*	J. Booth Alum.	Birmingham
Ekco	Southend*	T.J. Brooks	Leicester
Marconi	Basildon*	Ceramic aircraft components	Southall*
General Precision Systems	Aylesbury*	Darchem	Durham
Elliott Bros	Rochester	Diac	Croydon*
Kollsmans Instruments	Southampton	Electro-Hydraulics	Warrington
Vinten	Bury St Edmunds	GKN	Birmingham
Williamson Mfg.	Willesden*	Sir G. Godfrey & Partners	Feltham*
AGI	Croydon*	H.M. Hobson	Wolverhampton
Wray Optical	Bromley*	IMI	Birmingham
Fraser Nash	Kingston on Thames*	Lucas GTE	Birmingham
ML Aviation	Maidenhead		Liverpool
Microcell	Camberley*	D. Napier & Sons	Luton*
MB Metals	Portslade	High Duty Alloys	Redditch
Normalair	Yeovil	Firth Vickers	Sheffield
Stargate Engineering	Blackpool	Daniel Doncaster & Sons	Sheffield
Sperry	Bracknell*	Firth Derihon Stamping	Sheffield
Triplex	Birmingham	Mark Bridge Iron & Steel	Leeds
Palmer Aero Products	London	Hughes Johnson Stamping	Olbury
		Tubes Ltd	Birmingham
Serck Radiations	Birmingham		
Teddington Aircraft Controls	Merthyr Tydfil		
Ultra Electronics	Acton*		
Vactric	Morden*		
Ransome & Marles	Newark		

Note : * 'London-area' location

Source: G. Williams et al, Crisis in Procurement: A Case Study of the TSR-2, (RUSI, Whitehall, 1969), pp. 74-5.

Figure 5.2 : Distribution of Boeing 757 Work in the USA

Table 5.2 : International Suppliers to NATO/AWACS

Company	Location	Product
AEG Telefunken	Saarbrucken	racks,consoles, cabinets, flight-deck parts
	Ulm	radar components
Boeing of Canada	Winnipeg	tailcone
Diehl Elektronik	Nurnberg	special test equipment
Dornier	Oberpfaffenhofen	mission system installation and check
ESG	Munich	software development
Fleet Industries	Fort Erie, Ontario	vertical fin, rudder, nacelles, power pack
Liebherr-Aero	Lindenberg	antenna hydraulic drive
Litton Systems Canada	Rexdale, Ontario	on-board test monitor subsystems
Siemens	Munich	data displays and controllers
Standard Electrik Lorenz	Stuttgart	data processing system components

assemblies derive from company facilities in the US industrial heartland, a fact which speaks volumes in dismissing the relevance of material transfer costs for aircraft plants.

Labour

While locational costs incurred in obtaining material inputs may appear trivial for airframe operations, the same cannot be said of labour. Simply put, managers of airframe plants locate irrespective of the sites of their components suppliers but they are, in contrast, very conscious of labour supply in choosing to locate an airframe facility. Labour, in combination with agglomeration, plays an important part in determining plant locations. As long ago as 1939 the ratio of wages and salaries to value of product converted into percentage terms stood at 37.7 for the industry in the USA, and only 12 out of 71 main industries in the Census of Manufactures recorded a higher level.[28] This essential labour-intensive characteristic of the industry remains intact as modern economic-geography texts attest.[29] Several aspects of labour stand out as significant in the aircraft industry: first, the sizeable quantity required; secondly, the orientation towards higher skills; thirdly, the tendency towards stability of employment among the workforce and finally, the differential impact of those quantitative and qualitative considerations on firms' manpower costs and the resultant drive to cut labour costs. Confirmation of the sheer quantity of labour required is readily forthcoming from the 1.2 million or more currently engaged in US aerospace activities. However, a better intimation of the relative importance of labour is got from measures of manpower per plant. Table 5.3 shows, for example, that in the early 1960s, the typical UK Tier I airframe plant employed 2,692 workers when the aggregate manpower undertaking aircraft manufacture numbered 129,250.[30] Plants employing in excess of two thousand people are sizeable entities by any standards and necessitate, in consequence, a substantial labour pool to support them. As shall be shown in reference to government plant dispersal policies, a major concern was to find labour sheds with reserves of potential workers of this (or even greater) magnitude.[31]

The skill mix of the industry's manpower is equally distinctive. In World War II skilled labour constituted 41.3 per cent of all labour required in US airframe manufacture, whereas semi-skilled labour made up 46.5 per cent, unskilled labour contributed 7.7 per cent, and the residual 4.5 per cent consisted of clerical and managerial staff.[32] It was the presence of skilled and semi-skilled labour in abundance that induced many aircraft firms to establish themselves either in New York or the Los Angeles metropolitan area during the formative decades of the 1920s and 1930s. In recent years the bias towards quality manpower has kept pace with the tempo of technological change experienced by the industry. By the mid-1970s American aerospace workers were composed of 453,000 production workers, 165,000 scientists and engineers, 63,000 technicians and 253,000 'others' including clerical staff. Clearly, the number of 'technical' workers was encroaching on the traditionally-large factory workforce, skilled or otherwise. This pattern continues to the present day. It was noted, for example, that the employment growth for technicians in 1980 was a hefty 13 per cent, while for scientists and engineers the growth rate recorded a respectable 10.7 per cent. In marked contrast, however, demand for production workers had

Table 5.3 : UK Aircraft Firms and Plant Size, 1962

Firm	No. of plants	Average plant labour force
Aviation Traders	2	800
Beagle Aircraft	2	650
BAC	12	2,917
Handley Page	3	2,000
HS Aviation	20	3,275
Scottish Aviation	1	1,850
Shorts	3	2,333
Westland Aircraft	5	2,200
National Average		2,692

been a paltry three per cent.[33]

One consequence of the industry's need for skilled labour is its desire to retain it despite the fluctuations in activity levels imposed upon aerospace by the wave-cycle and business cycle. The essential defence nature of aircraft manufacture comes to the fore in this respect. Hartley and Corcoran have noticed that cancellation of government defence projects rarely results in a commensurate decline in employment. The two workers note that cancellation of projects in 1965 employing 30,000 in the UK aircraft industry should have resulted in the loss of 25,000 jobs and the closure of five plants. Yet, layoffs one year later only amounted to 7-8,000 and a single plant had been closed. The only conclusion to be drawn is that a substantial proportion of the 'redundant' workforce are intentionally retained and, in so being, perhaps under-employed. In line with the behaviour of the 'Iron Triangle' mentioned in the last chapter, they assert that firms might even overstate the scale of redundancies in order to "influence the decisions of vote-maximising governments".[34] At any rate, cost-based pricing whereby product price is determined by total outlays plus an agreed-upon profit margin is hardly conducive to production (labour) cost controls during activity slowdowns. However, the evidence indicates, in a circumstantial manner, that fixed-price contracts may induce firms to be more sensitive to production outlays, including a greater tendency to shed labour in periods of demand downturn. Yet, the relationship between reluctance to shed surplus labour and defence contracts should not be over-emphasised in view of the findings of Hartley and Corcoran that industries producing clocks, glassware, iron castings, ships and cars are even more reluctant than the aircraft industry to dismiss workers during lean times.[35] The common thread, shared by all those industries, is the need for at least a modicum of skilled labour which, by dint of its scarcity value, compels firms to procrastinate where layoffs are concerned.

Paradoxically in view of the just stated assertion that aircraft firms are loth to dispense with skilled (and thus, expensive) labour, they may still be amenable to tapping supplies of cheap labour if, by so doing, they materially reduce production costs (e.g. see Chapter 8 with respect to Boeing's agreement with Indonesia; also P & W has established duplicate production lines in the USA so as to overcome potential labour disruptions). Unsurprisingly, the attraction of cheap labour is especially telling for firms operating in civil aviation markets. In other words, firms of this kind may not enjoy the cost-based pricing endemic in defence markets and, therefore, are much more conscious of marginal savings in production costs. Among Tier III firms, for instance, the overhaul subsidiary of IAI - Bedek - stresses its competitive position as a result of the cheaper labour prevailing in Israel. During the 1970s this firm was bidding for airliner overhaul contracts on the basis of $6 per man-hour labour costs in contrast to the standard rate of $10 per man-hour in Europe and the $14.50 in the USA.[36] From a slightly different focus - that of chronic labour shortage at home - Pilatus Aircraft of Switzerland was obliged to have the wings for its B4 glider made in India.[37]

Entrepreneurship

Effective entrepreneurship continues to act as a main force in the aircraft industry, as is attested by the formation of new companies attempting to market appealing designs. In the UK in recent years, such entrepreneurs have set up firms to produce revolutionary observation aircraft (Edgley Optica), basic trainers (NDN Turbo Firecracker) and aerobatic light aeroplanes (Trago Mills SAH-1). In the USA, the achievements of entrepreneurs such as the late William P. Lear in both formulating new types of bizjet and forming companies to manufacture them are well-known and far-reaching. The desire of an entrepreneur to create a new aircraft company has obvious geographical repercussions. On the one hand, the new firm may be set up in the resident community of the entrepreneur, but, on the other, it may settle on a location which the founder has selected as a result of the persuasion and support of state authorities. This latter aspect comes to the fore in terms of regional policy and will be dealt with then. The former aspect, however, is best illustrated by highlighting the case of Wichita, Kansas. In the words of Rae:

> The astonishing rise of Wichita, Kansas, as the nation's principal center for the manufacture of private planes started in the early 1920s. Wichitans attribute the rise to the city's location in the heart of a vast plain constituting the largest natural airport in the country, but this claim could be made for any number of places in the same approximate longitude. The Wichita achievement was fundamentally entrepreneurial. A well-financed beginning attracted talent to the city and became the stem from which other companies proliferated.[38]

The process underway in Wichita combined pioneer entrepreneurial efforts with a 'copy-cat' effect which induced agglomeration of aircraft firms. The initial enterprise, the Wichita Airplane Company, attracted design talent of the likes of Lloyd Stearman and Walter Beech, both of whom later departed to form their own company in partnership with Clyde Cessna. By the 1930s all three were operating companies of their own, although Stearman's enterprise had been absorbed into the Boeing empire. Today, in addition to the Wichita division of Boeing which is integrated into the Seattle company's military and civil ventures, the two firms in Wichita, between them, account for the lion's share of the world's output of light aircraft. Only the Los Angeles area can challenge Wichita as a multi-firm aerospace centre of world stature, but this agglomeration centre grew to commanding importance largely as a result of firms relocating there from the US Eastern Seaboard. Of the numerous firms eventually locating in Los Angeles, Donald Douglas pioneered the way by intentionally choosing the area for its good climate (conducive to flight testing) and plentiful supply of skilled labour.[39] His actions in 1921, give him claim to being the first aircraft entrepreneur to actually engage in locational decision-making.

LOCATIONAL IMPLICATIONS

Douglas was, of course, searching for a suitable site for aircraft manufacture, a procedure which still occasionally distracts the attention of the industry's managers. Prior to Douglas's precedent, little consideration was given to determining special sites for plants and for good reason: space for landing grounds was scarcely a problem when aircraft were small enough to be trucked to a convenient piece of flat ground for aerial testing. Consequently, any industrial premises, more likely than not, the engineering shops or body-building works of the original diversifying firm, served to house aircraft assembly. Subsequently, of course, the drawbacks of cramped urban locations were recognised and firms tended to transfer to sites with plenty of room for airfields adjoining the airframe facilities. Nevertheless, these relocations were generally minimum distance moves: in the UK, for example, DH moved from London (Edgware) to one of its satellite towns (Hatfield), Gloster transferred from Cheltenham to its outskirts (Brockworth), while Armstrong Whitworth moved in two stages out from Coventry (Parkside to Whitley to Baginton). They fulfilled the purpose of seeking room for operations without undue change in locale. It is worth emphasising, though, that many firms persevered with cramped urban sites in spite of the mounting difficulties: Avro (at Manchester) and Handley Page (in London) persisted in building large bombers in subassemblies at urban factories and painstakingly transporting them to suburban airfields for reassembly (Woodford and Radlett).[40] In the UK, at least, very few firms relocated to sites at some remove from their original premises, but one of the few was Shorts which moved from Rochester to Belfast and is, incidentally, an integral component of the Northern Ireland regional policy case addressed later in this chapter.

In the USA relocations were much more common, especially those involving firms forsaking eastern sites for California in the 1930s. Since World War II, however, long-distance relocations have been rare. Chance Vought (LTV) opted to quit Bridgeport, Connecticut, for Dallas, Texas, in 1948 owing to the obsolescence of its old facilities and the prospect of existing newer facilities in Texas along with better flying weather.[41] Yet America has thrown up a contemporary example of site selection-cum-relocation; namely, the case of Piper Aircraft. The incentive for relocation occurred in the mid-1950s when the firm's existing plant at Lock Haven,

Pennsylvania, reached saturation point. Eventually a site for a new plant was chosen at Vero Beach, Florida. Four factors were influential in the decision. In the first place, the equable climate not only facilitated flight testing but also minimised heating costs in factories which are, of necessity, areally extensive one-storey structures. Secondly, the new plant was devoid of a design division (a function which was continued in Pennsylvania) and required a mainly unskilled workforce for which the nonunionised tradition of Florida conspired to present attractively-priced labour. Thirdly, the state was something of a tax haven, having no personal or corporate income taxes and inheritance tax, not to speak of the below-average property taxes. Finally, the Vero Beach site was a former naval air station and thus endowed with a well-equipped airport and suitable space to accommodate a 45,000 m^2 factory building. The enthusiasm of the local municipality in granting clear title and long-term leases to the land added to its attractions.[42] Indeed, the locational advantages of Florida impressed themselves upon Piper as the years unfolded. By 1973, it had decided to build another Florida plant - at Lakeland - to produce an aircraft type developed at Lock Haven.[43] Two years later, it was publicly musing over the possibility of abandoning Lock Haven in view of the lower labour productivity in the original centre.[44] By 1984 it took the plunge, so to speak, deciding to close its two Pennsylvania factories (the metal-parts plant at Quehanna as well as Lock Haven) and transferring to Florida in its entirety.[45] Interestingly, another denizen of the industrial-heartland, Bethpage (New York)-based Grumman has also chosen to expand in Florida. In this case, the company purchased the old Fairchild facility at St. Augustine in order to rebuild ex-military HU-16 amphibians as G-111 civil machines. The availability of an existing airport plus the nearby location of Grumman's other Florida factory at Stuart were reasons proffered for the choice of St. Augustine.[46]

Strategic Relocations

In truth, however, plant relocations undertaken as a consequence of private enterprise decision-making have been overshadowed by those undertaken as a result of government fiat. In these instances, strategic considerations far outweighed any issues of location cost. The USSR offers the supreme example of aircraft industry location and relocation on the basis of national security. As early as the second five-year plan of the mid-1930s, the government was aiming to decentralise the aircraft industry away from the Moscow area. This led to the construction of the Gorki fighter plant (GAZ No 21) and the Voronezh bomber plant (GAZ No 18) as well as three large aeroengine plants at Zaporozhe and Rybinsk.[47] The essential spur to decentralisation, however, arose out of the German invasion of the country in 1941. In spite of the exigencies of wartime, most plants west of the Leningrad-Moscow-Stalingrad line (including much of the plant in the first two cities) were evacuated to cities in the east which heretofore had not undertaken aircraft manufacture (Figure 5.3). Soviet railways are reputed to have carried 1.5 million waggonloads of plant, machinery and personnel to the new centres and transferred 1,523 factories, many of which were GAZ units.[48] Moscow, for one, was denuded of its aircraft plants: the fighter factory, GAZ No 1, and the aeroengine facility, GAZ No 24, were both transferred to Kuibyshev; Kazan received the bomber-maker GAZ No 22, Irkutsk became host to another bomber plant - GAZ No 39 - and Tashkent benefited from the re-establishment of GAZ No 84, the transport aircraft manufacturer. While aircraft production had regained its prewar level in Moscow by the end of the war, the region embracing Kuibyshev had experienced a five-fold rise in activity; the tempo of activity had increased eleven-fold in the Urals, while Eastern Siberia's production rate had increased by a phenomenal factor of thirty.[49]

Dislocations as a result of World War II were also widespread in the case of France, Britain and the USA. In these cases, however, the changes were less relocations than redistributions; which is to say, the original firms remained in situ but were responsible for operating government owned-plants as 'branch' establishments in regions outside of the 'war zones'. The French and British cases were bound up with capacity expansion during the phase of rearmamental instability prior to the war. Nationalisation of the French aircraft industry in 1936 was accompanied by initiatives to set up new capacity in the south, away from Paris. The efforts, such as they were, did not materially influence the French distribution of production until after the German occupation and postwar period of reconstruction. The present situation of Aérospatiale's orientation to Toulouse and Marignane (on the outskirts of Marseille) is an obvious legacy of those prewar efforts to integrate strategic considerations into aircraft production.

British attempts at plant dispersal also have

Figure 5.3 : Soviet Evacuations of Aircraft Plants

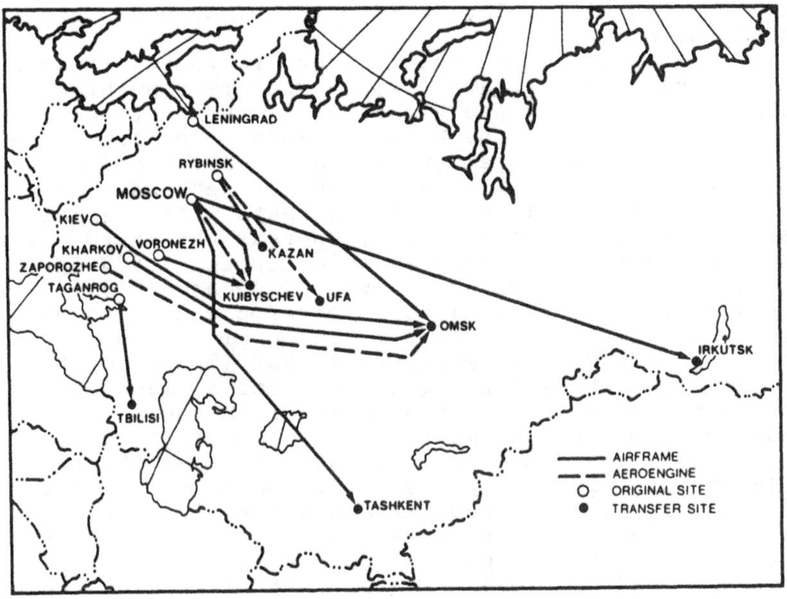

had far-reaching implications. The current focus of BAe military aviation is Preston - a product of a prewar-induced engineering firm's attempts to enter aerospace (i.e. English Electric) at government instigation provided it received a government-built aircraft factory (Samlesbury) in a 'safe' (from bombing) region. The UK Government was disturbed about the concentration of aircraft capacity in London and the South-east and, accordingly, drew up the so-called 'shadow' factory scheme in 1935.[50] Its aim was, quite simply, to decentralise defence industries, including aircraft plants. The new plants were to be devoid of R & D facilities: rather they would mass-produce standard designs of the established firms. The division of responsibilities meant that the private firms would design aircraft and initiate production in their own facilities, but should the design warrant wholescale adoption, this would be undertaken in state-built 'shadow' factories under the supervision of the original firm. The 'shadow' factories were, in fact, what the Americans came to call 'government-owned company-operated' plants. Added to the requirement of being outside easy bombing range was the criterion that they should be near (but not in) centres of population from which adequate labour could be drawn.

Figure 5.4 shows the 'shadow' factories managed by established aircraft firms. Vickers ran three complexes: Chester and Blackpool in the North and Castle Bromwich in the West Midlands. The first consisted of a main assembly line at Hawarden and a secondary line at Byley; the second was centred on a primary assembly line at Squires Gate with a supplementary line at Stanley Park, whereas the third was a massive centralised complex which built 11,939 Spitfires and 305 Lancasters between 1940 and 1945.[51] Such productivity required a correspondingly large investment in plant: Avro's Yeadon plant had a floor space of 136,277 m^2, employed 11,000 (53 per cent women), had three housing estates and a fleet of 160 buses to ferry the workers to and from their houses.[52] One of the most unusual (and temporary because it resided in a national park) was Shorts flying-boat plant at Windermere. Selected in view of its access to sheltered, inland waters for flight testing and access to towns (and labour) by courtesy of the railway, the plant produced 35 Sunderlands between 1942 and 1944. Another set of 'shadow' factories was turned over to the automotive industry when car-making firms were co-opted into the aircraft production programme. They, likewise, were located in the West Midlands and north of Britain: Rootes Securities, for example, ran large plants at Speke (Liverpool Airport) and Blythe Bridge near Stoke-on-Trent, whereas Austin Motors built Lancaster bombers at its Longbridge (Birmingham) Works and then assembled them at the Marston Green 'shadow' factory. Although most of these plants abandoned aircraft manufacture after the war, the current aerospace centre at Chester is really the Hawarden 'shadow' factory in disguise and complements Preston as an inheritance by BAe of the dispersal scheme.

The US version of strategic dispersal centred on a 'Defence Zone' which was at least 200 miles inland. Moreover, burgeoning growth of existing aerospace centres on the coast led to labour shortages and the desire to tap under-used manpower resources in the interior. The outcome was a number of 'branch' plants in the Great Plains and mid-West (Figure 5.5). Costing almost $4 billion ($3.5 billion of which was government funded), many of these plants were on a huge scale. The War Department's need for B-24 bombers resulted in three giant factories: Tulsa (ran by

Figure 5.4 : UK Shadow Factories of Aircraft Firms

Douglas), Fort Worth (managed by Consolidated, the precursor to GD), and Willow Run (operated, as in Britain, by the co-opted automotive industry - in this case by Ford). The last site employed 42,000 and necessitated the construction of an express highway from Detroit to Ypsilanti simply to get the workforce to the factory.[53] Two other large bomber-assembly plants were built by the US Corps of Engineers at Omaha (for Martin) and Kansas City (for North American). A number of Tier III factories were also built by the government. Known as 'modification centres', they were sites where aircraft off the production lines were finished in accordance with operational military requirements. Several locations new to the aircraft industry hosted such centres, including: Elizabeth City, North Carolina (managed by Consolidated); Daggett, California (under Douglas supervision); Phoenix, Arizona (ran by Goodyear Aircraft, a subsidiary of the tyre company); and Birmingham, Alabama (operated by the Bechtel-McCone construction company).[54] As with all the other countries engaging in strategic dispersal, many of the wartime US sites became permanent fixtures in the postwar aerospace sector.

REGIONAL POLICY

The government record of redistributing industry (and not least the aircraft industry) during the war was instrumental in stimulating regional industrial policy after 1945. Essentially, the policy adopted everywhere was to provide incentives to private firms to influence their choice of location. Italy went one step further by compelling public enterprises to locate a portion of their capacity in the depressed Mezzogiorno.[55] It was hardly surprising, therefore, that on the formation of Aeritalia as a result of merger, its headquarters were placed at Naples and the Italian Government promised the southern depressed region a new R & D centre and aerospace factory capable of employing 13,000.[56] The other principal Italian state-owned aircraft company - Agusta - was responsible for an expansion plan which explicitly recognised the need to shift aerospace investment to the south. The first outcome of this plan was the opening, in 1981, of the Industria Aeronautica Meridionale at Brindisi Airport. This subsidiary of Agusta was tasked with overhaul of aircraft and manufacture of helicopter parts as well as the fabrication of rudders and vertical stabilisers for the Lockheed L-1011 Tristar. Another subsidiary was to be set up for the production of aluminium and magnesium castings for use in airframe plants.[57]

The usual pattern with aerospace activities, however, is for regional incentives to emanate from regional authorities who proffer them with the intent of attracting private companies. The examples of Northern Ireland, British Columbia and Belgian Flanders are cases in point and are outlined below. Yet, even the USA has within it regions that have resorted to incentives aimed at attracting aircraft companies.

Figure 5.5 : US War-Built Branch Plants

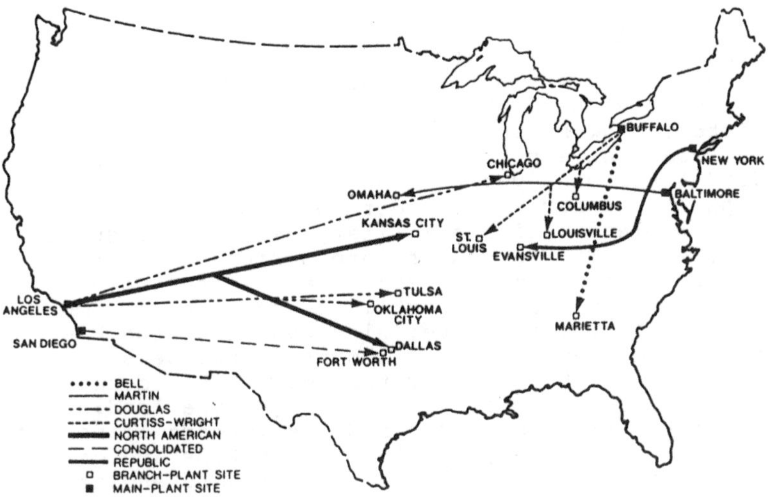

Mindful of the publicity associated with high-technology industries, the Government of Puerto Rico offered tax concessions (and the prospect of low-cost labour) to the Ahrens Aircraft Corporation of Oxnard, California. A new venture, Ahrens had developed a four-engined turboprop utility transport (the AR-404) almost to the flight-test stage when it agreed to transfer to Puerto Rico for certification and production of the machine. Housed at the former Ramey Air Force Base, the island government "arranged financing for an initial production run of 18 aircraft as part of an effort to offset the impact of the base's closing on local employment".[58] The second prototype flew in 1979 and the Puerto Rico Government appeared willing to provide loan guarantees to would-be customers. By the middle of 1982 about 65 staff were employed on the project and a factory was tooled up and poised for production. Certification difficulties, however, resulted in the failure of the venture and its abandonment of the island. That setback was not the end of the AR-404, though, for plans were afoot in 1984 to have the aircraft (renamed the KM 180) built in Sweden. Backed by the Malmo City Council and the Swedish Investment Bank, the project was to be implemented from a purpose-built plant in that city.[59]

Northern Ireland

Aircraft construction here effectively dated from the late 1930s when shipbuilder Harland & Wolff formed a partnership with the Shorts aircraft concern of Rochester, England and commenced to build bombers and flying-boats at a plant alongside its Belfast shipyard.[60] After many vicissitudes, Shorts was taken into public ownership in order to ensure its continuance. Completion of the military Belfast-transport programme in 1966 forced it into subcontract work: initially with Fokker and MBB in a collaborative effort to build the F-28 jetliner and then with MD for manufacturing the outer-wing panels of the F-4 fighter. Subcontracts kept Shorts in business throughout the 1970s and by the end of that decade it was making, in addition to F-28 wings, the landing gear doors for Boeing's 747 and the inboard flaps for the 757, the ailerons, spoilers, wing-tips and galley doors for the Lockheed L-1011, the forward engine nacelles for the R-R RB.211 engine, and the entire engine nacelles for the BAe 146. At the same time, its own series of light transports were coming to fruition; exemplified by the sale of 18 C-23A Sherpas to the USAF in 1984 which was worth $165 million and, best of all, guaranteed 1,000 jobs for a year. All these efforts required continual injections of government funds: the company received $43 million in 1980 from the UK Government in order to cover losses of $40 million in 1978-9 and to finance the development of its model 360. Similarly, the Northern Ireland Department of Economic Development (Shorts' controlling shareholder) committed £30 million in 1984 for the firm's role in developing the wing of the new Fokker F100 airliner.[61] Notwithstanding the difficulties of maintaining Shorts, the UK Government was keen to augment the province's aerospace sector by subsidising the ill-fated Lear Fan project. The brainchild of William Lear, this centred on the model-2100 twin-turboprop business aircraft; a revolutionary design entailing an airframe made almost entirely from graphite/epoxy and Kevlar composite materials, and an arrangement whereby the two engines independently drive a pusher propeller mounted in the tail. The UK division of the enterprise - Lear Fan Ltd - was a wholly-owned subsidiary of Lear Avia Corporation of Reno, Nevada. The intent was to pursue R & D and testing at the US location, leaving Northern Ireland responsible for manufacturing production aircraft. The initial capitalisation encompassed $80 million, of which $50 million derived from UK Government sources ($35 million for industrial grants and loans and the balance from loan guarantees).[62] By 1982, the enterprise employed 560 at Carmoney and Aldergrove in Northern Ireland and 400 at Reno. It was, however, desperate for development money, and there was talk of Beech Aircraft on the one hand, and a group consisting of American and Saudi investors on the other, coming forward to inject the necessary capital. The latter was sucessful and a reconstituted company - Fan Holdings Inc - was registered in Delaware and offered the prospect of 2,800 jobs in Northern Ireland by 1987. Minority shareholders included the Northern Ireland Department of Economic Development (with five per cent equity), Lear Avia, and the New York-based Oppenheim partnership. The UK operation was promised a further $30 million from the government on the understanding that private investment would be in the order of twice that amount. Consequently, Lear Fan Ltd purchased a 45,000 m^2 factory at Antrim which, owing to its previous use as a synthetic-fibre facility, was particularly well-suited with environmental controls for handling composite materials. Plans envisaged building of the first 42 aircraft in Northern Ireland as components and their subsequent dispatch to Reno for final assembly. With copy No 43, complete production and assembly would take place in the UK and the aircraft flown 'green' to the USA for outfitting: the Northern Ireland operation would represent about 70 per cent of total production man-hours. Unfortunately, structural problems with the airframe (ironically, not involving the revolutionary composites but the gearbox) in 1984 imposed delays on certification and forced the company to lay-off most of its UK workforce. A renewed attempt at certification was thwarted by cash-flow problems which led to the demise of the firm in 1985. The fact that the innovative nature of the project obliged Beech, Cessna, and Gates-Learjet also to introduce composite business aircraft projects was small consolation for the technical difficulties confronting Lear Fan as the pioneer in the field.

British Columbia.
The mixed results of Northern Ireland's attempts to build a regional aerospace industry can be compared with the even less auspicious experience of British Columbia. This Canadian province attempted to establish a regional aerospace core based on the Trident venture. The Trident Aircraft Company originated as

a private firm in Vancouver, formed in 1970 to manufacture a redesign of the US Republic Seabee amphibian which was renamed the Trigull. Encountering financial difficulties virtually from the outset, the provincial government rapidly stood in to provide, under the aegis of the British Columbia Development Corporation, enough resources to keep the project functioning. At its instigation, the federal government also became involved and later, in 1978, the federal Enterprise Development Board pledged support worth $6 million.[63] At the same time, British Columbia agreed to contribute another $1 million and the company claimed that it could find $950,000. However, the federal government could rescind its contribution if there was a 'material change in risk' and it was through such a loophole that the Enterprise Development Board withdrew its pledge. The decision of Trident to internalise components manufacture owing to difficulties with suppliers was interpreted by the federal government as an unwarranted risk burden. The direct result was the closure of Trident's new Victoria plant (paid for by British Columbia Development Corporation) in January 1980 and the dismissal of 100 employees. The attempt to create a regional aircraft industry from scratch had met with ignominious failure.

Belgian Flanders.

Undeterred by such experiences as those offered by Northern Ireland and British Columbia, the Belgian Government has designated Flanders as the site for future aerospace developments. The impetus for this stance follows from the perceptions of the Flemings that the Walloon-portion of the country has received disproportionate aerospace investments. In particular, they point to two projects: Belairbus and the F-16 offsets. The first embraces Belgium's participation in the Airbus and translates to a state funding of in excess of $30 million to SONACA for A310 wing-parts production. By the same token, the government (along with Fabrique Nationale) acquired SONACA in Wallonia in order to guarantee production of F-16 components. These initiatives were visualised as part of a regional development strategy for Wallonia which included the construction of a $12 million titanium-casting plant for aerospace products. In an attempt to arrive at regional balance, the Belgian Government had ordered Merlin transports from Fairchild on the understanding that the US firm would provide offsets which would be distributed 40 per cent to Flanders, 40 per cent to Wallonia and 20 per cent to Brussels. Such a sop to Flanders was regarded as insufficient with the result that 64 manufacturing firms combined to form FLAG - the Flemish Aerospace Group - in order to promote regional aerospace development. In February 1983 FLAG was vindicated when the Belgian Government announced that offsets from any military programmes must be directed to Flanders.

The main attention for regional development in the north, though, revolves round the Foxjet project. Emulating Lear Fan in many respects, the Foxjet ST-600 is a twin-turbofan business aircraft designed by an American, Tony Fox, the President of Foxjet International of Minneapolis. Conceived in 1977, the ST-600 was to be built in a planned 9,000 m^2 factory in Minneapolis. Its selling point was the fact that it was light (about one-third the weight of the competing Cessna Citation) and, therefore, cheap. It was powered, however, by two engines of revolutionary design which, as it transpired, led to teething troubles in the certification process. Plans to build the aircraft in the USA were abandoned and, instead, onus was shifted to Belgium. In 1984 the Belgian Government stated that a $80 million factory would be built at Zutendael in north-east Belgium to manufacture the ST-600. The Foxjet project in combination with a proposed helicopter plant employing 2,000 (a by-product of military offsets) is anticipated to form the core of the Flanders aerospace industry.[64]

CONCLUSION

In historical terms, the aircraft industry evolved as a 'spin-off' of other related engineering activities and, consequently, tended to locate in the same industrial milieu even to the extent of adopting inner-city premises ill-suited for extension. This pull of inertia was strong enough to retain many aircraft enterprises within the agglomeration after due allowance was made for the extensive space requirements of the industry and the virtual necessity of relocation to suburban sites. Agglomeration centres were also replete with appropriate supplies of labour, the only locational factor of any real significance to the industry. Certainly, the desire to minimise spatial linkages to supplier industries was not a cause for selecting a site in an agglomeration where this industry is concerned. None the less, the quest for labour was sufficient stimulus to engender interest in relocation and accounts, along with the climatic factor, for the rise of southern California as a main world centre of aerospace. When combined with state strategic interests, the labour requirement was a powerful instrument for geographic redistribution of the industry not only in the USA, but in the USSR, Britain and France as well. Today, governments continue to influence the location of the industry, although their interest is generally couched in the language of regional development and not that of defence planning. Interestingly, the forthcoming regional policy has often been incumbent on the action of entrepreneurs who have taken the active part of designing aircraft which are then built at public expense in return for the state having the right to locate the production facility in a preferred region. In itself, this fact highlights the continuing importance of entrepreneurship in the industry and, more so, the crucial role played by such people in technological advance. The equally self-evident fact that entrepreneurship and technological change are not always commercially rewarding is also extracted from the regional policy experience. Why technical change is vital to the fortunes of the industry is the subject of the next chapter.

NOTES AND REFERENCES

1. W. G. Cunningham, The Aircraft Industry: A Study in Industrial Location, (Morrison, Los Angeles, 1951), p.2.
2. Ibid, p.42.
3. See, for instance, M. J. Taylor, 'Industrial Linkage, "Seed-Bed" Growth and the Location of Firms', University College London, Geography Occasional Paper 3, September 1969.
4. Recall Chapter 2 for an overview of Vickers' aeronautical initiatives. Exceptions to this trend have occurred. Grumman, for example, built a new airframe plant at Savannah, Georgia in 1967: a site markedly removed from its principal plant at Bethpage, New York. The plant was subsequently sold to Gulfstream.
5. W. G. Cunningham, Aircraft Industry, p.18.
6. A fact brought out by Erickson, who points to the wideranging geographical effects of purchases made by Boeing. See R. A. Erickson, 'The Regional Impact of Growth Firms: The Case of Boeing, 1963-1968', Land Economics, vol.50 (1974), pp.127-136.
7. AW & ST, 17 August 1970, p.11.
8. In 1979 one European Currency Unit was valued at $1.37; in 1980 it stood at $1.39.

9. 'The European Aerospace Industry: Trading Position and Figures', EEC Commission, Staff Working Paper, Sec. (80), 1237, Brussels, 23 September 1980, pp.50-64.

10. FI, 1 January 1983, p.11.

11. FI, 16 January 1982, p.138.

12. AW & ST, 2 June 1980, p.9.

13. AW & ST, 6 October 1980, p.15.

14. AW & ST, 13 April 1981, p.52.

15. AW & ST, 29 March 1976, p.9.

16. FI, 11 September 1975, p.373.

17. AW & ST, 26 April 1982, p.82.

18. AW & ST, 25 May 1981, p.13. Note, the UK had, in 1975, a capacity of 2,500 tons of titanium per year; 1,000 tons of which was earmarked for the aircraft industry. The USSR produces 80 per cent of the world's sponge titanium, supplying the needs of Italy and West Germany in addition to its own requirements.

19. AW & ST, 26 April 1982, p.78.

20. FI, 11 September 1975, pp.375-6.

21. AW & ST, 2 August 1982, p.84.

22. R. A. Erickson, 'The Regional Impact', p.130.

23. R. A. Erickson, 'The Spatial Pattern of Income Generation in Lead Firm, Growth Area Linkage Systems', Economic Geography, vol.51 (1975), pp.17-26.

24. FI, 11 February 1984, p.388.

25. AW & ST, 20 February 1982, p.44.

26. AW & ST, 10 November 1980, pp.74-5.

27. All told, 58,000 people in 3,000 firms are expected to be working on the $20.5 billion contract. See AW & ST, 25 January 1982, p.19.

28. W. G. Cunningham, Aircraft Industry, p.29.

29. For example: R. C. Estall and R. O. Buchanan, Industrial Activity and Economic Geography (Hutchinson, London, 4th edition, 1980), p.105 and, incidentally, for the effect of climate see p.204.

30. Calculated from information in FI, 30 August 1962, pp.309 ff.

31. Cunningham asserts that wartime plants used 10,000 or more workers; some ballooning to require 30,000. As a result "location in or near a large city was essential". See W. G. Cunningham, Aircraft Industry, p.22.

32. Ibid, p.21.

33. AW & ST, 3 November 1975, p.16 and 6 July 1981, p.55.

34. K. Hartley and W. S. Corcoran, 'Short-run Employment Functions and Defence Contracts in the UK Aircraft Industry', Applied Economics, vol.7 (1975),

pp.223-233. Quote from p.223. It should be noted, however, that labour 'hoarding' is much less prevalent in the USA than in Europe - as is attested by the figures in Table 2.5.

35. Ibid, p.230.

36. AW & ST, 4 June 1973, p.56.

37. AW & ST, 29 October 1973, p.66.

38. J. B. Rae, Climb to Greatness, (MIT Press, Cambridge, 1968), p.15.

39. Ibid, pp.10-11.

40. Certain UK firms located in non-metropolitan centres from the outset and so space limitations were rarely an issue in their expansion, e.g. Westland at Yeovil.

41. J. B. Rae, Climb to Greatness, p.188.

42. Jane Lancaster, 'Piper Aircraft's Vero Beach Plant: An Analysis of Locational Determinants in Light Aircraft Manufacturing', The Southeastern Geographer, vol.7 (1967), pp.22-33.

43. AW & ST, 26 March 1973, p.67.

44. FI, 20 March 1975, p.445.

45. FI, 19 May 1984, p.1316. Ironically, concentration also entailed dispensing with the Lakeland facility.

46. AW & ST, 30 June 1980, p.69. Incidentally, the plant at Stuart, another former naval air station, had initially been chosen by Grumman for testing its E-2 AWACS aircraft as the lack of iron in the soil did not interfere with magnetic testing. In the early 1980s Stuart was rebuilding OV-1 aircraft and making parts for the F-14, E-2C, Boeing 767 and CH-53. See AW & ST, 14 September 1981, p.135.

47. Alexander Boyd, The Soviet Air Force since 1918, (MacDonald and Janes, London, 1977), p.36.

48. Ibid, p.187.

49. Ibid, p.203.

50. W. Hornby, Factories and Plant, (HMSO, London, 1958).

51. M. J. F. Bowyer, Action Stations 6: Military Airfields of the Cotswolds and the Central Midlands, (Patrick Stephens, Cambridge, 1983), p.101.

52. B. B. Halpenny, Action Stations 4: Military Airfields of Yorkshire, (Patrick Stephens, Cambridge, 1982), p.198.

53. J. B. Rae, Climb to Greatness, p.159.

54. W. G. Cunningham, Aircraft Industry, pp.94-5. It is interesting to record that strategic relocation is not quite dead: in the 1970s the Chinese were keen on transferring aerospace facilities away from the disputed border with the USSR. See AW & ST, 19 January 1976, p.19.

55. Good reviews of Italian regional policy

include: V. Cao-Pinna, 'Regional Policy in Italy' in N. M. Hansen (ed.) Public Policy and Regional Economic Development, (Ballinger, Cambridge, Mass, 1974), pp.137-179 and E. Nocifora, 'Poles of Development and the Southern Question', International Journal of Urban and Regional Research, vol.2 (1978), pp.361-78.

56. AW & ST, 31 May 1971, p.73.

57. AW & ST, 21 April 1980, p.141.

58. AW & ST, 15 November 1976, p.48.

59. The Ahrens story can be assessed from FI, 15 May 1982, p.1225; 17 July 1982, p.118; and 21 April 1984, p.1081.

60. An abortive attempt by Miles Aircraft of Reading, England to set up a second production line for Messenger aircraft at Newtownards was cancelled by the ending of hostilities after only a few aeroplanes had been delivered. See John Corlett, Aviation in Ulster, (Blackstaff Press, Belfast, 1981), pp.78-9.

61. See AW & ST, 14 April 1980, p.44 and 8 December 1980, p.52. Also FI, 10 March 1984, p.614; 24 March 1984, p.734; and 18 August 1984, p.96.

62. A series of articles deal with this issue. See AW & ST, 21 July 1980, p.22; 13 December 1982, p.27; 31 October 1983 and 4 June 1984, p.25. Also: FI, 11 September 1982, p.774; 25 September 1982, p.923; 14 January 1984, p.65; 28 January 1984, pp.277-9 and 3 March 1984, p.561. It is of interest to note that the enticements of regional development planners nearly resulted in another American aircraft firm moving to the province in 1980. Cabair Sales Ltd, the UK distributors for Gulfstream American, announced that the US manufacturer would relocate part of its production process to the UK - "probably Northern Ireland". The relocation never came to pass. See Air Pictorial, April 1980, p.122.

63. Financial Post, 29 December 1979.

64. Information germane to Flanders is found in: FI, 18 September 1975, p.402 and 31 March 1984, p.797. Also: AW & ST, 16 May 1977, pp.57-9; 31 March 1980, pp.92-3; and 2 February 1981, p.11. In addition: Toronto Globe and Mail, 5 July 1984.

Chapter Six

TECHNOLOGY AND INDUSTRIAL ORGANISATION

The crucial interaction between technical change and the evolution of the aircraft industry was recounted in Chapter 2. The object of this chapter is one of refinement, that is to say, to specify the ways in which typical aircraft enterprises rely on technology for their well-being. What is more, the vital dependence on technical change necessitates certain strategies on the part of enterprises, as business organisations, in order to vouchsafe their own survival. That subject is also the purview of this chapter. In short, corporate ploys for gaining access to, and making use of, aerospace technology will be highlighted. To that end, the chapter is divided into two broad areas: the first outlines a conceptual framework wherein the interaction between technology and business organisation can be accommodated, the second reviews the practical means for sharing technology which have been adopted by aircraft firms. Accordingly, the former stresses the importance of the interplay between endogenous R & D and exogenous R & D in the operations of a characteristic aircraft firm, whereas the latter considers such matters as international and national co-production arrangements and subsidiary ventures. Reference to the role of the state in these considerations is unavoidable.

Clearly, the fortunes of industrial organisations are inextricably bound up with the rate of technical change, or, the degree of 'technological-imperative', to put it in terms familiar to the aircraft industry. Yet, equally apparent is the 'environmental' milieu within which the industrial organisations are found. Environmental factors include a temporal dimension; namely, fluctuations in demand imposed by the wave-cycle and business cycle, as well as a political factor which embraces the influence of the state both directly in terms of regulating demand and indirectly by way of influencing industrial location. The structural contingency model intentionally postulates that 'environment' and technology have the effect of determining the shape of industrial organisations as a result of their interaction.[1] In according technology a central role, it can reconcile both motivations for technical change: the 'technology-push' whereby innovations from within the aircraft industry determine subsequent market activity and the 'demand-pull' by which the market imposes specifications delimiting new designs produced by the industry.[2]

A STRUCTURAL CONTINGENCY FRAMEWORK

The essence of the structural contingency model is that technology bridges the environment and the industrial organisation. In other words, technology can be a component of the environment when it is construed as emanating from a source external to the enterprise in question. Alternatively, technology can be part-and-parcel of the enterprise when it forms a dynamic component of the focal organisation. Advocates of the structural contingency model have tended to adopt mutually-exclusive stances, claiming that technology is either exogenous or endogenous to the enterprise; but, conceptually, there is no reason to suppose that technology cannot be envisaged as being part-exogenous and part-endogenous. Indeed, a comprehensive view of the importance of technology to the aircraft industry necessitates such a compromise view. In practical terms, it means that attention must be directed evenly to endogenous R & D and exogenous (to the firm) R & D.

Of equal significance is the allowance for feedback effects between industrial organisation and technology. Put otherwise, the simple proposition that technology (R & D) leads to product or process innovation which, in turn, shapes the production activity and organisation of the firm needs to be placed in context. On the one hand, the format of the firm has some bearing on the generation and acceptance of technical change: conceivably, for example, a large firm well-endowed with resources will be more susceptible to promoting R & D and then adopting the resultant innovations than would a small firm strapped for resources. On the other hand, the economic attributes of the firm - the fact that it is specialised or diversified, an independent operation or subsidiary operation - also greatly influence the attitudes to technology. Diversified firms, for instance, may be in a position to take risks with innovations that would not be contemplated by specialised firms: the former can divert resources from other arms of the organisation to cover the losses that may ensue; that is, they can pursue a strategy of cross-subsidisation unavailable to the latter. In sum, the type of feedback, or modification imposed on technology (R & D) by the firm, is dependent on the history and environmental conditions within which individual enterprises operate. It is impossible to predict deterministic behaviour applicable to all firms in the aircraft industry: at best, general strategies which firms may follow are made logical when related to the interactions outlined by the structural contingency framework.

The basic framework within which all aircraft firms have to function is outlined in Figure 6.1. The unbroken lines connect the origins and destinations of primary stimuli while the broken lines indicate that the format of technological change is, at one and the same time, incumbent on demand and a determinant of it. The first case arises from the specifications - military operational requirements, for example - defined by the customer and passed on to the R & D team for bringing to fruition. The desire for technical supremacy expressed by air forces has obliged aerospace R & D teams to compete in terms of performance increments wherever warplane contracts are concerned. The second is occasioned by innovations formulated by aerospace engineers and designers which have an immense impact on the perceptions of the customer: introduction of the jetliner convinced airlines of the need to obtain such equipment virtually overnight and created a new market at the expense of that for piston-engined machines. In short, the opposing stimuli between technological change and demand conform to 'demand-pull' and 'technology-push' motivations for innovation. The direct edge linking technological change to industrial organisation allows for the possibility of the formation of aircraft firms as speculative ventures to market an innovative product: the example of Lear's companies in the bizjet field are cases in point. Most aircraft enterprises, however, evolve and grow as a result of their access to the market; hence, the link connecting technological change to industrial organisations via the demand intermediary. The other major 'environmental' player is, of course, government. It can come to bear either as a main force in formulating demand or alternatively, as the direct instigator of the aircraft firm when the latter is set up as a state undertaking. Feedback effects emerge from these primary relationships: the firm can invest in

Figure 6.1 : A Structural Contingency Framework

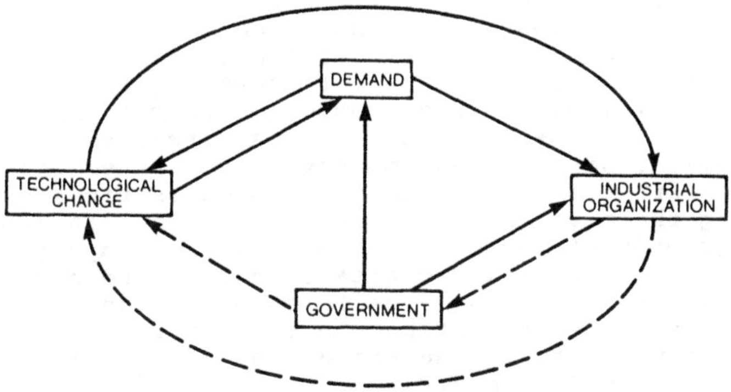

technological change by independently summoning resources for the purposes of R & D, or, it can do so by way of government subsidies. Whichever route is adopted, the outcome is a fresh round of technical advance which, in turn, triggers a new set of circumstances for the markets and the firms.

Missing from such a framework is the distinction between exogenous and endogenous R & D on the one hand, and the explicit manner in which the form of industrial organisation influences the firm's attitude towards adoption of subsequent innovations. Is the 'technological change' box of Figure 6.1 ensconced within the firm or does it function partly inside and partly outside of it? Does the size of the enterprise influence the receptiveness of management to succeeding innovations? These questions have already been aired, but the structural contingency framework needs adjustment to expressly account for them. The precedent set by Phillips is germane here.

The Phillips Eclectic Model

Phillips noted that aerospace belonged to a select group of industries (electrical equipment, communications, chemicals, motor vehicles, machinery, and instruments) which were characterised by high market concentration and rapid technical progress. Rather than concluding that large firms propagate technological change, he averred, after studying the US civil aircraft industry, that changes in the technological environment were key players in altering the structural arrangement of the industry. In other words, the size of aircraft firms was not a significant factor in promoting technological change: instead, such change was the outcome of adjustments in the market which arose out of technological advance and which, in turn, compelled firm expansion to meet customer needs. The impetus forwarded by technological advance was, moreover, generated for the most part outside of the focal organisations constituting the civil aircraft industry. Only in subsequent rounds of technical change, market adjustment and reaction of firms, did size of enterprise become an issue. At that point, the firms of commanding stature could ensure that barriers to entry were imposed on new firms. The whole line of thinking is systematised in Figure 6.2.[3]

The important distinction in this, Phillips' Eclectic Model, is that between the two boxes representing technical change: one box, building on the work of Schumpeter and Galbraith, allows for exogenous R & D undertaken quite independently of corporate goals for market control; the other, accommodates endogenous R & D undertaken by the firm in order to further its market penetration. In Phillips' conception, the former encapsulates the work undertaken by private inventors, government establishments, private research institutions and universities. It is, therefore, outside of the control of the firm and, possibly, dissociated from any sense of belonging to the concerned group which identifies itself as serving the interests of the aviation community. The R & D pursued by the aircraft firm, however, is done to counter the efforts of other firms which might eventually conspire to undermine its market position. As a risk-reducing activity, commitment by firms to endogenous R & D is always tempered by the thought that 'short-cutting' and using exogenous R & D is an expedient ploy which can save on development costs. At any rate, exogenous R & D enriches the R & D efforts of existing firms and also induces the entry of new ones: the two forms of business organisation together formulating the product and process innovations that shape the market.

The resultant market structures proceed to thrive on the strength of the performance advantages gained as a consequence of the application of new technology (provided, of course, that the innovation does not represent a 'false-start').[4] Aircraft firms, or at least some of them, also benefit from the adoption of the innovation and the incorporation of its

Figure 6.2 : Phillips' Eclectic System

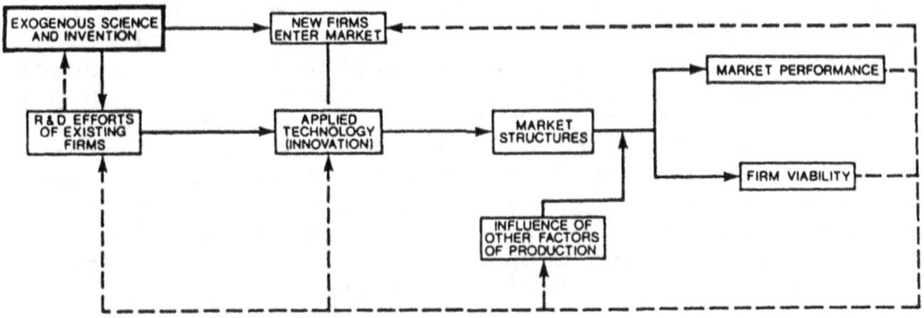

advantages into the aeroplane product. Yet, the eclectic nature of the accomplishments of firms needs underscoring. Harking back to the Schumpeterian creative-destruction argument, Phillips maintains that new firms tend to displace older firms in as much as they offer a dynamic new competitive force in the market. Indeed, only the innovation-adopters among the old firms will tend to survive: the others will be driven out of business owing to their tardy commitment to technological advance. This pattern is subject to modification, however, if the existing firms have had ample time to corner a portion of the market which remains loyal to their product. In this case (and now technical change is de facto a subsequent round of innovation application) the advantages of firm size can come to bear. The broken lines in Figure 6.2 comprise the feedback system. In effect, two loops close the model. The first trends back from market performance - that is, the emergence of demand opportunities - to new firm formation. A dynamic, growing market which has shown itself receptive to innovations can elicit entrepreneurial initiatives that take material form in the establishment of new firms geared to incremental innovations. Enhancement of the stock of competing firms serves to heighten the competition for customer allegiance among the aircraft producers and leads to further market improvements. The second feedback loop extends via the achievements-of-firms box to the motivation for continual replenishment of endogenous R & D. Quite simply, firms that have prospered from prior innovation will be encouraged to try again.

Some of the rewards of that prior effort could be passed on to sources of exogenous R & D in order to facilitate the process of cross-fertilisation. As stated, a goodly proportion of the exogenous R & D emanates from government, and the role of the state in both moulding market performance and underwriting the success of firms is accommodated in this feedback loop within the rubric of 'other non-technical supply and demand factors'. That somewhat amorphous category also allows for general 'environmental'factors. All in all, the steady stream of innovations germane to the aeronautical field, combined with an unstable market situation, led to the outcome whereby industrial concentration became paramount and the major firms were heavily committed to spending on R & D.

The Evidence

After analysing the stream of innovations affecting US civil aircraft operations between the late-1920s and the mid-1960s, Phillips was convinced that, firstly, the numbers of airliner manufacturers had declined sharply over the years in question and, secondly, that the surviving manufacturers have experienced wide swings in market shares. Without the palliative of massive orders for warplanes, the probability of many more exits from aircraft production could not be discounted.[5] The US aircraft industry was, in effect, benefiting from the subsidies flowing from a giant defence establishment and the military R & D commensurate with that military stance. The overwhelming trend towards industrial concentration and the consonant disinclination of new entries into the market was traceable from an examination of the product innovations - the successful airliners - which garnered an element of market control for their manufacturers. Pinpointing in chronological order the Ford Trimotor, Douglas DC-2, DC-3, Lockheed L-10, Douglas DC-4, DC-6, DC-6B, Lockheed Constellation series, Boeing 707, 720, Douglas DC-8 and Boeing 727, Phillips demonstrated that, at the time of their entry into airline service, these aircraft offered definite operating-cost advantages over alternative machines. In consequence, their impact on the market was such as to induce 'copy-cat' effects. In Phillips' words, operating savings "supplemented in most instances by other performance improvements and by the demonstrated effect of new types of planes on passenger demand, were such that the new aircraft were demanded for replacement of existing models as well as for fleet expansion".[6] It is abundantly clear that 'technology-push' innovations are seen as the prime movers in US civil aircraft development.

The firms fortunate enough to marshal the innovations reaped the accompanying benefits and acted to thwart the successful entry of newer, smaller aircraft manufacturers. Nevertheless, the maxim of 'once successful, always successful' did not seem to apply, as the failure of Ford (propagator of that early success, the Trimotor) duly attests. Also, the highly successful Lockheed and Boeing companies, formulators of a string of innovative airliners, were not immune from backing market failures. Boeing, for example, produced the models 307 and 377 piston-airliners which were commercial disasters, losing out to the Douglas DC-6 family, and would have bankrupted the company if alternative defence contracts had not saved the day. Lockheed, for its part, virtually failed with the burden of the L-1011 Tristar and relied upon government for salvation. The roles were reversed later. Boeing more than recouped its share of civil markets when it introduced the 707: Douglas which had dominated the piston-engined field had to resort to defence production to stave off collapse. The fact remains, though, that firms were deterred from entering the airliner market: GD refrained after approaching financial disaster with its ventures into the jetliner arena (the Convair 880 and 990), settling instead for more lucrative warplane programmes.

Exogenous R & D. In terms of civil aircraft, Phillips points to the crucial part played by US government agencies in providing the basic R & D for innovation development. All of the formative work on aeroengines, for example, came from government-funded research. Much of the incentive for state support came, in fact, from the desire to underpin military technology but it sufficed, none the less, to cross-fertilise civil aircraft developments. The affinities of Boeing's C-97 military transport and its model 377 airliner for one, and the KC-135 aerial tanker and the model 707 for another, are cases in point. However, perhaps the best example of the reliance of existing US aircraft manufacturers on exogenous R & D was the inception of the turbojet. This technological breakthrough was pioneered in the UK and Germany and was taken up in the USA (and USSR) as a derivative innovation.[7] Development of jet engine technology emphasised a persistent feature of aeronautical innovation; namely, that so much of it derived from the efforts of individual inventors. Indeed, Miller and Sawers are altogether dismissive of the record of endogenous R & D in the formulation of effective product innovations in aeronautics. They proffer the stark comment that of the principal innovations "only those of two types of flap can wholly be credited to the employees of aircraft manufacturers".[8]

Highlighting three major phases of innovation in aircraft design, Miller and Sawers ascribe the frantic years 1908-12 and, again, 1930-33 to the stimulus emanating from the civil aircraft market, leaving the fruitful 1942-47 period as the sole representative of military-led development. The earliest period was congruent with the flowering of pioneer inventors and aviators: men who responded in particular to the potential for private aircraft in France. The second phase was largely triggered by the competition among American airlines, while the third was, naturally enough, a product of the exigencies of war. Among the major innovations coming to the fore at the end of the 1920s were the variable-pitch propeller and the stressed-skin metal airframe. The former was largely the outcome of inventors working privately - Hele-Shaw, Beacham, Turnbull and Caldwell - while the latter was the outcome of combined private research and company R & D (Junkers and Northrop both formed their own companies to exploit the advance after pioneering it; while Dornier and Rohrbach pioneered the process innovation while working for the Zeppelin company). The major product of the 1940s phase was, as intimated, the jet engine and its associated wing redesign (swept-back wings). As with the others, individual initiative was crucial. Whittle, working on his own, was a major pioneer in jet technology as was von Ohain, whereas wing innovation rested mainly on the work of Busemann and Betz at the University of Göttingen.[9] Even where product innovations result from R & D endogenous to the industry, they do not necessarily arise out of the efforts of firms ensconced in the market. According to Miller and Sawers, many innovators in airliner design were warplane producers who wished to diversify into civil aviation. Prior to its DC-2 success in 1932, Douglas had only built military aircraft while Vickers, the designer of the world's first turboprop airliner (the Viscount), had (as recounted in Chapter 2) based its aviation interests on defence products.[10] Those examples might, figuratively speaking, coincide with the entry of new firms as posited in the Eclectic Model but, in reality, they were established aircraft firms whose evolution and R & D impetus had stemmed from the military branch of the market.

Entry of New Firms. The aforementioned examples of Douglas and Vickers emphasise the relative ease whereby firms can enter the civil aircraft market should they be blessed with resources acquired from other markets (defence, in this instance) and a general familiarity with aircraft R & D (the indivisibility of civil and military R & D noted in Chapter 3). The situation can apply in reverse of course, with airliner manufacturers breaking into the military market. In this respect, the sale of bizjets to air forces has been mentioned and, by the same token, manufacturers of light aircraft for general aviation purposes have also prospered from defence contracts. The Canadian DHC concern, for instance, received modest prosperity from the development of STOL 'bush' planes after World War II. It leapt to prosperity, however, when those light aircraft were adopted by the US forces during the Korean War as utility transports. A total of 980 Beaver planes, nearly 58 per cent of total output, were bought by the USAF and US Army and this precedent led to purchases of DHC-3 Otter, DHC-4 Caribou, DHC-5 Buffalo and DHC-6 Twin Otters in large numbers by the US forces.[11]

As a result of protection accorded by governments, some enterprises are given the opportunity to develop designs which will challenge the supremacy of existing market leaders. Nowhere is that situation more apparent than in the current market for light airliners, the so-called 'commuterliners'. In the market for small commuterliners (10-20 passengers), the market leaders of the 1970s (Beech, DHC, Government Aircraft Factories, PBN, Piper, and Shorts) have been faced by the competition of 'new' entries in the 1980s (BAe, Cessna, Dornier, Fairchild) compelling some of them to retaliate by innovating 'follow-on' products. As Table 6.1 shows, the original innovators Beech, PBN and Piper responded by introducing new aircraft designs to coincide with the introduction of 'new' entry products. Other original firms, however, have stuck to their 'tried-and-tested' designs and hoped to retain their market share by a combination of marginal improvements applied to the aircraft and financial inducements offered as a result of scale economies realised over sizeable production runs. The table indicates that, on the whole, the older designs are lower-priced than the newer products of the same firms or 'new'-entry firms. Where this is not the case, the higher price tends to indicate a successful product enjoying price 'inelasticity' within a well-established market

Table 6.1 : Small-Commuterliner Market

Type	Company/Source	First Flight	Basic Price ($m,1984)
Super King Air	Beech (US)	1972	1.87
Twin Otter 300	DHC (Canada)	1965	2.10
Nomad N24A	Government Aircraft Factories (Australia)	1975	1.20
Islander	PBN (UK)	1965	0.38
Chieftain	Piper (US)	1973	0.46
Skyvan	Shorts (UK)	1963	1.20
Jetstream 31	BAe (UK)	1980	1.70
Caravan 1	Cessna (US)	1982	0.65
228-200	Dornier (W. Germany)	1981	1.70
Metro III	Fairchild (US)	1981	2.20
C99	Beech (US)	1980	1.45
1900	"	1982	2.85
B300	"	1983	2.34
Turbine Islander	PBN (UK)	1980	0.73
T-1040	Piper (US)	1981	0.87

Source: Flight International, 1 September 1984, p.412.

Table 6.2 : Medium-Commuterliner Market

Type	Company/Source	First Flight	Basic Price ($m,1984)
212 Aviocar	CASA (Spain)	1971	2.40
Bandeirante	Embraer (Brazil)	1968	2.10
330	Shorts (UK)	1974	3.30
Dash 8	DHC (Canada)	1983	5.20
340	Saab-Fairchild (Sweden/US)	1983	5.30
Brasilia	Embraer (Brazil)	1983	4.70
360	Shorts	1981	4.10

Source: Flight International, 1 September 1984, p.412.

niche. None the less, some of the original market leaders have opted to divert their efforts to a different market because either the competition in the first market is becoming too intense or the firm feels that better prospects will be forthcoming from 'new'-entry status in a fresh market. This trend is discernible in the medium-commuterliner market. As evinced from Table 6.2, both DHC and Shorts redirected their subsequent design efforts to the 'up-market' commuter sphere once their initial commuterliner ventures (the Twin Otter and Skyvan) had been brought to maturity. The far fewer competing products in this market is a pointer to the less-intensive competitive environment (and also to the greater R & D cost involved in designing a larger aircraft). Interestingly, however, the original market leaders in the medium-commuterliner field have responded in a manner comparable to some of their counterparts in the small-commuterliner market, that is, they have brought out 'follow-on' designs. Embraer and Shorts itself are cases in point.

Role of the State. The state has had far-reaching consequences in two respects: first, by facilitating the provision of exogenous R & D for the ultimate betterment of aircraft firms and, secondly, through deliberately restructuring those aircraft firms to make them more amenable to technological progress. The first aim is achieved both directly and indirectly. In the indirect sense, governments maintain state research institutions whose mandate is to pass on aeronautical findings to aircraft designers: the US NASA, the British Royal Aircraft Establishment (RAE), and the Soviet Central Institute of Aerodynamics and Hydrodynamics (TsAGI) all fulfil this function. It is not always a particularly fruitful relationship, however, as the nature of pure research is not easily grafted onto product design.[12] Consequently, governments resort to the provision of specific R & D monies as a second, less indirect way of fomenting innovation in aircraft design. As to be expected in view of the symbiosis between the state and defence contractors brought out in Chapter 4, public monies are particularly munificent in warplane development. Table 6.3 lists the top ten recipients of RDT & E awards from the US DoD in 1983 and it also gives examples of the budget requests put forward by the firms for 1984. Three companies each received in excess of one billion dollars in state-aid for military aerospace development, and a further six benefited to the tune of over half a billion dollars each. A single project, the B-1B, was the subject of a request for three-quarters of a billion dollars in RDT & E support. Multiplied over a number of years-the ten years typically required to design a modern combat aircraft - and the level of exogenously funded R & D is truly staggering. While the gigantic American MIC devours vast sums of public funds for military aviation, the more modest aircraft industries of the EEC are not sluggards where state-supported R & D is concerned. The £2 billion A320 Airbus programme has been mentioned, and will be again in Chapter 7, but the amount of public money put into the UK industry is illustrative of government backing for national aerospace R & D. Even twenty or more years ago, the UK Government was reputed to be averaging £9 million per year in support of civil aviation projects.[13] A paper presented to the House of Commons in the mid-1970s suggested that in the previous nine years, sums of £300 million and £350 million had been made available by the state to support civil airframe programmes and military aviation R & D respectively. The then Minister responsible for the aircraft industry stated to the House that in the period since 1965 some £350 million had gone to subsidise civil aircraft while £450 million had been sunk into warplane R & D.[14] For its part, the industry suggested that the lion's share of state support had been earmarked for just two projects: Concorde (absorbing £548.4 million since 1964) and the RB.211 aeroengine produced by R-R for the Lockheed L-1011 Tristar (£189.4 million). Excluding those two programmes, they implied that state largesse had been confined to an investment of £52.8 million in a decade, £36.7 million of which was repaid.[15] Arguably, most projects stood or fell on their commercial merits and the willingness of firms to take risks in backing them: a significant few, however, were brought to completion as a result of government intervention. Clearly, the risk-burden associated with product innovation was being shouldered entirely by the state in those instances.

Governments have agreed to absorb the risk burden in direct proportion to the rise in project development costs. In a telling passage, Miller and Sawers highlight the escalation in cost of engineering development (Table 6.4). The rise seems inexorable: the £2 billion price tag put on the A320 Airbus and the sum in the order of $4 billion that Boeing attributes to the development of the 757/767 new-generation of jetliners are mere continuations of past trends. Unable to summon the resources necessary to cover development costs, firms have either to go

Table 6.3 : US Aerospace RDT & E Awards

Firm	Award ($'000)	Examples of Budget Requests
Boeing	1,703,491	
RI	1,171,720	B-1B bomber, $749.9 million
Martin-Marietta[1]	1,048,660	
TRW[1]	669,331	
MD	647,323	AV-8B tactical fighter, $118.2 million
		F-15 fighter, $117.8 million
		F-18 fighter, $27.2 million
GE[2]	645,426	
GD	643,504	F-16 fighter, $107.4 million
Hughes	627,333	AH-64 helicopter, $28.3 million
Lockheed	509,219	
UTC[3]	339,431	

Notes: 1. missiles and avionics only
2. aeroengines only
3. helicopters and aeroengines

Source: Aviation Week, 14 March 1983, pp.10-11 and 18 June 1984, p. 85.

cap-in-hand to the state for subsidies or, alternatively, they may be forced out of the airframe business. Prior market success is no guarantee for smoothing the progress in overcoming obstacles where development costs are concerned. The failure of Britten-Norman is salutary in indicating the consequence of a shortfall in development funds. This British firm had spent about $3 million on R & D associated with its highly-successful Islander light transport. Nevertheless, it owed $600,000 of a $1.32 million production loan from the UK Government, not to speak of $6.72 million to a commercial bank. Inability to service the bank loan resulted in receivership for the firm in 1971. Britten-Norman, the organisation established by a duo of entrepreneurs, was subsequently purchased by the Fairey engineering company and, on its bankruptcy in 1976, by Pilatus Aircraft of Switzerland. The original firm had been capitalised for only $250,000 and was unable to finance R & D without incurring a loan burden which eventually crippled it.[16] Ironically, the Islander was built in four countries (the UK, Belgium, Romania and the Philippines) largely to contain aircraft production costs. The machine was commercially successful, PBN handing over copy number 1,000 to the customer in April 1982, but 'follow-on' product innovations were clearly beyond the financial capabilities of the original innovating organisation.[17] Another firm confronted by similar cash-flow problems was R-R, but its size prevented the stoppage commensurate with commercial failure which was the lot of Britten-Norman. The aeroengine giant had over-extended itself in attempting to develop the RB.211. On its entering receivership in 1971, it was immediately nationalised by the UK Government in order to maintain its commitments (and ensure a national aeroengine capability). Prior to collapse, the state had invested $213.6 million in the RB.211 programme, but a further $72 million was needed simply to fulfil development targets. Problems with the development programme had pushed up individual engine costs from the $840,000 agreed with Lockheed as the sale price to $1,104,000: resulting in a whopping loss to R-R for each engine built.[18] The scale of the dependence of R-R on subsidies to cover development costs is apparent from the bill introduced in the UK House of Commons in 1980 which aimed at immediately raising the borrowing limit of the company from £750 million to £1.5 billion with the prospect of another £500 million over the succeeding five years.[19]

<u>Merger</u>. Governments have actively intervened to promote restructuring of aircraft firms in an attempt to make them more competitive all round. A significant aspect of the augmented competitiveness is the ability to command greater resources for R & D. The merger of separate business organisations into a single, larger enterprise is a tactic much favoured by governments. In Britain, government encouragement of mergers came about in the 1950s when a combination of reduced defence contracts after the 1957 Defence White Paper and increasingly expensive project development costs compelled a rationalisation of the industry. Already UK aircraft production had fallen from a figure of 2,000 completed airframes in 1953 to 510 by 1960 and the Government was no longer prepared to support a large number of airframe manufacturers either with production contracts or R & D subsidies for the next generation of aircraft. Of its own volition, the industry commenced merger steps in the phase of demobilisational instability after World War II. Two groups coalesced: General Aircraft and Blackburn forming an airframe group and Cierva and Saunders-Roe (Saro) forming a helicopter combine.[20] The Government began to force the pace when in 1957

Table 6.4 : Escalation in Engineering Development Costs

Period	Type	Cost ($'000)
1920s	Lockheed Vega airliner	25
1930s	Douglas DC-3 airliner	300
1940	Douglas DC-4 airliner	3,300
1945	Douglas DC-6 airliner	14,000
1947	Boeing B-47 bomber	29,000
1950s	Douglas DC-8 airliner	112,000
1950s	MD F-4 fighter	468,000
1960s	RI XB-70 bomber	1,500,000

Source: Miller and Sawers, The Technical Development of Modern Aviation, p.267.

it insisted that a contract to produce a jetliner for BEA be split 67.5 per cent to DH, 22.5 per cent to Hunting and 10 per cent to Fairey, with the three companies forming a working consortium (the Trident eventually materialised).[21] A similar consortium-arrangement to produce the only major new warplane requirement was used as an excuse by the Government in 1959 for forcing the creation of BAC. Centred around the TSR-2 programme, BAC was based on the merger of English Electric Aviation and Vickers-Armstrong (Aviation) Ltd. Junior partners which joined in 1960 to officially launch BAC were Hunting and Bristol (the ownership breakdown being in the ratio of 40:40:20 English Electric - Vickers - Bristol; later the first two bought out Bristol). At the same time, Hawker Siddeley Aviation Ltd was prodded into becoming an integrated manufacturing organisation rather than the loose holding company it had been hitherto. Figure 6.3 summarises the merger process which culminated in 1960 with two large UK airframe producers and five smaller manufacturers which remained immune from the larger mergers (Beagle, Handley Page, Scottish Aviation and Shorts - as aeroplane producers - and Westland as a helicopter specialist).[22]

It is not without irony that BAC, the product of government machinations, should have virtually foundered in the succeeding decade as a result of government-project cancellations (TSR-2, PT428 missile and OR351 next-generation combat aircraft).[23] Cancellation of missile R & D led to the closure of the Luton factory inherited from English Electric in 1962 while

Figure 6.3 : The UK Pre-Nationalisation Mergers

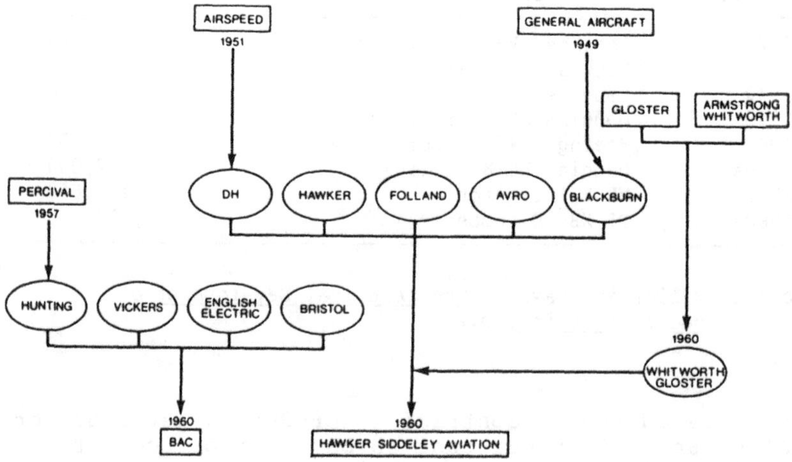

the scrapping of TSR-2 resulted in the abandonment of military work at Weybridge and Bristol and its concentration on Preston. Fortunately, the firm persevered with a civil project, the BAC-111, and by a judicious allocation of parts manufacture to Bristol, Luton (Hunting's plant), Hurn and Weybridge was enabled to keep these facilities operating. A problem that arose as a by-product of merger became evident in connection with the TSR-2 cancellation. Observers felt that the programme was delayed by up to two years owing to the distraction of management with issues of organisational restructuring.[24] The delay might have contributed to the cost escalation which was used by the Government as the basis for cancellation. In the final analysis, though, BAC and HS survived because they were large enough - as a consequence of merger - to absorb losses on the scale of TSR-2 (which employed 20,000 men).[25] Other firms, devoid of either the extra resources consonant with merger or state predilection to support them, were unable to survive. The examples of Britten-Norman and Handley Page have been touched on elsewhere, but Beagle had also collapsed by 1970 and Shorts was only kept in being because of its sensitive Northern Ireland location. Therefore, in a European context, merger appeared to be the only option capable of overcoming the problem of acquiring the resources necessary for innovating major aircraft programmes.

The French certainly subscribed to this view. About 70 per cent of that country's aircraft industry was owned by the state in any event. However, the French Government forced the merger of its two airframe undertakings, Nord Aviation and Sud Aviation, along with a rocket R & D establishment (SEREB, or Société pour l'Étude et la Réalisation d'Engins Balistiques), into a large, integrated concern, namely, Aérospatiale.[26] The reasons put forward to justify the enlarged corporation were three-fold: first, to muster an increased resource base for launching new projects, secondly, to streamline management, and finally, to render the French industry more competitive in relation to the US aerospace giants. At the same time, the Government promoted merger in the private sector (Figure 6.4). The outcome was the union of Breguet and Dassault in the airframe sector and the acquisition of Hispano-Suiza by state-owned SNECMA in the aeroengine sector.[27] By the end of the 1970s the state-aeroengine enterprise had formed an alliance with GE of the USA to muster the requisite resources for large turbine development (CFM International).

The West Germans accomplished wholesale merger only in 1980. Yet, the formation of MBB-VFW was the outcome of a long process of government-induced rationalisation (Figure 6.5). By the end of the 1960s, two airframe producers of consequence had emerged in the Federal Republic: MBB and VFW. Unfortunately from the point of view of the West German Government, VFW had teamed up with Fokker of the Netherlands in order to access airliner technology. This, the pinnacle of foreign penetration of the German industry, was perceived by the Government as detrimental to a national, state-sponsored aerospace sector. Consequently, the Government made the separation of VFW-Fokker a precondition for subsidising the merger of Bremen-based VFW and Munich-based MBB.[28] It had already staved off bankruptcy for the former in 1977 (the result of the failure of the model 614) by advancing credits amounting to $250 million. However, by 1979 VFW was making sales in excess of $575 million whereas MBB's sales were in the order of $1 billion and the Government believed that a merged company would be able to compete on equal terms with BAe and Aérospatiale. In 1980 Fokker formally dissociated itself from VFW and the US firm, UTC, agreed to sell its 26.4 per cent holding to Fried. Krupp GmbH. The threat of withholding state funds for the Airbus programme was sufficient incentive to bring together VFW and MBB in that year.

Figure 6.4 : French State and Private-Sector Mergers

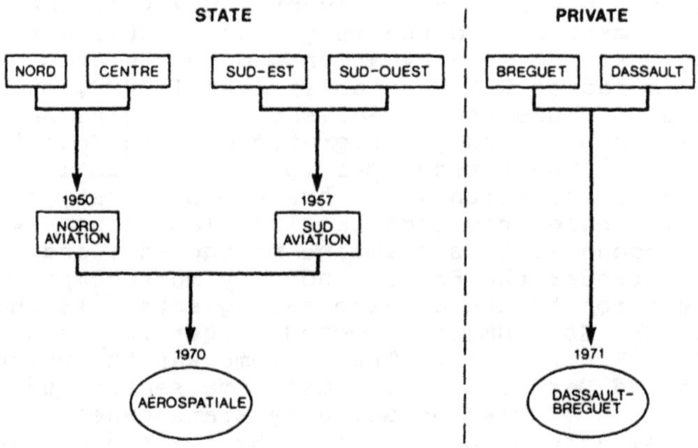

The unified corporation inherited a range of international programmes giving the German industry access to the spectrum of aerospace technology, viz: the Tornado MRCA (42.5 per cent share), Airbus (37.5 per cent share), Euromissile (50 per cent share), PAH-2 helicopter (50 per cent share) and Eurosatellite (24 per cent share).[29]

Emulation of the British-French mania for mergers was not confined to West Germany. At the beginning of the 1970s, the Italian Government instituted merger proceedings for the same reason: the need for an entity large enough to participate in new-generation aircraft developments. An invigorated state undertaking, Aeritalia, was created out of the aircraft interests of Fiat and Aerfer (Finmeccanica-IRI), and was soon joined by Aermacchi. The helicopter-producer Agusta also expanded by acquiring SIAI-Marchetti.[30] A major rationalisation underway in the 1980s consolidated the state's role in Italian aerospace. In terms of the airframe sector, the results included the take-over of Partenavia by Aeritalia and the partial acquisition of Aermacchi by this dominant aircraft firm. In return, however, Aeritalia transferred its Nerviano (Milan) factory to Agusta, the state-owned helicopter and light aircraft group. Comparable mergers in the aeroengine field in both West Germany and Italy followed the precedent set by R-R and SNECMA. Thus, as the 1980s unfolded,

Figure 6.5 : West German Mergers

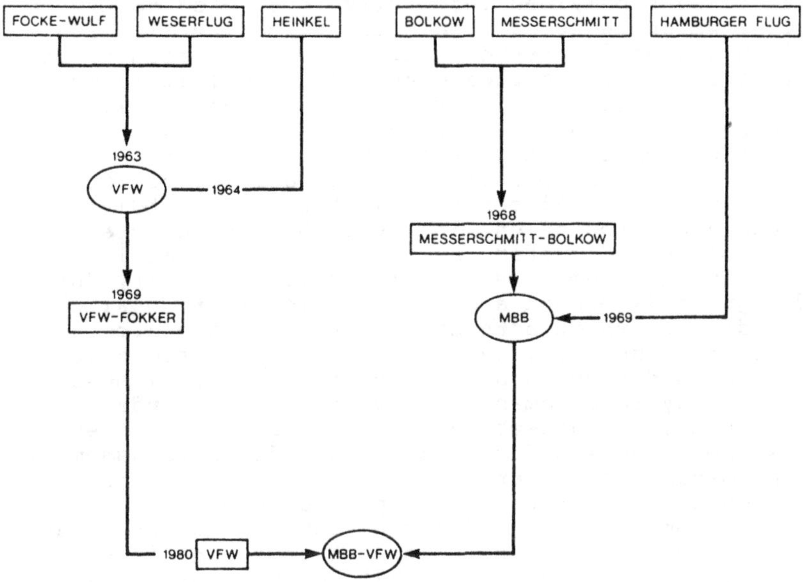

EEC Governments felt that their national industries were better placed to compete with US corporations in aircraft development.[31] To facilitate that competitiveness, they also fostered co-operative international aircraft projects with each other, but that topic deserves addressing from the viewpoint of technology transfer.

TECHNOLOGY TRANSFER

Technology transfer is a mechanism used by some industrial organisations in order to overcome the problems associated with innovating new aircraft or production technology. It involves the transfer of technology developed by one enterprise to another enterprise in return for a fee, royalty, or other kind of remuneration. The conduits for technology transfer are three in number: first, by way of interfirm co-production agreements, secondly, through the provision of licence-production agreements, and thirdly, by virtue of the operations of subsidiary companies established to utilise the R & D efforts of the parent firm.[32] Co-production occurs when two or more firms participate in roughly equal proportions in the development and/or manufacture of aircraft. It can be subdivided into fully-integrated co-production, which is to say, each participating firm is given production responsibility for a particular part or aircraft system regardless of the multiplicity of assembly lines (i.e. 'world product mandates'). If the agreement is international in scope (as in many EEC programmes), this means that one firm supplies the needs for a specific item for all the collaborating countries. Alternatively, the other subdivision, licence co-production, involves the manufacture of assemblies and systems by a variety of firms in roughly equal amounts but with prime authority for design, development and modification resting with the 'lead' firm which acts as licensor for the aircraft. Licence-production, per se, entails the production of a foreign design in a country without the licensee having any involvement in 'world product mandates' for particular assemblies or systems. More often than not, the licence-production reduces to assembly (and minimum fabrication) of subassemblies built in the country of origin and imported into the licensee's premises. Subsidiary operations may be established by enterprises in foreign countries in order to boost the technological base of the host's aerospace industry. As with licence-production, it tends to act as a mechanism for transferring technology from AICs and NICs.

Co-Production

In a nutshell, the fully integrated variant has been characteristic of European efforts whereas the licence variant has typified American ventures into the co-production arena. Frequently, European co-production initiatives have involved the creation of a holding company to act as focal organisation for the project: Airbus Industrie (initially for the A300) and Panavia (for the Tornado MRCA) are cases in point. Examples of prominent fully-integrated co-production projects are presented in Table 6.5 while some of the principal licence co-production programmes are proffered in Table 6.6.

The Europeans favour co-production not only because it reduces duplication in R & D and therefore cuts the unit costs of aircraft to the individual enterprise, but also because it offers the prospect of economies of scale with the longer production runs that follow from several guaranteed customers.

Table 6.5 : Fully-Integrated European Co-Production Programmes

Project	Prime Airframe Contractor	Other Airframe Contractors
Atlantic patrol plane	Breguet (1959)	Dornier SABCA (Belgium) Fokker Aérospatiale Aeritalia (after 1968)
Transall transport	Aérospatiale (Nord) (1959) MBB (Hamburger Flug)	
G.91 tactical fighter	Aeritalia (Fiat) (1956)	Dornier Heinkel Messerschmitt
Alpha Jet trainer	Dassault-Breguet (1970) Dornier	SABCA
Jaguar strike fighter	SEPECAT holding company (1967) BAe (BAC) Dassault-Breguet	
Tornado MRCA	Panavia holding company (1969) BAe (BAC) MBB Aeritalia	

Moreover, some enterprises stand to gain from access to technology developed by a partner organisation, a major factor in West German involvement in Panavia and Airbus as mentioned. One of the earliest co-production agreements, that for the Atlantic maritime-patrol aircraft, was the outcome of a NATO competition of 1958.[33] Based on the winning design of Breguet and funded by the USA, the machine was built for France, West Germany, the Netherlands and Italy. The Belgian ABAP group (Fairey SA, FN, SABCA) produced components, Aérospatiale (then Sud Aviation) built the outer wings, Fokker was responsible for the centre section and nacelles, Dornier for the rear fuselage and tail, and Breguet for the forward fuselage and final assembly. Later Aeritalia was brought into the programme as a reward for an order from the Italian Air Force.[34] The aircraft's engines - R-R Tyne Type 21s - were also the subject of collaborative production: R-R, SNECMA, FN and MTU all being involved. A more recent illustration is provided by the Tornado. This MRCA is managed by Panavia, a Munich-based holding company which accommodates the interests of the partners from the UK, West Germany and Italy (divided in a ratio of 42.5 per cent each to BAe and MBB, and the remaining 15 per cent to Aeritalia). A parallel holding company, Turbo-Union, oversees development and manufacture of the RB.199 engine for the Tornado (shared 40 per cent each by R-R and MTU and 20 per cent by Fiat). The complicated allocation of work-sharing stemmed from the commitment of each nation to purchase batches of aircraft: the larger the procurement, the greater the weight in airframe and aeroengine work.[35]

The US licence co-production agreements listed in Table 6.6 embrace foreign designs (UK, as it happens) built, after due modification, in the USA and American designs built by NATO European consortia. Under the proviso that all major items of equipment for the US armed forces must be domestically produced, the general rule is for the DoD to purchase American-designed and made aircraft. Exceptions occur wherever US manaufacturers are tardy in innovating particular weapons systems, e.g., the light jet bomber (causing the adoption of the British Canberra as the B-57) and the V/STOL tactical fighter (filled by adaptation of the BAe Harrier). In 1949 the Martin XB-51 attack bomber failed to meet USAF operational requirements and was scrapped in favour of the Canberra to which Martin was entrusted with redesigning to US standards. The initial model - the B-57A - was virtually a copy of the 'B2' version of English Electric's original Canberra; subsequent models, however, incorporated increasingly novel features. The engine incidentally, was a US Wright-built version of the UK Armstrong-Siddeley (later part of Bristol) Sapphire. A total of 403 B-57s emerged from Martin's plant at Baltimore. With the AV-8 project, licence-production of the British original followed the purchase of an initial batch of Harriers (AV-8A) from HS in the UK. The US Marine Corps purchased a dozen for $48 million and then requested $96.2 million for another 18. A quarter of the latter sum was required to provide for partial assembly at St. Louis by MD - the surcharge, as it were, of insisting on domestic production.[36] The updated AV-8B was a true co-production venture with 60 per cent of the airframe work assigned to MD and the residual to BAe. The British firm manufactures the rear and centre fuselage as well as the fin and rudder and ships them to the USA for completion.[37] By the same token, the R-R Pegasus engine for the AV-8B is jointly built by its designer in the UK and P & W in the USA. Continuing the US-UK co-production formula is the BAe Hawk, due to fulfil the US Navy jet trainer role from 1987 onwards. Shared in a 55:45

Table 6.6 : US Licence Co-Production Programmes

Project	US Prime Contractor	Other Airframe Contractors
B-57 bomber	Martin (1953)	English Electric
F-104G fighter	Lockheed (1959)	MBB VFW Fokker SABCA Aeritalia
F-16 fighter	GD (1975)	Fokker SABCA/SONACA
AV-8B V/STOL fighter	MD (1981)	BAe

ratio between MD and BAe, the former's Long Beach, California, plant will build the forward and rear fuselage sections and assemble the finished aircraft, leaving the latter's Kingston plant to make the wings, centre fuselage, canopy and empennage.[38]

Both the F-104G and the F-16 were US designs widely adopted by NATO and built as collaborative efforts on both continents. Designed with West German needs in mind, the F-104G update of the USAF Starfighter was also adopted by Belgium, the Netherlands and Italy. Consequently, four production consortia were established (German, Dutch/German, Belgian, Italian) and produced 947 machines for the four air forces, added to which were a further 290 shipped direct from Lockheed. A vital spin-off of this project was the augmentation of the aerospace manufacturing capabilities of the European participants.[39] In 1975 the F-16 was adopted as a replacement by Belgium, the Netherlands, Denmark and Norway.[40] Regardless of a unit cost penalty ($4.55 million each if built entirely by GD, but $6.091 million each if co-produced), the Europeans opted to establish production facilities for co-producing the F-16.[41] One American engineer surmised that the higher unit costs entailed by such a move would be compensated by technology transfer. He averred that the Europeans "are really interested in procedures, quality control, configuration management - all practical things such as precise machining and close tolerances".[42] In other words, they wanted to gain access to process innovations as much as the F-16 product innovation. Fokker, for instance, obtained new milling machines, SABCA got new plant for building wings, and Kongsberg Vapenfabrik (of Norway) was able to use F-16 technology in developing new lines of shipboard navigation systems.

Co-production is becoming increasingly popular outside of the NATO context. Both West Germany and Japan have used it to boost their respective aerospace capabilities. This is especially pertinent to helicopter technology, an area in which MBB has been prominent. Its BO105 was the world's first twin-turbine helicopter (flying in 1967) and also it pioneered the use of rigid titanium hubs with feathering blades in the rotor system, not to speak of rotor blades made of composites. Assembly of the BO105 began in the Philippines in 1974 and its manufacture was commenced in Indonesia in 1976. It was with Japan, however, that co-operation was to bear most fruit. In February 1977 MBB and Kawasaki agreed to develop the BK-117, a scaled-up version of the BO105 and having many interchangeable parts with the earlier aircraft. Development costs were to be shared equally between the two partners, with MBB retaining responsibility for the dynamic and hydraulic systems, tail boom and empennage, and power-amplified controls, while Kawasaki dealt with the airframe, landing gear and equipment. The innovating forte of MBB earned it the right to participate with Aérospatiale in the PAH-2 project to develop an Army helicopter for France and West Germany in the late 1980s, and has also given it design leadership in an agreement with India's HAL to develop a twin-turbine helicopter for the Indian military.[43] Before concluding the co-production section, the present trend in aeroengine development deserves mention. Since the agreement between GE and SNECMA leading to the CFM56 turbofan (referred to earlier), all large engines have tended to become collaborative efforts by virtue of their huge development costs.[44] R-R, for instance, engineered the establishment of International Aero Engines in 1983 to develop the V2500 (for the A320 Airbus) along with P & W, MTU, Fiat and a Japanese consortium.[45] P & W, for its part, has allowed MTU, Volvo and MHI a minority stake in its JT8D-200 turbofan which powers the MD-80 series of jetliners.[46]

<u>Licence-Production</u>

Table 6.7 lists the major US warplanes built under licence elsewhere. Notable among the AICs are Canada, Italy and Japan which repeatedly adopt American

designs and therefore circumvent the problems associated with innovating their own aircraft (Britain has followed suit with helicopters). Also present in the table are a scattering of NICs - Taiwan and South Korea in particular - and this pattern of licence-production typifies the classic way in which 'underdeveloped' aircraft industries acquire technological know-how.[47] Historically, the pattern of accumulating expertise progressively through licence-production until indigenous R & D comes of age is best exemplified by the postwar experience of Japan. Abetted by the Japanese Government which was willing to pay uneconomic prices for licence-built aircraft solely to enable the native producers to gain access to American know-how, Japanese companies started building light aircraft in the early 1950s (Fuji's contract for Beech T-34 piston-engined trainers and Kawasaki's for Bell 47 helicopters). However, after a remarkably brief learning period, they were capable of copying relatively advanced designs. From 1956 they built the Lockheed T-33 jet trainer (Kawasaki), North American F-86 jet fighter (MHI) and Lockheed P-2 patrol plane (Kawasaki).[48] By 1962, Japan could face the prospect of building the supersonic F-104 with equanimity. Experience derived from this programme and the replacement F-4, built under licence from MD, gave MHI the technological base to develop its own fighter and jet trainer. By the mid-1970s, Japan was interested less in licence-production than in partial co-production. As recounted elsewhere, it was a partner (albeit junior) in the Boeing 767 and had attained equal status with R-R in the development of the RJ500 engine. Nevertheless, it persisted in licence-building US designs in areas where its technological expertise was lacking. However, the current MD F-15 and Lockheed P-3C programmes are widely distributed among Japanese contractors in order to disseminate technological know-how. With respect to the F-15, the nose, forward and centre fuselages and final assembly are the province of MHI, whereas IHI produces the engine (under P & W licence) and Kawasaki the aft fuselage and wings. The P-3C programme is even wider dispersed: Kawasaki (centre fuselage and final assembly), Fuji (wing), Shin Meiwa (nose and tail), Nihon Hikohki (nacelles) and IHI (Allison T56 turboprops) all having a part to play.[49] The fact that Japan was prepared to find an extra $1.8 billion to domestically-produce the F-15s instead of buying them direct from the USA has caused some unease among American aviation circles which express dismay at the prospect of rising Japanese competition in the aerospace field fuelled, ironically, by the results of US

Table 6.7 : US Aircraft Subject to Multiple Licensing Agreements

Type	US Licensor	Licensee Country (Year of agreement)
F-86 fighter	North American	Canada (1949) Australia (1952) Italy (1954) Japan (1955)
S-55 helicopter	Sikorsky	UK (1950) Japan (1958)
T-33 trainer	Lockheed	Canada (1951) Japan (1954)
47G helicopter	Bell	Italy (1952) Japan (1953) UK (1957)
T-34 trainer	Beech	Canada (1955) Japan (1957) Argentina (1958)
S-58 helicopter	Sikorsky	UK (1956) France (1960)
F-104 fighter	Lockheed	Canada (1959) Japan (1960)
UH-1 helicopter	Bell	Italy (1961) Japan (1964) Taiwan (1969)
S-61B helicopter	Sikorsky	Canada (1962) Japan (1962) Italy (1963) UK (1963)
F-5 fighter	Northrop	Canada (1965) Spain (1965) Taiwan (1973) Switzerland (1976) South Korea (1979)
OH-58 helicopter	Bell	Italy (1967) Japan (1971)
OH-6 helicopter	Hughes	Japan (1968) Italy (1969) Argentina (1973) South Korea (1976)

Source: Derived from M. Rich et al, Multinational Corporation of Military Aerospace Systems, Appendix A.

R & D.[50]

Several countries insist on technology-transfer as a return for ordering foreign aircraft, and this usually entails a combination of process technology and the licence-production of some or all of the aircraft in question. Such offset agreements are now the order of the day. Thus, Australia was introduced to titanium hot forming and chemical milling and machining in return for its $2.75 billion order to MD for F-18 fighters. The engine manufacturer, GE, also allowed Australia to make 20 per cent of the aircraft's F404 high-performance engine.[51] The sheer extent of such technology-transfer can be gauged from the offsets dangled before Greece in an attempt to get that nation to buy the Panavia Tornado. In its final (unsuccessful) offer, Panavia was prepared to let Greece assemble the aircraft and engine for the Greek order and build components for all future Tornadoes regardless of customer. Additionally, the Greeks were to build the Mauser aircraft cannon under licence and co-produce the aircraft's missiles; they were to build a trainer aircraft selected by Panavia, obtain gas-turbine overhaul capacity, an aircraft tyre retread facility, and an ejection seat overhaul facility, and last but not least, to benefit from the repair and maintenance of Tornadoes sold to other countries.[52] The package of benefits clearly extended from Tier I to Tier III operations, of which airframe assembly was but one constituent.

Subsidiary Operations

Perhaps one of the more historically crucial examples of a subsidiary firm established to funnel the transfer of technology was the Junkers venture in the USSR of the 1920s. Founded in the wake of the Soviet-German Trade Agreement of 1921, this German enterprise erected a factory at Fili on the outskirts of Moscow and passed on metal-monoplane technology to the uninitiated Soviet aircraft industry.[53] Since then, the use of subsidiaries to trigger national aircraft industries has not been uncommon. Canada is an obvious example: its first supplier for a nascent RCAF was a subsidiary of British Vickers. Some contemporary NIC aerospace sectors are virtual subsidiary operations in spite of official state guardianship. Spain's CASA for instance, hides a minority foreign shareholding under the dominant 65.62 per cent stake held by the state. Northrop of the USA holds 20.8 per cent of CASA while MBB of West Germany and Dassault-Breguet of France have nominal shares (2.25 and 1.47 per cent respectively) reflecting their technical assistance.[54] To take another example, Israel's Bet-Shemesh aeroengine maker is also ostensibly a government enterprise, but the state's 49 per cent holding was overshadowed by the majority stake of Turboméca of France. In fact, the French company built the Israeli plant to licence-produce Marboré turbojets required for the Magister aircraft then being manufactured under licence by IAI. In view of Israel's desire to power the indigenously-designed Lavi fighter with P & W engines, the engine-maker's parent company, UTC, was intent on buying a 40 per cent share of Bet-Shemesh in 1984 presumably with the object of facilitating technology transfer.[55] Even enterprises in AICs sometimes contain a foreign shareholding. The generally successful Fokker organisation in the Netherlands is one-fifth owned by Northrop Corporation.[56] The former holding of UTC in West German VFW has already been mentioned and much of the postwar revival of Italian aerospace depended on American involvement.

Often, foreign shareholding goes hand-in-hand with licence-production. The licensor forms a pact with a national concern - usually the government - in order to set up from scratch the facilities for aircraft assembly. The peripatetic Northrop Corporation was involved in the creation of an aircraft industry in Iran. Under the auspices of Iran Aircraft Industries (IACI), a firm owned 49 per cent each by Northrop and the Iranian Government and two per cent by the Imbdi Iranian Bank, the US enterprise embarked on an ambitious plan at Mehrabad. Commencing with airframe and engine overhauls, IACI was to graduate to aircraft assembly and, in due course, design its own types.[57] Before disruption as a result of the Iranian Revolution, IACI had completed two sites totalling almost 32,000 m^2 and was underway with a personnel training programme.

CONCLUSION

Technological change is the quintessence of evolution for the aircraft industry and at its heart is the commitment to R & D. Under the rubric of the structural contingency framework, the rationale for viewing technological change as the cornerstone of a particular firm soon becomes apparent. Both markets and relations with the state depend, ultimately, on the firm's technical initiatives. In turn, the manner in which those 'environmental' forces respond to the firm's technical initiatives reverberate to mould its form of business organisation. Made specific by Phillips, frameworks of this nature can accommodate distinctions between exogenous and endogenous R & D on the one hand, as well as allowing for interfirm competition (manifest through the entry of new firms) on the other. Throughout, however, the key role of technological change remains sacrosanct.

The chapter summoned evidence to support the basic precepts of such a framework. It established the trend towards market concentration as a result of the inexorable rise in development costs of aircraft. Yet, even firm enlargement was no guarantee either of finding the necessary resources to innovate new aircraft types or innovating a saleable product should the resources be forthcoming. In other words, the risk burden associated with continual product innovation is tending to become untenable. Only massive backing by the state offers inducement to persevere. The Americans accomplish this aim through defence RDT & E and large aircraft contracts. The Europeans, conversely, call upon formal state involvement in the industrial organisations themselves.

Technology-transfer can lighten some of the burden of development costs for firms determined to maintain technical initiatives. Such firms resort to collaborative measures, apportioning the development load among the partners and thus dividing both the costs and risks. Large EEC firms, devoid of the security of the 'follow-on' system enjoyed by US companies, have been especially prominent in this respect. Alternatively, technology transfer can be used in its traditional sense; as a means of acquiring know-how when the donor firm is technologically superior to the receiver. Used by the smaller NATO countries to acquire American process technology, co-production has emerged as a major form of international warplane manufacture. Technology-transfer in the guise of licence-production remains the norm for instituting aircraft manufacture in NICs.

NOTES AND REFERENCES

1. P. McDermott and M. Taylor, Industrial Organisation and Location, (Cambridge University Press, Cambridge, 1982). Note, 'environment' is a deliberately vague concept here which can embrace everything outside the focal organisation.

2. For a review of the salient features of technical change, see: E. Mansfield, The Economics of Technical Change, (Longman, London, 1968); J. Schmookler, Invention and Economic Growth, (Harvard University Press, Cambridge, Mass., 1966).

3. Almarin Phillips, Technology and Market Structure: A Study of the Aircraft Industry (D. C. Heath, Lexington, Mass., 1971).

4. The adoption of passenger-carrying airships in the 1920s can be put forward to illustrate the idea of 'false-start' innovations: the product is either faulted or before its time and therefore is ultimately rejected by the market. The post-1945 attempt to resurrect flying-boat airline services is another case in point.

5. A. Phillips, Technology and Market Structure, p.127.

6. Ibid, p.90.

7. Ibid, pp.115-126.

8. R. Miller and D. Sawers, The Technical Development of Modern Aviation, (Routledge & Kegan Paul, London, 1968), p.246.

9. Ibid, pp.248-9.

10. Ibid, p.263.

11. K. M. Molson and H. A. Taylor, Canadian Aircraft since 1909, (Putnam, London, 1982), p.268.

12. The historical experience of the RAE supports this criticism. See P. Fearon, 'The British Airframe Industry and the State', Economic History Review, vol.27 (1974), pp.236-251, and especially p.247.

13. FI, 29 March 1962, p.489.

14. FI, 23 January 1975, p.83.

15. FI, 30 January 1975, p.122.

16. AW & ST, 1 November 1971, pp.18-19.

17. Air Pictorial, vol.44 (July 1982), pp.266-7.

18. AW & ST, 8 February 1971, p.25.

19. AW & ST, 1 December 1980, p.37.

20. Charles Gardner, British Aircraft Corporation: A History (B. T. Batsford, London, 1981), p.15.

21. Ibid, p.22.

22. The helicopter specialist, Westland, had emerged as an enlarged company in 1960 when the helicopter interests of Bristol, Fairey and Saro were merged into it. Note, the aeroengine companies were collapsed into two companies about this time also (i.e. R-R and Bristol Siddeley Engines Ltd).

23. C. Gardner, British Aircraft Corporation, p.63.

24. G. Williams, F. Gregory and J. Simpson, Crisis in Procurement: A Case Study of the TSR-2, (Royal United Services Institute, London, 1969), p.50.

25. Contemporaneous with the TSR-2 cancellation was the ending of the P.1154 supersonic V/STOL fighter and HS.681 STOL transport projects of HS. HS responded by closing its Whitworth-Gloster division and its accompanying airframe plant at Coventry.

26. More properly, Société Nationale Industrielle Aérospatiale.

27. AW & ST, 26 January 1970, p.21-2.

28. Prior to the merger, state interest in VFW was reflected through Bremen's 38.4 per cent holding, while MBB was owned by Bavaria (22.65 per cent) and Hamburg (20.25 per cent). Currently, MBB is about 50 per cent state owned.

29. The events leading up to the merger of MBB-VFW are dealt with in AW & ST, 18 February 1980, p.24; 6 October 1980, p.28; 20 October 1980, p.115 and 8 June 1981, p.94.

30. AW & ST, 9 March 1970, p.50 and 30 March 1970, p.11.

31. The UK experienced another bout of merger in 1977 leading to the formation of BAe, but that story is bound up with nationalisation and, as such, is reserved for Chapter 7.

32. There is a fourth possibility; namely, that firms purchase the specialised expertise from other organisations. Such technology transfer is akin to tapping specialist sub-contractors for a specific purpose within the overall project development. CASA, for example, invited MBB to produce the rear fuselage section for its prototype C-101 jet trainer in 1974. Similarly, Saab-Scania contracted BAe to design and develop the carbon-fibre composite wings for the JAS 39. See AW & ST, 27 March 1978, p.41 and 29 November 1982, p.28.

33. The programme, renamed 'Atlantique 2' was resuscitated in 1984 to provide for the needs of the French Navy into the 1990s.

34. AW & ST, 10 August 1970, p.51.

35. The combined orders for in excess of 800 aircraft allow for production economies despite the fragmented international input and enable unit costs of Tornado aircraft to match those of comparable US programmes. See Trevor Taylor, Defence, Technology and International Integration, (St Martin's Press, New York, 1982), p.89.

36. AW & ST, 5 January 1970, p.19 and 2 March 1970, p.17.

37. AW & ST, 31 August 1981, p.18.

38. FI, 28 November 1981, p.1604.

39. M. Rich et al, Multinational Coproduction of Military Aerospace Systems, (Rand Corporation, Santa Monica, October 1981), p.3.

40. Denmark and Norway were supplied with F-104s built by Canadair. This Canadian firm built 200 for the RCAF and then a batch of 140, paid for by DoD, to be distributed to NATO countries.

41. The first batch of 650 F-16s for the USAF (as opposed to 348 for the four NATO countries) are expected to be five per cent more expensive as a

result of European participation in the US domestic production system. The programme covers three assembly sites: GD in the USA, SABCA in Belgium, and Fokker in the Netherlands. See Rich et al, Multinational Coproduction, pp.82-104.

42. AW & ST, 2 May 1977, pp.47-9. Quote from p.47.

43. See Air Pictorial, vol.43 (April 1981), pp.128-133; AW & ST, 1 May 1978, p.15 and 20 August 1984, p.21. The BO105 is also to be built under licence in Canada.

44. FI, 17 January 1981, p.142.

45. AW & ST, 21 May 1984, p.33.

46. AW & ST, 18 June 1984, p.43.

47. This is not to say, of course, that advanced aerospace nations are not sometimes prone to undertake licence-production. The USA adopted Euromissile's (i.e. Aérospatiale and MBB) Roland 2 for manufacture under the auspices of Hughes. Fairchild also built a small number of Swiss Pilatus Turbo-Porters for the USAF and Thai air force.

48. AW & ST, 12 January 1970, pp.56-66.

49. AW & ST, 24 April 1978, p.16.

50. AW & ST, 19 April 1982, p.11.

51. AW & ST, 26 October 1981, pp.22-3.

52. AW & ST, 11 October 1982, p.22.

53. A. Boyd, The Soviet Air Force since 1918, (MacDonald and Jane's, London, 1977), p.9.

54. FI, 17 January 1981, p.173.

55. AW & ST, 18 June 1984, p.28.

56. AW & ST, 8 February 1982, p.55.

57. AW & ST, 21 May 1973, pp.60-1. Note, Bell-Helicopter-Textron was to undertake a similar project, this time for helicopter assembly, at Isfahan.

Chapter Seven

THE STATE AND THE AIRCRAFT INDUSTRY

Throughout this book the point has been repeatedly made that the aircraft industry cannot be considered independently of the actions of the state. The fact that the industry relies for the bulk of its market on military customers was brought out in Chapter 2 where the dependence of aircraft manufacturers on the whims of government (as manifest through the wave-cycle) was affirmed. By the same token, the reliance of aircraft firms on government financing schemes in the civil market became apparent in Chapter 3. The formal structure enabling state co-operation with aircraft firms which functioned as defence contractors was evinced in Chapter 4 where the MIC was construed, in the American context, as a government-private enterprise partnership. The aircraft industry was shown to be inordinately dependent on government even in the selection of its plant locations and was, indeed, a prime candidate for use in regional policy (Chapter 5). Finally, Chapter 6 elicited the seeming truism that innovation cannot be effective in aerospace enterprise unless bolstered by the state. The object of this chapter is not to reiterate that material, but instead to focus on the state's involvement in the industry from its inception, that is, the nurturing of aerospace as an 'infant' industry; to consider the state's maintenance of aircraft enterprises on the grounds that they are national assets; and to examine the attitude of European states who foster joint aerospace ventures in the name of enhanced competitiveness of their own national aircraft industries.

Before pursuing those themes, it will not go amiss to remind ourselves of the ubiquitous interference of the state in aerospace affairs. At one extreme is the model of the communist bloc, followed, wittingly or otherwise, by most NIC aircraft industries; namely, the state asserting the right to own and operate the industry in its entirety. One need only point to the Soviet Ministry of Aircraft Production which has under its jurisdiction about 400 Tier I, II and III plants and which, moreover, designs, manufactures and markets all the aircraft required by the USSR.[1] This, the world's largest aerospace enterprise, is a far cry from the state sponsored fledgling aircraft industries of Chile or the Philippines: but the essential ingredient of state intervention remains common to all of them, and for the obvious reason that, without it, the chances of a national aircraft industry emerging at all are likely to be very slim indeed. By way of contrast, the US approach is fundamentally different. The state is, in truth, the chief market (in the manifestation of the DoD) and the chief supplier of R & D funds: it is not, however, officially involved in the organisation of the aircraft industry. None the less, even the US Government feels obligated to sponsor the export efforts of private US aerospace corporations. In 1974 the Department of Commerce singled out the industry as one of fifteen 'target' industries eligible to receive government support for staging displays and trade shows around the world. Furthermore, the US Government began to stand as official backer of offset warplane deals struck between US corporations and foreign governments (e.g. the F-16 NATO venture).[2] When it is recollected that US firms also benefit from a de facto protected domestic market - the effect of the 'Buy America Act' - then the ostensible non-intervention of the US Government is seen to be largely a chimera.[3]

Adopting a position mid-way between that of the USSR and the USA is the array of EEC countries and Japan. In most instances, state involvement in the aerospace business is officially countenanced through state-owned enterprises, although this pattern is eschewed in Japan. That country, in marked contrast, tolerates only private aircraft firms but it ensures, for all that, a close regulation on the part of the state. Notwithstanding the fact that Japan does not allow export of arms nor officially maintains offensive forces, and despite its firms having the highest dependence of any upon warplane orders, the Japanese Government has emphasised the need for its aerospace sector to hinge on civil aircraft projects. Accordingly, MITI is prepared to advance 50 per cent of new product development costs, insists that Japanese firms are accorded full-partner rights in international programmes, and sets up holding companies whenever appropriate.[4] The first of these - Nihon - received passing mention in Chapter 1, but the latest arrangement, the Civil Transport Aircraft Development Corporation, is subsidised by MITI to fulfil Japan's input into the Boeing 767 and the next-generation YXX project.[5] Regardless of ideological outlook, all states foment the creation of national aircraft industries and it is to that theme that we now turn.

THE INFANT INDUSTRY CASE

The state's role in nurturing a domestic aircraft industry is as old as the industry itself. The rudimentary British aircraft designs of World War I were, for the most part, pioneered by government establishments in Britain and, to a much lesser extent, built in them too. Formation of the Royal Flying Corps in 1912 meant that along with the military air arm came a joint R & D and production facility; namely, the Royal Aircraft Factory at Farnborough. The hiving off of a naval branch, the Royal Naval Air Service, was not complete without the foundation of its Experimental Construction Depot at Port Victoria near Chatham. A combination of ineffectual production mobilisation, some poor designs, and jealousy from the newly-ascendant private firms, led to the demise of aircraft production at those two sites in 1918. Instead, the pattern was set whereby the UK public sector was to confine its attention to R & D; to become the source, in fact, of exogenous R & D for use by the private aircraft companies. Interestingly, however, the UK Government had no qualms about establishing 'National Aircraft Factories' (albeit under private management) at Aintree(Liverpool), Waddon(Croydon) and Heaton Chapel(Manchester) in that same year when the supply of warplanes fell short of requirements on the Western Front (they were precursors of the 'shadow factories' run by private firms in World War II).[6] That bastion of private enterprise, the USA, also toyed with state airframe facilities in the formative era. The Naval Aircraft Factory was founded in 1916 at Philadelphia in order to provide the plant, unavailable in private firms, required to build large flying boats. It lingered on through to the end of World War II designing some aircraft (latterly, target drones), but mainly building standard aeroplanes under licence from Grumman and other major private contractors. By then it was an anomaly, as US practice had conformed to the British pattern, which is to say, the state provided the firms with exogenous R & D through the likes of NASA and its predecessors.

Several other AICs emulated the British and

American experience in the years following World War I. Unlike the precursors, however, they maintained state enterprises throughout. One of the more constant in this respect is Switzerland. The Federal Aircraft Factory at Emmen began by building foreign combat aircraft under licence for the Swiss Flugwaffe, but in 1934 shifted to indigenous design. Curiously, an indigenous type, the C-36 dating from World War II, was rebuilt in 1968-72 with US Lycoming T53 turboprops rather than the original piston engines.[7] True to minor aircraft industries, however, most of Emmen's efforts were directed to building foreign types (e.g. DH Vampire, Dassault Mirage and Northrop F-5). Belgium, likewise, relied on the state for the inception of its aircraft industry. SABCA was founded in 1920 on the promise of a monopoly supply of all government aircraft. While engaging in indigenous design from the outset, most of the enterprise's energies have been expended on licence production.[8] By the late 1970s its Haren factory was busy with components manufacture for the F-104G and Fokker F-27, whereas its airframe plant at Gosselies was assembling Mirage 5 fighters and Alouette II helicopters for the Belgian forces. To facilitate technology transfer, the Belgian Government had connived at minority participation by Fokker and Dassault.[9] The other lodger at Gosselies, SONACA, had been set up in 1931 as Avions Fairey and was to be integrated with SABCA in the 1970s on the failure of its foreign parent company. At government insistence, the UK Fairey company had established the subsidiary in order to build the Firefly and Fox aircraft for the Belgian Air Force, providing, as it were, an alternative means of procuring an aircraft industry to the state establishment.[10]

Infant Industries in NICs

Development of state aircraft industries in NICs has had mixed results. While reasonably adept at licence-production, they have, with few exceptions, been unable to formulate marketable indigenous designs. The experience of Argentina is typical. Created at Cordoba in 1927, the Military Aircraft Factory (FMA or Fabrica Militar de Aviones) is a constituent part of the Argentine Air Force. Employing 8,000 and occupying factory space of 263,000m^2, FMA has built Cessna light planes under licence and also undertakes 'in-house' design; the latest product of which is the IA 63 jet trainer.[11] Two designs of merit warrant mention. The IA 50-G II is a twin-turboprop light transport (powered by French Turboméca Bastan engines) and a total of 41 were built for the air force from the late 1960s. The IA 58 Pucara of Falklands War fame, is a twin-turboprop (i.e. Turboméca Astazou) counter-insurgency combat aircraft based on the IA 50. Deliveries began in 1975 for an initial air force requirement of 100 and it has subsequently been exported to other Latin American and African nations in modest numbers. The fact that it can operate from rough airstrips of about 700m in length, plus its turboprop power, makes it a cost-effective machine for cash-starved air forces.

Taiwan is another NIC whose aircraft industry is a branch of the air force. Commencing aircraft construction in 1968, the Taiwan enterprise (which became the AIDC in July 1969) built a slightly modified US Pazmany PL-1 light aeroplane in small numbers. This was followed in short order by licence-production of the Bell UH-1H helicopter and, since 1973, by the much more sophisticated Northrop F-5E. The Taichung airframe plant progressed through five phases in this fighter programme. The first of these merely entailed acceptance of shipments of major airframe structural components built in the USA and then assembled by AIDC. In the second phase, Northrop transferred more of the subassembly finishing work to Taiwan. By the third phase, AIDC was in a position to assume responsibility for manufacturing and assembling the forward fuselage. The fourth phase extended AIDC responsibility to the fabrication of the aircraft's rudder, leading edge extensions and nose landing gear doors. Before the programme culminated in 1980, AIDC fabrication also embraced fuselage dorsal covers, trailing edge flaps and ailerons.[12] The engines were beyond Taiwanese capability and this constraint has hindered development of the AT-3 indigenous jet light-attack aircraft (only the Avco Lycoming T53 turboprops are built under licence in Taiwan).[13] The much desired autonomy of warplane supply (in the manner of Israel) thus continues to elude the Taiwan Government.

As mentioned in Chapter 1, the Egyptian attempt at creating a fully-fledged aircraft industry highlighted the pitfalls associated with forced industrialisation. Dating from 5 July 1950 when the Defence Minister, El Ferik Muhammed Haydar Pasha, announced that an aircraft enterprise would be established at the cost of E£400,000, the General Aero Organisation was formed to make the German Bucker Bestmann trainer under licence. Emanating from 'Factory 72' at Helwan near Cairo, the Bestmann was restyled the Gomhouriya and remained in intermittent production up to the 1980s. Initially powered by Czech-made Walter Minor engines, later batches of this primary trainer were equipped with imported US Continental and Lycoming piston engines. At the forefront during the Nasser years, the aircraft industry extended its efforts to the licence-production of jet trainers (the Spanish Hispano Saeta, retitled the Ha-200 Al Kahiras) after 1960 and also embarked upon an ambitious scheme to build a lightweight supersonic air-superiority fighter. Importing a team from Spain led by Willi Messerschmitt (the designer of the Ha-200), Egypt built new plant at Helwan for the Ha-300 programme. Simultaneously, it hired Austrian engineer Ferdinand Brandner to develop the E-300A turbojet for mating with the Ha-300 airframe. Difficulties with both the airframe and engine resulted in the abandonment of the programme in 1967 but not before 17 engines and four aircraft had been assembled. At the same time, development problems with the missiles designed by 'Factory 333' at Helwan meant that the small Kahir, larger Zafir and two-stage Ared surface-to-air missiles were never put into production.[14] For well over a decade, Egypt remained disillusioned with indigenous R & D and confined its aircraft enterprise to overhaul of Soviet-built hardware. Only since the rapprochement with the West has the industry been retooled for assembly of French-designed machines (Alpha Jets and Gazelles along with SNECMA engines) and latterly, the Embraer Tucano from fellow NIC, Brazil. Ultimately, the industry wishes to gear up to co-production of the Mirage 2000 fighter.[15]

The problem of marshalling the correct resources to produce viable aircraft designs is endemic to infant aircraft industries notwithstanding the full backing they receive as state enterprises. India is salutary in this respect. Upon achieving independence, the Government of India authorised HAL to supply the needs of the air force. Licence-production of light trainers (the UK Percival Prentice) began in 1948 and was followed in 1950 by assembly of the DH Vampire light jet fighter, again of UK design. The first indigenous design, the HT-2, appeared in 1953 and it was a satisfactory, if unsophisticated, primary trainer.[16] More sophisticated work stemmed from modifications to the licence-built HS Gnat (the Ajeet) and its various jet trainer derivatives in the 1960s and 1970s. However, Indian attempts to design a supersonic combat aircraft were doomed to disappointment. The HF-24 Marut was ready (after a gestation period of eight years) in its Mark 1 form in 1964, but was found to be underpowered. The brainchild of the German engineer Kurt Tank, the HF-24 was tried with two R-R Orpheus engines (then being made under licence for the Gnat) and about 100 were built by 1977. Scarcely capable of reaching Mach 1, let alone the hoped-for Mach 2, the HF-24 was refitted with the Egyptian E-300A prior to the abandonment of that engine. A Mark 3 Marut has been projected, equipped with the same engines as those powering the Panavia Tornado (RB.199), and this machine should be capable of realising the original performance requirements specified thirty years ago. In the meantime, Indian Air Force needs have been met through licence-production of Soviet and Western supersonic types (e.g. Mig-21, Mig-27, SEPECAT Jaguar). Clearly, successive experience of licence-production, no matter how sophisticated the aircraft, is no guarantee that the transition to indigenous design of high-performance aircraft will be plain sailing. India continues to subscribe to the classic NIC pattern as the Jaguar programme attests, that is, a progression from the initial phase where the aircraft are supplied by the licensor (BAe) in kit form for assembly by the licensee (HAL) to a final (in this case, seventh) phase when the complete aeroplane is manufactured in the NIC.[17] Otherwise, production of indigenous designs is limited to the Kiran 2 jet trainer and the HPT-32 piston-engined trainer: a situation not too far removed from the 1950s when the Indian aircraft industry was in its infancy. Nothing daunted, however, India intends to develop a new fighter for the 1990s from its own resources which includes design and production of an appropriate engine.

Protected Markets

The proclivity of governments to protect their aircraft industries by reserving civil aircraft orders for state airlines was commented upon in Chapter 3. Air France and British Airways' predecessors, BEA and BOAC, were all state owned and compelled, as a result, to operate domestically-made transports. The French carrier complied by introducing the Sud Caravelle jetliner, BEA was induced to pioneer the service life of the Vickers Viscount, while BOAC was primary user of the DH Comet jetliner and Bristol Britannia turboprop airliner. While providential for the aircraft manufacturers, this policy had mixed results for the airlines and, consequently, was abandoned in the 1960s. It has been estimated, for example, that BOAC suffered capital losses of $21 million on its Comet fleet and $63 million on its Britannia fleet, whereas the Vickers VC-10 jetliner inflicted operating costs on BOAC variously estimated at ten to fifteen per cent higher than the comparable Boeing

707.[18] With respect to military aviation, government protected markets have become institutionalised through the 'follow-on' system and, without it, the US aerospace sector would most likely collapse. The point to be made, however, is that protected markets are part-and-parcel of the infant-industry approach to the aircraft industry: in other words, establishment of a state airframe constructor demands government connivance in the provision of guaranteed markets. Historically, even where the state has eschewed formal government-owned aircraft enterprises, it has been obliged to maintain private aircraft firms as informal national production and design facilities, and contemporary American practice is not an aberration in this respect. The British post-World War I record bears out this assertion as well.

The onset of demobilisational instability cut a swath through the aircraft firms, so much so, that the industry was in danger of disappearing. The UK Government had no choice but to bolster the survivors - even though it had officially disparaged state involvement in aircraft manufacture - just to ensure a reserve capacity in the national interest. In 1920 it decided to designate a number of firms as official defence contractors, that is to say, they alone would be allowed to tender for military aircraft contracts. Furthermore, in order to ensure a degree of competition among suppliers, the state disbursed R & D contracts to the firms so that more than one could respond to each operational specification issued by the military. The resultant 'fly-off' of prototypes would determine the best machine but would also, incidentally, underwrite the survival of the losers at least as design bureaux if not as recipients of major production contracts. Holding to a 'ring' of sixteen firms, the Air Ministry claimed that any diminution in the number would reduce the technical competitiveness among the warplane enterprises. Moreover, winning designs were contracted out to firms other than the innovating enterprise just to maintain their manufacturing plant in workable order and hoard key workers.[19] One firm, Handley Page, was on the verge of collapse in 1922 when the Air Ministry, in response to a desperate letter from the firm's founder, sent some RAF aircraft (DH-9A) to the plant for reconditioning.[20] Production contracts, such as they were, just sufficed to keep the 'ring' firms in existence; but this accomplishment rested on the willingness of the firms to cater to special RAF needs. Table 7.1 identifies the firms comprising the 'ring' and notes their warplane specialisation in the 1920s and 1930s. Thus, whenever a fighter

Table 7.1 Protected Firms and their UK Warplane Specialisation

Firm	Location	Aircraft	Example
Armstrong Whitworth	Coventry	Fighter	Siskin IIIA
Boulton Paul	Wolverhampton	Bomber	Sidestrand
Bristol	Bristol	Fighter	Bulldog
Blackburn	Brough (Hull)	Marine aircraft	Perth
DH	Hatfield	Trainer	Gipsy Moth
Fairey	Hayes (London)	Carrier-borne aircraft	Seal
Handley Page	Cricklewood (London)	Transport/Bomber	Hinaidi
Hawker	Kingston (London)	Fighter	Fury
Gloster	Cheltenham	Fighter	Gamecock
A.V.Roe (Avro)	Manchester	Trainer	Tutor
Supermarine	Eastleigh (Southampton)	Marine aircraft	Southampton
Short	Rochester	Flying-boat	Rangoon
Saunders Roe (Saro)	Isle of Wight	Marine aircraft	Singapore
Vickers	Weybridge	Transport/Bomber	Valencia
Westland	Yeovil	Army co-operation aircraft	Wapiti
G. Parnell	Bristol	Carrier-borne aircraft	Plover

specification was formulated, Hawker and Gloster would invariably tender a design, whereas Handley Page and Vickers were generally forthcoming with designs whenever a multi-engined aircraft (bomber or transport) order was in the offing. Should the design fail to win the contract, it might be revamped as a private venture and offered for export.[21]

Aircraft exports acted as 'bonuses' for the firms, but they also served as direct competition to the indigenous aircraft industries of the importing countries. The extent of the competitive edge enjoyed by AIC aircraft exports can be gauged from Table 7.2 which lists the additional costs required to build comparable aircraft in the importing country (in this case India). With the examples cited, domestic production of aircraft cost from half as much again as equivalent imports to almost double the AIC amount. Indeed, India's insistence on licence-production of Jaguar strike fighters means that the country has to absorb a cost penalty of 100 per cent over and above what would have been the price if the machines had been imported.[22] The cost differential arises out of inefficiencies in the 'learning curve' experienced by NIC constructors, but it is equally attributable to the costs of purchasing engines, avionics and parts which are generally beyond the manufacturing capabilities of NIC aerospace sectors. Consequently, governments must assimilate excessive costs and attempt to partially recoup them through extended production runs for state air arms and airlines. This is the route adopted by India. Production contracts for the Mig-21 have run to over 500 while, at 69 aircraft in the initial batch, HAL's production of the BAe 748 has amounted to about one-third of the effort devoted to the programme in Britain. As noted elsewhere, such 'protected markets' have enabled NIC enterprises in Brazil and Indonesia to overcome initial start-up problems.

PERMANENT RECEIVERSHIP

An integral part of being a defence contractor in the USA is the guarantee of government support whenever certain circumstances arise; namely, a financial crisis visited upon the organisation in the first place and an indispensable position within the DoD procurement system in the second. Known as the 'bail-out imperative', the government commitment is to ensure the ongoing viability of the enterprise as a supplier entity, regardless of whether that entails organisational restructuring or simply the revitalising of the firm through state subsidies. In fact, this process can be generalised to apply to most non-communist nations and is best subsumed under the guise of 'permanent receivership'. Coined by Lowi, the term refers to those organisations, be they officially private or public enterprises, which are the recipients of state attention in order to guarantee their continued stability and success.[23] In vouching for organisational stability through the underwriting and socialisation of risk, the "government maintains a steadfast position that any institution large enough to be a significant factor in the community" shall not be permitted to founder.[24] As vital elements of national defence, aircraft firms of any stature are automatically accorded the status of permanent receivership.

This condition pertains in the USA as elsewhere, but the American version of permanent receivership is stripped of any public enterprise connotations. An obvious indirect way of underwriting risk for the companies is to provide them with plant and premises on 'loan'. While common practice in periods of re-armamental instability and wartime equilibrium, the phenomenon of government-owned, company-operated plants is still widespread in the US aerospace sector. Table 7.3 elicits the amount of fixed capital made available in this way. Evidently, some firms rely on government premises to a much greater extent than average (e.g. GD), whereas others (e.g. UTC) make use of no government plant at all.[25] However, the US Government has directly intervened to rescue ailing aircraft companies. The most notable venture was the 1971 decision of President Nixon to provide $250 million in loan guarantees to Lockheed Corporation in a successful attempt to prevent its bankruptcy. Overextended on the L-1011 Tristar airliner, Lockheed had invested $1.4 billion ($400 million in bank loans, $240 million in advance payments from airlines, $350 million from sub-contractors and the balance from its own resources) and had still been unable to bring the project to fruition. At the same time, it was faced with a $200 million loss on the C-5A cargo transport for the USAF. Collapse of the company would have meant the loss of 10,000 jobs (not to speak of 7,000 R-R workers in the UK who were also adversely affected by the L-1011) and a negative spill-over cutting another 14,000 employed by sub-contractors in 25 states. Under pressure from the UK Government, disturbed at the prospect of the demise of R-R, the Nixon administration felt obligated to keep the Tristar programme operational virtually at any cost - ideological as much as pecuniary.[26]

Table 7.2 Costs of Indigenous Designs versus Imported Aircraft as Exemplified by HAL

HAL Production	Total production cost ($'000)	Cost of importing comparable aircraft ($'000)	Indigenous-Import ratio
Kiran basic trainer	340	200	1.7:1
Mig-21 (Soviet licence) fighter	1,520	830	1.8:1
HF-24 Marut fighter	940	600	1.6:1
Alouette (French licence) helicopter	270	170	1.6:1
BAe.748 (UK licence) transport	1,490	1,000	1.5:1
Gnat (UK licence) fighter	380	200	1.9:1

Source: H. Tuomi and R. Väyrynen, Transnational Corporations, Armaments and Development, (Gower, Aldershot, 1982), p. 204.

Table 7.3 : Plant Leased by Aircraft Companies from the US Government

Company/main site	Total Factory Area ('000 m^2)	Proportion leased from Government (%)
Boeing/Kent, Wa.	3,404.6	1.1
GD/Fort Worth, Texas	1,199.1	54.9
Grumman/Bethpage, N.Y.	932.2	24.3
Lockheed/Burbank, Calif.	2,278.6	31.8
MD/St. Louis, Mo. and Long Beach, Calif.	2,409.0	13.4
RI/El Segundo, Calif. and Columbus, Ohio	4,509.0	13.0

Source: Derived from G. Adams, The Politics of Defense Contracting: The Iran Triangle, (Transaction Books, New Brunswick, 1982).

Despite the furore at the time, the Lockheed subsidy was not unprecedented. The company itself pointed out that in the immediate postwar years the Reconstruction Finance Corporation had provided the Glenn L. Martin Company with credits of $26.6 million after that firm had almost gone bankrupt over a disastrous venture into civil aviation (the Martin 2-0-2 airliner, a departure from Martin's previous experience with USAF bombers and US Navy flying-boats). Similarly, Lockheed justified its own federal support on the strength of the $75 million provided by the US Government to Douglas Aircraft in 1967 when that firm was in financial trouble as a result of development problems associated with the DC-8 and DC-9. Last but not least, Lockheed hinted that airliner manufacturers such as Boeing were persistently receiving subsidies by virtue of the $600 million in loan guarantees provided, up to that time, by the government-owned Export-Import Bank which induced foreign airlines to purchase US products.[27] Availability of civil aircraft orders enabled firms such as Boeing to survive regardless of cutbacks in military programmes.

Nationalisation

Unlike the US variant, European approaches to permanent receivership have been characterised by state acquisition of industrial organisations. The French have been particularly prominent in this respect, for, the country's aircraft industry has experienced piecemeal acquisition over more than four decades. The first foray into nationalisation occurred in 1936 and, in the years prior to World War II, about 70 per cent of the industry was acquired by the state. Effected in order to maintain a viable defence industry, this initial nationalisation did not result in a monolithic state enterprise: rather, organisations centred in distinct regions were established. Initially numbering six, the Sociétés Nationales de Constructions Aéronautiques (SNCA) were reduced to four in 1941 when the Vichy regime forced the merger of SNCA de l'Ouest with SNCA de Sud-Ouest (assuming the latter title) and SNCA du Midi with SNCA de Sud-Est (under the mantle of Sud-Est).[28]

A second nationalisation spree came on the heels of Liberation when private firms accused of collaborating with the Germans were summarily taken into public ownership. The better known of those firms were Amiot, Caudron and Farman; the first being retitled Ateliers Aéronautiques de Colombes. State ownership did not prevent liquidation of enterprises, it should be noted, for SNCA du Centre collapsed in 1949. A typical state aircraft manufacturer of the 1950s, SNCA du Nord ('Nord'), was constituted from the original 1936 acquisitions (Potez, CAMS, Les Mureaux, and part of Breguet), a forcible 1945 acquisition (Caudron-Renault), the SNCA du Centre assets transferred in 1949, and the SFECMAS (Arsenal de l'Aéronautique) assimilated in 1954.[29] In 1957 the state decided to 'rationalise' its aircraft enterprises, that is to say, to consolidate them into larger focal organisations. Sud-Ouest (the former Bloch and Bleriot concerns) and Sud-Est (centred on the former Potez firm) were combined into Sud Aviation in that year. Yet it was not until 1970 that rationalisation was taken to its logical conclusion: the formation of Aérospatiale with the merger of Sud and Nord airframe manufacturers and other aerospace elements (recall Figure 6.4). Interestingly, the state had felt obliged to take over Morane-Saulnier when it had failed in 1966: the former Sud subsidiary becoming the SOCATA light aircraft branch of Aérospatiale in the consolidation exercise of 1970. In so doing, the French Government was ensuring a domestically-owned competitor to the country's only other significant light aircraft manufacturer, Reims Aviation, which concentrated on Cessna licence-production and was, to boot, 49 per cent owned by that US firm.

The final phase in the nationalisation of the

aircraft industry in France began in 1978 when the government took 21 per cent of the shares of Dassault-Breguet, the only sizeable private aircraft company remaining in operation. That company is, of course, esteemed for its export success with warplanes (Mirages), and the state's acquisition of part of it was actuated by a desire to be "better able to co-ordinate all French aerospace efforts".[30] Spurred on by ideological commitment, the new Socialist Government effectively nationalised Dassault along with the Matra missile firm in 1981.[31] Officially, the state boosted its holding of Dassault stock to 46 per cent, but by virtue of double-voting rights accorded to some shares, it obtained majority control of the company.[32] The 1981 acquisitions, however, have not been incorporated within the Aérospatiale structure. The distribution of the main aircraft plants in France is shown in Figure 7.1.

The French record of nationalisation renders it possible to discern various catalysts to permanent receivership. The first is associated with the desire to augment national defence capability, the reason why the industry was partly nationalised in 1936 and also, incidentally, the grounds upon which the US Government subsidises 'surge capacity' among its defence contractors. Secondly, the state has intervened as a 'punitive' measure, acquiring those firms that defy the national interest (by analogy, communist states have also commandeered private firms in the name of the public interest) and this rationale accounts for the 1945 acquisitions. The nationalisation of foreign-owned DHC (an HS subsidiary) in 1974 and Canadair (a GD subsidiary) in 1976 by the Canadian Government can perhaps be viewed in the same light, that is, as a sign of the displeasure of the state at the strategies adopted by private industrial organisations. Thirdly, the state intervenes to rationalise capacity under the supposition that the international competitiveness of the industry will not otherwise be forthcoming. It was on this count that Aérospatiale was created in 1970 and the industry 'co-ordinated' in 1981. Finally, firms may be acquired by the state simply to ensure their survival, as the acquisition of SOCATA amply testifies. This last is, of course, a pure expression of the bail-out imperative at work and is resorted to whenever private interests cannot be shored up (à la Lockheed) or have shied away from further investment owing to the excessive risk burden. The Belgian Government, for example, was forced to nationalise the bankrupt UK-owned Fairey SA at Gosselies and reconstitute it as SONACA because insufficient private

Figure 7.1 : French Aircraft Plants

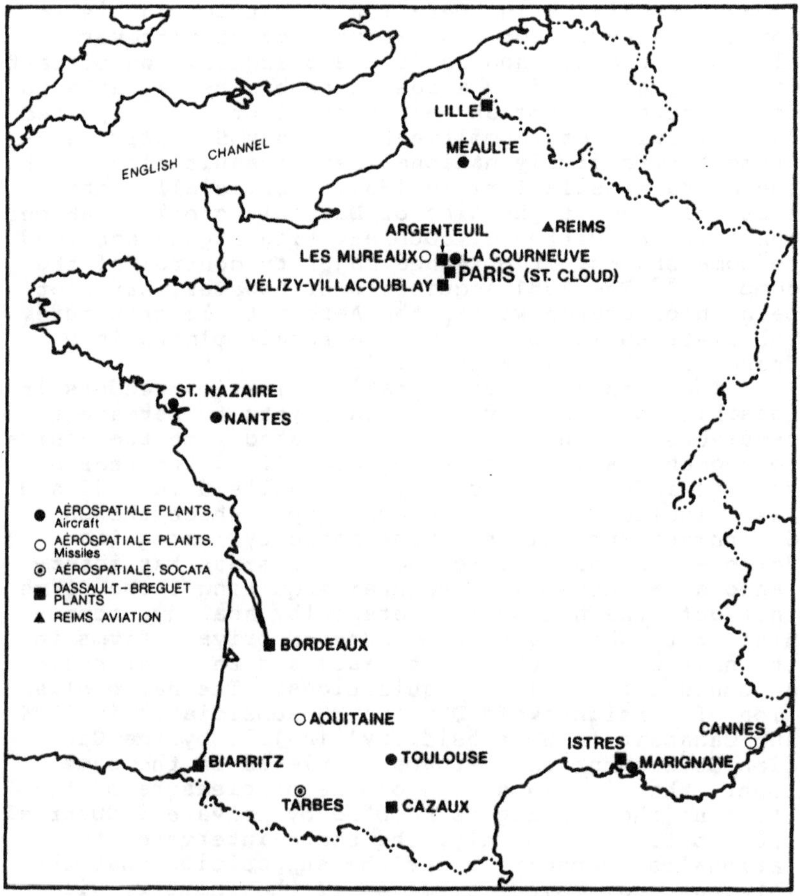

investors were willing to continue the firm's commitment to the F-16 co-production programme.[33]

The UK nationalisation experience reflects some of these symptoms. In short, it has been motivated, by and large, through a desire to combine rationalisation with the bail-out imperative. As a result, government involvement has proved to be somewhat contradictory. On the one hand, firms have been taken into public ownership in order to vouchsafe their survival - and the communities that depend upon them

- most notably the state's take-over of Shorts in Northern Ireland. But, on the other, the government has not demurred at the decisions of state enterprises to close aircraft factories which, inevitably, exacerbate local unemployment (e.g. the decision of BAe to axe its Bournemouth/Hurn airframe facility in the early 1980s). Indeed, a lack of clear purpose in UK nationalisation is all too evident. The intent of the Labour Government to acquire the bulk of the industry in the mid-1970s was surrounded by controversy. For one thing, the principal airframe manufacturers were profitable entities: BAC, for instance, consistently recorded profits throughout the 1970s.[34] 'Inside' opinion was convinced that nationalisation was the outcome of the ideological bent of the government of the day. In answering its opponents, the UK Government claimed that the industry must be taken into public ownership bacause of its overwhelming reliance on the public purse. State control would provide greater public accountability and, by dint of fresh management, lead to a restructuring of the industry along more effective lines, and incidentally, centralise the firms' chaotic missiles divisions. More specifically, the aims of the new state enterprise were: (1) the securing of long-term viability, (2) the 'unification' of production units, (3) integration of the industry's interests with those of the country, (4) the furthering of flexible operations, (5) the development of worker participation and (6) the pushing ahead with diversification.[35] All companies with turnover in excess of £20 million were to be incorporated in British Aerospace. Curiously, the helicopter sub-sector was excluded (i.e. the Westland firm) and the existing state firm in Northern Ireland (Shorts) remained outside the mainland conglomerate. Consequently, when it finally appeared in 1977, BAe was the product of merging BAC, HS Aviation, HS Dynamics (the missiles branch of HS) and Scottish Aviation. At that juncture, therefore, the UK Government controlled most of the airframe industry and, through its Rolls-Royce interests, the aeroengine industry as well.

The argument that state ownership would facilitate 'viability', 'unification', 'flexibility' and 'diversification' as variously proffered, was seen as promoting rationalisation in all but name. It will be recollected that it was under this banner that the UK Government had urged the private-enterprise mergers of 1960. Yet, the merits of rationalisation seemed inconclusive in theory and turned out to be somewhat elusive in practice. Some doubted the argument that increasing size of enterprise was conducive to economies of scale. Referring to the earlier merger episode, one commentator stated that the case for rationalisation was not proven despite the size advantages enjoyed by competing US enterprises.

> On the assumption that size was, in fact, synonymous with efficiency and (the second basic fallacy of rationalisation) that size in itself would be sufficient to attract new orders to the industry from overseas, which meant, of course, that Government expenditure need not be increased, the reshaping of the industry was enforced by the stick-and-carrot process of making contracts conditional upon amalgamation.[36]

In other words, the state had realised a degree of success (as manifest through profitable merged private firms) in forcing rationalisation on the aircraft industry of 1960, but had also imposed costs on those firms which flowed directly from unwieldy organisational units; to be blunt, organisations too large to be efficient. The prospect of further economies of scale from an even larger organisation was, therefore, very questionable. Besides, US firms were large owing to their organisation around large DoD contracts, something which could not be replicated in Britain which had a defence effort amounting to only a fraction of the US effort.

American critics were even more scathing of the move to acquire profitable HS and BAC, claiming that "the Labour Government's chief motive in grabbing control of a thriving and prosperous industry is to solidify its role as a job source for the government's union supporters".[37] This view must be tempered, however, by the thought that rationalisation also carries with it the prospect of plant closure; a condition scarcely compatible with the maintenance of jobs (sinecures or otherwise). In any event, BAe became a modestly profitable enterprise which, with a change in government and ideological complexion, was partially denationalised in 1980 (the state retaining a 49 per cent holding) and offered for almost complete 'privatisation' in 1985. It made pretax profits of £52.8 million in the year prior to this volte-face, and £70.6 million in the year immediately following it (its main plants are distributed as in Figure 7.2). Regardless of formal ownership, BAe is still heavily incumbent on the state for development monies, as indeed is Westland which had never been taken into state ownership during the rationalisation mania (in 1984, for example, this latter was promised £60 million in state aid to develop the EH-101

Figure 7.2 : Distribution of UK Aircraft Plants

anti-submarine helicopter with Agusta of Italy).

Contrasting with the ambiguity surrounding the rationale for nationalising the UK airframe industry, the reasons for taking R-R into public ownership owed much more to the bail-out imperative. Reconstituted out of the gas-turbine interests of the old private company which had gone bankrupt with the Lockheed Tristar venture, Rolls-Royce (1971) Ltd had the UK Government as its sole shareholder. At its inception, it employed 62,000 at factories located, in the main, at Derby, Glasgow, Bristol, Coventry and Leavesden(Watford).[38] In addition to the large RB.211 engine designed for the Tristar, R-R had major programmes for powering the Concorde (based on the Olympus two-shaft turbojet jointly developed with SNECMA), the Tornado (using the RB.199 under the aegis of Turbo-Union), the Vought A-7 for the USAF and Navy (in co-operation with the Allison Division of General Motors on the TF41 version of the Spey engine) and the Jaguar (for which it produces the Adour in collaboration with Turboméca). Table 7.4 lists the engine programmes underway at R-R in the 1970s. To them must be added the collaborative ventures initiated with the Japanese to develop the experimental RJ500 in 1979 and the 1983-formed International Aero Engines, set up to offer an alternative powerplant for the A320 Airbus.[39] Such a diverse effort was monumentally expensive and R-R was repeatedly turning to its government paymaster for extra funds, for example, the £364 million for the ongoing development of the RB.211 between 1979 and 1984, and £60 million for the V2500 that R-R is designing in co-operation with International Aero Engines.[40] Notwithstanding subsidies of this magnitude, the enterprise continued to make losses: £134 million in 1982 and £193 million in 1983.[41] The state persisted, however, in wholeheartedly backing R-R on the score that it was a national asset. By the same token, it had stepped in to inject £15 million into the Ferranti avionics firm in 1974 (in return for 62.5 per cent of the equity) using a similar rationale; namely, that the firm possessed invaluable technical capabilities and, besides, was an important source of employment in job-scarce Scotland.[42] State commitment of this kind is instrumental in fomenting the multinational 'mega-projects' which characterise much of European aerospace initiative in the 1980s. Those ventures are, in effect, the culmination of permanent receivership as conceived by national governments.

GOVERNMENT-INDUCED INTERNATIONAL CO-OPERATION

The inspiration for state-sponsored European-wide aircraft projects came out of the crisis facing individual European industries in the early 1960s. On the one hand, they were effectively denied access to the crucial US civil aviation market as a result of the protection afforded US manufacturers by the 'Buy America Act'. On the other hand, they were having difficulties competing with large, efficient US aircraft enterprises cushioned by lucrative defence R &

Table 7.4 : R-R Engine Programmes

Engine	Type	Representative User Aircraft	Production/Development Centre
TF41	turbofan	A-7	Indianapolis (Allison), Derby (R-R)
M45	turbofan	VFW-614	Bristol (R-R), Paris (SNECMA)
Olympus	turbojet	Concorde	Bristol (R-R), Paris (SNECMA)
Adour	turbofan	Jaguar	Derby (R-R), Tarnus (Turboméca)
RB.199	turbofan	Tornado	Bristol (R-R), Munich (MTU), Turin (Fiat)
RB.162	turbojet	Trident 3B	Derby
RB.211	turbofan	L-1011	Derby
Spey	turbofan	BAe.111	Derby
Dart	turboprop	Fokker F-27	Derby
Tyne	turboprop	Atlantic	Derby
Viper	turbojet	Soko Jastreb	Bristol
Pegasus	turbofan	Harrier	Bristol
BS.360	turboshaft	Lynx	Leavesden

Source: Jane's All the World's Aircraft, various editions.

D and production contracts. Even with state-induced mergers creating larger organisations, the average European firm was not comparable in size to the giant US aerospace companies (Table 7.5). Furthermore, structural problems unique to Europe exacerbated matters. In the first place, Britain and France were curtailing their military commitments as a consequence of reduced imperial responsibilities: the resultant "cancellation of major defence projects; the increase in project cost to the point where the relative smallness of the home market became a limiting factor" compelled some form of drastic state action to save industries inordinately dependent upon defence contracts of which aerospace was the prime example.[43] Secondly, employment policies, in insisting on retaining underemployed labour, made European plants less productive than their US competitors who showed much less reluctance in dismissing unwanted labour (witness the violent fluctuations in Boeing's workforce).[44] Thirdly, European civil aircraft were accused of being tailor-made for national airlines which were, in any event, obliged to buy them; but

Table 7.5 : Contrasts in Enterprise Sizes, Europe and America

Europe: Company	Employment[1]	Turnover[2]	USA: Company	Employment	Turnover
BAe	75,000	2,260	Boeing	98,300	8,130
R-R	56,600	1,680	MD	82,700	5,280
Aérospatiale	37,200	2,710	GD	81,600	4,060
Dassault-Breguet	15,600	1,700	Lockheed	66,500	4,060
SNECMA	10,700[3]	540[3]			
Turboméca	4,500	220			
MBB	26,500[4]	1,450			
VFW	12,000[4]	560			
Dornier	8,000	480			
MTU	6,200	280			

Notes: a. 1979 figures
b. Millions of 1979 dollars
c. 1978 figures
d. 1980 figures

Source: M. Rich, et al, Multinational Co-production of Military Aerospace Systems, (Rand, Santa Monica, 1981), p. 19.

the machines were, in consequence, ill-fitted to compete in international markets.[45]

To directly confront these problems, European Governments attacked on two fronts: inducing merger of their domestic firms often under the rubric of state acquisition (as recounted above), and forcing the restructured enterprises to co-operate with each other across international lines. The latter strategy was adopted largely to prevent American dominance of European civil and military aviation markets. It would, moreover, have specific political and technical advantages; not least of which were a reduction in national contributions to joint R & D projects as the share of the overall cost (admittedly, boosted as a result of the duplication inherent in collaboration) would be spread among several partners, and a larger guaranteed market - the outcome of several states committing themselves to buying the product - enabling economies of scale in production costs (which, in turn, would lower the unit cost of aircraft and enhance their marketability elsewhere).[46]

As the worst affected by the structural problems coming to a head, the British were the first to formally embrace international collaboration as an escape route for a purely national aircraft industry. According to the Plowden Report of 1965, salvation was to be sought in collaborating with other European aircraft industries because the UK Government was simply in too straitened circumstances to continue the level of support which it had hitherto provided the industry. It foresaw, in addition, a direct government stake in the recently-merged BAC and HS undertakings.[47] In certain respects, the official report - accepted without demur by the Government - was merely endorsing existing trends as manifest through the Concorde programme.

Concorde

The Anglo-French SST was the progenitor of a string of collaborative aircraft programmes that dominate European aerospace today. In the 1960s, it led to a series of European airliner projects (Table 7.6), some successful and others less so. Without doubt, however, Concorde was the most momentous of them all, not only for the technical innovation entailed in developing a supersonic airliner, but also in terms of the sheer size of the capitalisation involved. At £2.2 billion, the level of public funding was not matched in a civil aviation project until the A320 Airbus of the mid-1980s. Agreement on Concorde was reached in 1962 on two levels: between the manufacturers, BAC (inherited by BAe) and Sud Aviation (as it then was), and between their respective governments. In detail, the agreements called for an equal division of work between the airframe companies and an even split in development costs between the two countries. Six RDT & E aircraft were covered under the agreement: two prototypes, two pre-production models, and two complete airframes for static and fatigue testing. Co-production guaranteed the absence of any duplication in production jigs, but two assembly lines were set up: Toulouse and Bristol(Filton). Similarly, the aeroengines were to be the outcome of joint enterprise, R-R and SNECMA, and production was to be, once again, equally divided between the partners.[48]

Flight testing of Concorde was begun in 1969 and the first production machine was ready at the end of 1971. BAC's Weybridge plant was responsible for manufacturing the nose and forward fuselage of the production aircraft which were then sent to Toulouse or Filton for final assembly. Other BAC works undertook

Table 7.6 : State-Backing of International Programmes

Aircraft	Development Cost (millions of pounds)	Participating Countries (State enterprise in parentheses)	Government support (%)
Concorde	2,200	France (Aérospatiale)	100
		UK (ultimately BAe)	100
A300	595	France (Aérospatiale)	100
		West Germany	90
		UK (ultimately BAe)	100
		Spain (CASA)	-
		Netherlands	90
Mercure	171	France	80
		Italy, Spain, Belgium, Switzerland	-
VFW-614	69	West Germany	80
		Netherlands	100
		Belgium, UK	-
F-28	50	Netherlands	100
		West Germany	40
		UK	-

Source: Derived from Flight International, 20 November 1982, p. 1522.

to build the rear fuselage, vertical tail surfaces, engine nacelles, electrical system, fuel system and engine installation. Aérospatiale (the erstwhile Sud) was responsible for the rear cabin section, wings and wing control surfaces, hydraulic system, flying controls, navigation system, radio and air conditioning systems. The finished product was capable of 2,300 km/h, had a passenger capacity of 100 over a range of 4,900 km, and cruised at a service ceiling of 18,200 m. The aircraft entered service with Air France and British Airways in 1976 but only 16 production models were built: all the provisional orders (originally 74) evaporating when escalating fuel costs made the aeroplane an uneconomic proposition.

Airbus

It was in the spirit of the Plowden Report that Britain and France entered negotiations in 1965 into the desirability of producing a 250-300 seat jetliner as a collaborative effort. Conceived as a European answer to the American DC-10 and L-1011 'wide-bodies',the 'Airbus' was intended to be a major innovation in the Concorde tradition. From the outset, however, British attitudes were clouded by the priority accorded to Rolls-Royce as the prime medium for advancing aeroengine technology. The company's new, heavy turbofan had been thwarted in the bid to have it accepted as the engine for Boeing's 747 and, accordingly, pressure was placed on the UK Government to have it diverted to the Airbus.[49] Under a Memorandum of Understanding of September 1967, aeroengine leadership for the Airbus would be assigned to R-R while airframe leadership would be the province of Aérospatiale, and the Germans would contribute a secondary input. Airframe costs would be shared equally by the UK and France, but the former would assume responsibility for the lion's share (75 per cent) of aeroengine costs. However, in May 1968 R-R scored a triumph in winning the contract to supply the engines for Lockheed's L-1011 and soon ran into capacity constraints. As the 1971 collapse was to illustrate so graphically, R-R was in no position to simultaneously develop two advanced-technology engines. At UK Government connivance, it opted to develop the RB.211 for the L-1011, and the RB.207 for the Airbus was allowed to wither. Official UK Government involvement in the first-phase of Airbus was thereby curtailed.

Rebounding, the European partners in Airbus Industrie redesigned the A300 jetliner round the CF6-50 engine, a product of GE which was manufactured under licence by SNECMA and MTU. Construction of the first aircraft began in 1969 by a consortium of aircraft constructors. The main contributor was Aérospatiale, which apart from design leadership, manufactured the nose, lower centre fuselage and engine pylons, and undertook final assembly at Toulouse. Deutsche Airbus (centred on MBB) built the forward and rear fuselage as well as the vertical tail surfaces, CASA manufactured the horizontal tail surfaces, fuselage main doors and landing gear doors; while HS Aviation was entrusted with the wing. After a series of delays (the aircraft did not enter service until 1975), the success of the project was assured and no fewer than 246 A300s were on order or had been delivered by mid-1984. Market breakthrough (notably by US major airline, Eastern) encouraged the French Government to redirect resources into the programme in 1978, "including an immediate order from Air France for 24 A300s".[50] Moreover, the UK Government had second thoughts and, at the cost of some $600 million, bought itself a 20 per cent share of the A300 programme.

From this point onwards, Airbus Industrie committed itself to producing a family of jetliners, of which the A310 and A320 have so far materialised from the A300 stable (Table 7.7). The A310 is a smaller version of the A300 (with 210 to 234 passengers rather than the 300 or so of the earlier machine) which made its first flight in 1982. At its roll-out, it had already accumulated 90 orders and 90 options: a better record than the A300 when at a comparable stage of development (on the eve of the A300's first flight it had only achieved 14 sales). In view of formal British participation, the A310 workload was apportioned as follows: Aérospatiale and Deutsche Airbus (37.9 per cent each), BAe (20 per cent), CASA (4.2 per cent); while Fokker, along with Belairbus, enjoyed subcontractor status as 'associate' members of Airbus Industrie. As before, final assembly takes place at Toulouse but minor changes have been made to the A300 consortium arrangements with, for example, the Aérospatiale plant at Les Mureaux being called in to produce the A310's flight deck, and more fitting-out work being undertaken at MBB's Bremen facility.[51] A major order from Pan American World Airways in 1984 confirmed the viability of the type in global markets.

The A320, meanwhile, is a 150-180 passenger airliner, launched with much fanfare in 1984. Intended to fly in 1988, a production rate of 60 aircraft per year is planned. Costing in excess of £2 billion for development, BAe's contribution is put at £637 million.[52] In many respects an innovative machine, the A320 will, for example, be the first airliner with fly-by-wire primary flying controls (i.e. the ailerons and elevators respond to electrical signals rather than being activated by mechanical cables and pulleys). What is more, extensive use will be made of CFRP and aluminium-lithium in its construction: the latter is not only lighter, stronger and stiffer than conventional aluminium but is far less corrosive. Initial aircraft will be powered by the CFM 56-5, jointly developed by GE and SNECMA, and later aircraft may be fitted with the V2500 of International Aero Engines (e.g. those on order for Pan Am). At launch date, 51 A320s had been ordered with another 45 held on option.[53] Table 7.8 lists the financial and production responsibilities of each of the participating enterprises.

As Table 7.7 evinces, there is no shortage of planned successors to the A300, 310 and 320. The first of these, envisaged to enter service in 1992, is the four-engined 230 seat TA-11. It will occupy the long-range slot omitted from the present Airbus offerings. Replacement for the A300 will take two forms: the TA-9 which is a stretched, rewinged variant of the A300 for the short-range high-density (up to 400 passenger) market, and the TA-12 which will be a hybrid aircraft combining the A310/TA-11 fuselage

Table 7.7 : Family of Airbus Industrie Jetliners

Aircraft Size	Aircraft Range: Short	Type Designator Medium	Long
Small	A320	A310	TA-11
Medium	A310	A300	modified TA-11
Long	TA-9	enlarged TA-9	-

Source: Derived from Flight International, 1 September 1984, p. 391.

Table 7.8 : A320 Programme Breakdown

Enterprise	Share (%)	Responsibility
(Production)		
Aérospatiale	36.0	front fuselage, lower centre fuselage, pylons, nacelles, power plant integration, final assembly (at Toulouse)
Deutsche Airbus	31.0	upper centre fuselage, rear fuselage, fin and flaps
BAe	27.0	wing (at Chester), slats, flaps, ailerons, spoilers (at Hatfield)
CASA	6.0	CFRP tailplane
Belairbus	associate	slats
(Financial)		
Aérospatiale	37.6	
Deutsche Airbus	37.6	
BAe	20.0	
CASA	4.8	

Source: Flight International, 24 March 1984, p. 738.

with the wing and engine of the TA-9 and be optimised for routes of up to 4,500 nautical miles. These projects are being designed around fuel consumption targets one-quarter less than is the case with the

A300.[54] Eventually, modified versions of the new designs will cater for all size/range categories with the single exception of the large, long-haul class.

Tornado

The two aforementioned programmes are civil aviation initiatives, but the monumental Tornado tri-national programme is military inspired. Born out of the disarray created in the UK aircraft industry with the cancellation of the TSR-2 strike aircraft in 1965, the MRCA project was finalised as a collaborative effort between Britain, West Germany and Italy. Panavia Aircraft GmbH formulated a design which received government approval in 1970 and production authorisation in 1974. The MRCA (i.e. Tornado) was conceived as a twin-engined, two-seat supersonic strike fighter equipped with a variable-geometry wing having a sweep of 25° in the fully forward position and 66° when swept fully backward. It is powered by the RB.199 turbofan made by Turbo-Union, a consortium of R-R, MTU and Fiat formed in 1969. Panavia itself uses facilities provided by BAe, MBB and Aeritalia, with work-sharing apportioned according to the size of order from each government. Planned procurement called for nine prototypes, four from the UK (Preston/Warton), three from Germany (Manching) and two from Italy (Caselle). They would be followed by 809 production machines - 385 for Britain, 324 for West Germany and 100 for Italy - with final assembly of each nation's consignment at the appropriate one of the three international Panavia sites.[55] At £11.25 million a copy (1981 prices), the scale of the programme is truly staggering and has been frequently slowed to prevent the over-taxing of national defence budgets. By August 1984, the programme was less than half complete with 349 Tornadoes issued.[56] The sheer expense of such a complex aircraft has deterred export orders.

CONCLUSION

This chapter has stressed the pervasive nature of state involvement in the aircraft industry, not merely as an interested on-looker, but as an active ingredient in the formation of many aircraft enterprises and a guarantor of their continuance. Political ideologies are obviously of crucial import in determining the form of direct government involvement. Nationalisation has been a gambit of both capitalist and communist states, but its record of continuity has been much more discordant in the liberal democracies. Britain and France, for example, have tolerated at various times mixed public and private sector influence in the aircraft business, state monopoly control, and (in the British case) retrenchment of direct state involvement. The USA, for its part, is consistent in rejecting a direct role for the state in aircraft manufacture (apart from the 'infant' industry phase). The American alternative is, of course, the 'Iron Triangle', an indirect approach to government supervision of the aircraft industry.

All governments lay great store on the inception of domestic aircraft manufacture and the nurturing of aerospace as a classic infant industry goes on apace. To give but one example, the Philippines established the National Aero Manufacturing Corporation at Manila in 1973. On the strength of orders from the military, this enterprise is engaged in assembling MBB BO105 helicopters (44 by 1983) and PBN Islander light transports (57 by 1983) under licence from West Germany and the UK respectively. In accordance with the usual route to indigenous design, it is building a prototype light piston-engined trainer; in this instance strongly influenced by the Italian SIAI-Marchetti SF-260 aircraft.[57] Continuance of the trainer programme depends upon state generosity both in subsidising its development and in creating a protected market through military orders. The process whereby states furnish the means for aircraft industry expansion within the greater context of national industrial development is the subject of the next chapter.

NOTES AND REFERENCES

1. A. Boyd, The Soviet Air Force since 1918, (MacDonald and Jane's, London, 1977), p.227.

2. AW & ST, 2 September 1974, p.19 and 14 October 1974, p.7.

3. Two instances bear out the basic protectionist mentality prevailing in the USA. The first concerns the protest of New York Senator Alfonso D'Amato who felt aggrieved at the loss by Grumman (of Bethpage, New York) of a US Navy trainer contract to BAe. On the evocative cry that 43 per cent of the work on the T-45 Hawk would go to the UK and thus deny 16,000 jobs to Americans, D'Amato almost succeeded in blocking the MD/BAe contract (see FI, 26 December 1981, p.1880). The second, mentioned in Chapter 4, revolves around British protests at American bad faith when their Martin-Baker ejection seat was rejected by

Congress after winning the competition to fulfil the requirements of the F/A-18.

4. FI, 10 October 1981, p.1065.

5. AW & ST, 9 November 1981, p.164.

6. Peter Fearon, 'The Formative Years of the British Aircraft Industry, 1913-1924', Business History Review, vol. 43 (1969), pp.476-495.

7. Jane's All The World's Aircraft 1972-73, (Jane's Yearbooks, London, 1972), p.181.

8. Air-Britain Digest, vol. 32 (November-December 1980), pp.127-131.

9. FI, 10 April 1969, p.603.

10. Air-Britain Digest, vol. 33 (May-June 1981), pp.63-7.

11. Jane's, pp.3-4.

12. AW & ST, 5 June 1978, pp,14-16.

13. AW & ST, 21 May 1984, p.24.

14. Air Pictorial, vol. 38 (January 1976), pp.26-9.

15. FI, 9 January 1982, p.46.

16. Pushpindar Singh, Aircraft of the Indian Air Force, 1933-73, (The English Book Store, New Delhi, 1974).

17. FI, 18 December 1982, pp.1771-4.

18. Mahlon R. Straszheim, The International Airline Industry, (The Brookings Institution, Washington, D.C., 1969), pp.22-3.

19. Peter Fearon, 'The Vicissitudes of a British Aircraft Company: Handley Page Ltd Between the Wars', Business History, vol. 20 (1978), pp.63-86.

20. Ibid, p.71.

21. Peter Lewis, The British Fighter since 1912, (Putnam, London, 1979), p.165.

22. H. Tuomi and R. Vayrynen, Transnational Corporations, Armaments and Development, (Gower, Aldershot, 1982), p.205.

23. T. J. Lowi, 'Towards a Politics of Economics: The State of Permanent Receivership', in L. N. Lindberg et al (eds.), Stress and Contradiction in Modern Capitalism: Public Policy and the Theory of the State, (Lexington Books, Toronto, 1975), pp.115-24.

24. Ibid, p.117.

25. Some California aircraft firms realised 'windfall' subsidies as an outcome of the Watts race riots in 1965 and 1967. The Economic Resources Corporation used US Department of Commerce funds to set up factories in Los Angeles for employing unskilled, 'minority' labour. Lockheed made use of a $2.5 million factory to produce L-1011 parts while MD had one for making wire harnesses, bulkheads, floor beams, ash trays and pulley brackets for installation in its

airliners. See AW & ST, 18 May 1970, p.65 and 9 November 1970, p.61.

26. AW & ST, 10 May 1971, p.26.

27. AW & ST, 24 May 1971, pp.15-16.

28. *Air Pictorial*, vol. 39 (June 1977), pp.212-13.

29. *Air-Britain Digest*, vol. 36 (May-June 1984), p.59.

30. H. Tuomi and R. Vayrynen, *Transnational Corporations*, p.36.

31. E. A. Kolodziej, 'France', in N. Ball and M. Leitenberg (eds.), *The Structure of the Defense Industry*, (St. Martin's Press, New York, 1983), pp.81-110.

32. *Jane's All The World's Aircraft 1983-84*, (Jane's Publishing Company, London, 1983), p.59.

33. AW & ST, 1 September 1980, p.99.

34. In detail, the profits were (in millions of pounds): 4.1, 6.5, 13.7, 24.2, 30.0 and 40.0 for 1971-6. See H. Evans, *Vickers: Against the Odds 1956-1977*, (Hodder and Stoughton, London, 1978), p.185.

35. *Air Pictorial*, vol. 37 (March 1975), pp.92-3.

36. M. Hardy, 'Rationalise and Forget?', FI, 11 January 1962, pp.48-50.

37. AW & ST, 6 September 1976, p.23.

38. *Jane's 1972-73*, p.684.

39. AW & ST, 21 May 1984, p.33.

40. FI, 25 August 1984, p.178.

41. FI, 5 May 1984, p.1223.

42. FI, 22 May 1975, p.812.

43. R. L. Nobbs, 'A Note on Aerospace Collaboration', *Journal of Common Market Studies*, vol. 14 (1976), pp.368-71. Quote from p.368.

44. The stark contrast between Dassault which kept its workforce between 14,693 and 15,161 throughout most of the 1970s and Boeing which cut its payroll by about 60 per cent from 1968 to 1971 is indicative of transatlantic differences. See M. Rich et al, *Multinational Coproduction of Military Aerospace Systems*, (Rand, Santa Monica, California, 1981), p.15.

45. Joseph Rallo, 'The European Community's Industrial Policy Revisited: The Case of Aerospace', *Journal of Common Market Studies*, vol. 22 (1984), pp.245-67.

46. Keith Hayward, 'Politics and European Aerospace Collaboration: The A300 Airbus', *Journal of Common Market Studies*, vol. 14 (1976), pp.354-67.

47. Plowden Report, 'Report of the Committee of Inquiry into the Aircraft Industry', (HMSO, London,

Cmnd. 2853, 1965).

48. Jane's 1972-73, pp.104-106.

49. K. Hayward, 'Politics and European Aerospace Collaboration', p.359.

50. J. Rallo, 'The European Community's Industrial Policy Revisited', p.254.

51. Air Pictorial, vol. 44 (May 1982), pp.172-8.

52. FI, 10 March 1984, p.615.

53. Air Pictorial, vol. 46 (September 1984), pp.332-3.

54. FI, 1 September 1984, pp.391-3 and 8 September 1984, p.520.

55. Air Pictorial, vol. 38 (January 1976), pp.11-16.

56. Air Pictorial, vol. 46 (October 1984), pp.364-5.

57. Ibid, p.385. See also Jane's 1983-84, p.168. Note, the Philippines Aerospace Development Corporation - the holding company into which NAM was merged - manufactures the glass reinforced plastic parts for both types.

Chapter Eight

AEROSPACE AND DEVELOPMENT

The purpose of this chapter is simply to provide a broad overview of the general relationship between the aircraft industry and national economic development. The preceding chapter has loosely categorised the variety of relationships extant between the state and the major airframe manufacturers. These relationships, ranging from the classic infant industry case to the permanent receivership case and incorporating a number of institutional forms, must be set within the broader political-economic context of their emergence. In other words, the policy instruments utilised to cultivate the variety of state-industry links and the relationship of these to national development strategies warrant special attention. This chapter, then, will briefly highlight the general theoretical setting in which national aircraft industries are nurtured, and secondly, will examine a number of national examples deemed representative of the forms in which the industry may occur. Since much of the discussion hitherto has focused on the already established aircraft industries of the world, especially those of the USA and EEC; by way of contrast, the following examples will be drawn from those countries attempting to initiate aircraft industries.

THE THEORETICAL SETTING

The international economic system may be conceptualised as a hierarchical structure based on the division of labour, and is made manifest in the form of uneven accumulation among nation-states (ranging from the advanced industrial economies through to the low-income countries). The structure is not static, but rather is characterised by at least three important tendencies: concentration of political and economic power; 'transnationalisation' of markets, production and finance; and the importance of control over technology since, "Control over technology is an instrument to accumulate economic and political power and to steer transnational relations. Technological power is an important factor in determining the nature of the international hierarchy".[1] The unfolding of these general tendencies is plagued with crises, which frequently results in structural change, and necessitates an expanding state role (in capitalist economies). In the wake of poor economic performance during much of the 1970s coupled with changing international economic relationships centring on the concerns of technological change and the labour process, virtually all governments have turned towards industrial policies and strategies as means to foster industrial expansion and international competitiveness.[2]

In general, and along with fiscal and monetary policies, industrial policies constitute one element of a nation's basic economic policy framework. Simply, "industrial policy may be generally defined as any government measure or set of measures, to promote or prevent structural change" and in contrast to earlier experiences, "modern industrial policy aims at more than merely setting a general framework"; rather, "it descends increasingly into the microeconomic sphere of economic decision-taking that was formerly left to the price mechanism".[3] Two broad types of industrial policy may be discerned; namely, negative policies which are designed to slow down structural change and positive policies which are designed to facilitate the expansion of industries and firms at the forefront of technological development and/on experiencing rapid growth.[4] A number of types of industrial policy may be identified depending on their scope, time and intensity dimensions.[5] For example, policies may be broad based and apply across-the-board to all industries, albeit with differential impacts. The objective of this type of general industrial policy is to enhance the aggregate resource allocation of the economy. Frequently in conjunction with these broad based policies are a variety of selective policies aimed at realising specific objectives, as is the case with R & D policies. Similarly, sector-, industry-, and firm-specific policies may be formulated to achieve industrial development objectives. In practice, a number of industrial policy types are usually enacted at any given moment.

A prominent industrial strategy adopted by many developing and developed nations is import substitution.[6] Basically, this strategy calls for the domestic production of goods that were previously imported. The strategy depends, for the most part, on protection, principally through tariffs or quotas on competing imports; and often on the transfer of technology from established industries as well. In so far as a logical extension of import substitution strategies is to penetrate export markets for these goods, and thus diversify exports, the desire to produce goods experiencing growing demand inevitably follows. Moreover, given the paramount importance generally accorded technology, a salient feature of these industrial strategies has been to 'target' specific high technology industries and firms as recipients of special state attention and largesse. The aircraft industry is one such 'target' industry. As outlined in the foregoing chapters, there are a number of features of this industry which invariably make it a part of many national industrial programmes. Specifically, it is an important industry in the major industrial economies, it is a technologically-intensive industry which generates substantial multiplier effects and offers sizeable balance of payment gains, and furthermore, is potentially capable of bestowing important external economies on the national industrial environment as a whole. Of perhaps equal importance, the desire to develop an indigenous aircraft capability emanates from the strategic importance for national sovereignty allotted to it by virtue of its military function. Perhaps ironically, however, it is the military function which circumscribes the possibilities of developing a domestic aircraft industry. The defence market, as Chapter 4 made clear, is pivotal to virtually all aircraft firms. Thus a nation's defence policy, and in particular its procurement procedures, has important ramifications for fostering an indigenous aircraft industry. At the same time, since the control of aircraft technology (particularly with military applications) is highly concentrated in a few countries, and since the transfer of military technology is tantamount to foreign policy statements, a nation's geopolitical position in the world order conditions the direction of the development of its aircraft industry. Finally, whereas the realisation of industrial policy objectives may be attained through private sector initiatives and/or direct state involvement, the nature of aircraft production (substantial barriers to entry, especially in terms of front-end capital) has, in most cases, precluded the former option, and overwhelmingly favoured direct state participation.

JAPAN

Among the AICs, Japan's economic performance has stood second to none for much of the postwar period. Growth of GDP over the 1960s and 1970s exceeded that of all other AICs while, simultaneously, Japanese exports grew at an average annual rate of 17.5 per cent between 1960 and 1970 and 9.1 per cent over the following decade.[7] Manufacturing sector growth exceeded that of the economy as a whole and averaged 10.9 and 6 per cent respectively throughout the 1960s and 1970s.[8] In light of the country's limited endowment of natural resources, the Japanese Government has, since the 1950s, promoted industrial development as a means to sustained national accumulation. At the heart of Japan's industrial policy is MITI; the provider of administrative guidance in terms of the allocation of resources. In consultation with the private sector, it offers 'visions' which serve as general policy targets for the direction of industrial growth.[9] A salient feature of these so-called visions has been the choice of strategic industries as harbingers of long-run industrial expansion. The selection of specific priority industries is generally based on four key criteria: an industry's potential international competitiveness; the propensity of the industry to benefit from economies of scale and technological change (the efficiency of capital criteria); the nature of the industry's income-elasticity in terms of export demand and world real income; and the ability of the industry to generate linkages.[10] As a result, the government rejected the dictates of static comparative advantage as a guidepost to industrialisation; rather, MITI:

> Decided to establish in Japan industries which require intensive employment of capital and technology, industries that in consideration of comparative cost of production should be the most inappropriate for Japan, industries such as ... aircraft ... From a short-run, static viewpoint, encouragement of such industries would seem to conflict with economic rationalism. But, from a long-range viewpoint, these are precisely the industries where income elasticity of demand is high, technological progress is rapid, and labour productivity rises fast.[11]

In 1945, the once formidable Japanese aircraft industry was dissolved under the American occupation. However, with the outbreak of the Korean War and the signing of the 1952 Peace Treaty, the Japanese aircraft industry was again revived under a government decree, the Aircraft Manufacturing Law (later revised as the Aircraft Manufacturing Industry Law) which was designed to provide a foundation for future aircraft development and production.[12] Stimulated by demand for repair and overhaul work on USAF aircraft, the decree distributed airframe production contracts to seven factories, component-supply contracts to 41 factories and overhaul contracts to an additional 12 factories. Subsequently, characteristic of the economy as a whole, the Japanese Government has played a critical role in fostering the development of the industry.

First and foremost, this support has come by way of state procurement, and especially through the Japanese Defence Agency (JDA). Prior to 1954, Japan was prohibited from maintaining national armed forces; a provision which did not augur well for the promotion of an aircraft industry.[13] However, in 1954, the Diet assented to the Self-Defence Law which provided for the re-establishment of the armed forces and, moreover, served as an important catalyst in the development of Japan's aircraft industry. The need to equip the Self-Defence Forces (SDF) with aircraft provided the requisite demand to expand the industry's manufacturing capacity. The desire to develop a broad industrial base was entrusted to MITI which allocated JDA contracts among the principal aircraft producers.[14] In concert with Japan's propensity to rely upon foreign technology transfer, the lead programmes at the key manufacturers tended to be licensed production of US designs. Frequently building on prior overhaul experience, technology transfer generally proceeded in a phased process beginning with the licensee assembling 'knock-down' aircraft followed by the incorporation of locally-manufactured parts as production tooling was completed, and finally leading to the assumption of full manufacturing responsibility.[15] As recounted in Chapter 6, licence production of warplanes embraced Kawasaki's responsibility for Lockheed T-33 and P-2 aircraft, and Bell 47 helicopters; Fuji's manufacture of Beech T-34s and Cessna L-19s; and, in particular, the entrusting of F-86F jet fighter production to MHI. By 1969, MHI had delivered 300 F-86s to the armed forces (with domestic content finally reaching about 77 per cent of airframe components).[16] Although virtually all of the production technology (e.g. production data and tooling) associated with F-86F manufacture was imported, the programme (as was the case with the other licensing arrangements mentioned) proved invaluable in terms of elevating the firm's (and industry's) basic technological capabilities.

In order to facilitate production continuity, the phase-out of F-86F manufacture was co-ordinated with the phase-in of production of the more sophisticated Lockheed F-104 Starfighter at MHI. With Kawasaki as the major subcontractor, the JDA and MHI signed an agreement in March 1961 calling for the purchase of 200 F-104s (with the Japanese designation F-104J), including 20 trainer versions, (F-104DJs), at an estimated cost of $269 million (of which the US Government agreed to contribute $75 million). Typical of previous licensing arrangements, technology transfer progressed in a phased fashion: after the delivery of three complete airframes from the USA, 17 F-104J and 20 F-104DJ knock-down kits were supplied by Lockheed to MHI, with 160 F-104Js assembled and increasingly manufactured in Japan.[17] A follow-on order for 30 additional F-104Js in 1966 also increased the proportion of Japanese involvement. Similar to the F-86F experience, the F-104J avionics systems had to be imported from the USA owing to their complexity and high cost of transfer. Besides, a myriad of other parts were imported because the limited production run precluded economic manufacture (in contrast to the various European F-104 programmes). Complementing the transfer of product technology, Japanese industry was also exposed to important process technology, including chemical milling techniques, the spray-mat process to control icing, and improved techniques to form and handle high-heat treatment steel.[18] In addition to acquiring airframe technology, the F-104J programme also augmented Japan's aeroengine manufacturing capabilities, as IHI acquired the licence to produce the GE J-79 jet engine. Overall, it was estimated that Japanese-made F-104 airframes were cheaper to produce than US ones ($620,000 instead of $789,000), but Japanese aeroengines were more expensive ($232,000 as opposed to $184,000).[19]

The propensity to engage in licence production of front-line combat aircraft has since remained unabated. As a follow-on programme to the F-104J, licensed production of the MD F-4EJ fighter again witnessed MHI selected as the prime contractor and Kawasaki as the main subcontractor, with IHI responsible for the manufacture of the powerplant, an upgraded J-79. As was the case with previous co-production arrangements, technology transfer evolved in a step-wise format, with initial delivery of two F-4EJs from St. Louis being followed by Japanese production. Improved capabilities, however, ensured that almost 100 per cent of the F-4EJ airframe, avionics and engine were manufactured in Japan (in contrast to the F-104J, where main avionics systems were imported).[20] Analogous to the follow-on imperative discussed in Chapter 4, the JDA and MITI ensured Japanese production continuity with the decision to produce 100 MD F-15 air-superiority fighters at a projected cost of $3.3 billion.[21] A second memorandum of understanding, signed in December 1983, called for the purchase of an additional 55 F-15s scheduled for delivery over the 1986-90 period. Paralleling earlier programmes, MITI distributed production contracts among the three manufacturers with MHI as prime contractor and responsible for final assembly and production of the nose and forward and centre fuselage sections, Kawasaki overseeing aft fuselage and wing manufacture, and IHI again building the aeroengine (the P & W F100 in this instance). Following delivery of the last F-4EJ in May 1981, the first Japanese assembled F-15J (from a knock-down kit) rolled off MHI's Komaki South production line in August 1981.[22] Prior to Japanese assembly, the first eight F-15s were procured through US Foreign Military Sales credits while the remaining aircraft are to be progressively manufactured in Japan, with local content expected to reach 55 per cent.[23]

A second major military programme designed to carry the Japanese aircraft industry through the 1980s is the licensed production of the Lockheed P-3C patrol aircraft. By way of a technical assistance agreement struck between Lockheed and Kawasaki in 1973, the latter acquired the rights (through an initial payment of $16.5 million and a $270,000 per aircraft royalty fee thereafter) to produce the P-3C to meet an SDF requirement.[24] On the basis of a JDA order for 45 aircraft (since raised to 75), and consistent with its ambitions to develop a broad industrial base, MITI allocated production contracts to the major firms; namely, Kawasaki (as prime contractor), MHI, Fuji, Shin Meiwa, Japan Aircraft Corporation, and Sumitoma Precision Products.[25]

Although the majority of defence output is attributable to licensed-production programmes, experience and technology gained through these projects have spurred indigenous design efforts in the military field. These efforts have proceeded in two directions: on the one hand, Japanese firms have designed derivatives of aircraft produced under licence, and on the other, Japanese firms have undertaken more extensive design efforts which have led to new aircraft. In terms of the former, Fuji developed a modified version of the Beech T-34 trainer, the LM-1 Nikko liaison aircraft, of which 27 were delivered to the SDF.[26] Similarly, Kawasaki, designed the P-2J derivative of the Lockheed P2V-7 Neptune patrol aircraft.[27] With respect to truly indigenous designs, most Japanese efforts have focused on trainer aircraft (a characteristic which typifies many contemporary NIC aircraft efforts). To this end, the first postwar jet aircraft entirely of Japanese design was the Fuji T1F1 (T-1B) trainer powered by an imported UK engine initially, and then by an IHI designed J3-IHI-3 turbojet engine.[28] Built to a JDA requirement to replace US North American T-6s, some 60 T1F1s and T1F2s were procured for use by the SDF. A second trainer programme sponsored by the JDA was the Mitsubishi T-2. Initiated in the late 1960s, the T-2 was the first supersonic aircraft developed by the Japanese aircraft industry. Powered by two R-R Turboméca Adour turbofans, T-2 production began in the mid 1970s, with MHI receiving orders for 92 aircraft.[29] The T-2 programme subsequently spawned two offshoot projects. In the first of these, the T-2 was redesigned as a close-air-support fighter and restyled the F-1. After completion of design work and flight testing in 1976, deliveries of F-1s began in 1977, with orders numbering 74 by mid-1984. A second spin-off arose in 1978, when the JDA's Technical Research and Development Institute selected the T-2 as a testbed with which to develop active flight control technologies, and subsequently redesigned the T-2 to control configured vehicle (ccv) configuration. Finally, the JDA initiated a third trainer programme (XT-4/T-4) to replace Lockheed T-33As and Fuji T-1A/Bs. Based on Kawasaki's KA-850 design, the programme is a joint development/production project shared by Kawasaki (prime contractor and a 40 per cent share), Fuji (30 per cent) and MHI (30 per cent), with the SDF expected to procure 200 T-4s into the 1990s.[30] In addition to the foregoing, notable indigenous designs destined for the military market include: the Shin Meiwa PS-1 patrol flying boat and its air-sea-rescue derivative the SS-2A, of which 23 and 8 respectively were procured by the SDF; and the C-1 twin-jet transport which was designed under the auspices of the Nihon Aeroplane Manufacturing Company (NAMC), with Kawasaki, Fuji, MHI, Shin Meiwa, and Nihon Hikoki assuming production responsibility.

The government's prime policy measure for supporting the development of the aircraft industry has been military procurement. The JDA and MITI have utilised defence expenditure, in a manner reminiscent of the American follow-on system, as a means to sponsor licence-production programmes virtually irrespective of their economic feasibility. Indeed, "The government has been willing to support licenced production programs of clearly uneconomical projects simple to gain the technological know-how for reviving its industry."[31] Thus, the Japanese Government procured only 24 Fuji-built Cessna L-19 observation aircraft, when a production run of at least 120 aircraft was required to provide a minimum economic basis for the programme. Similarly, the Japanese Government was willing to pay $1.8 billion more for 90 F-15s in order to build the aircraft in Japan and gain access to the most sophisticated aircraft technology in use.[32] Clearly, the liberal expenditure of defence monies serves not only to secure markets for Japanese firms, but also acts as an outright subsidy to the industry. However, the acute dependence on defence contracts, which in 1977 accounted for 88.6 per cent of total aircraft production, presents serious challenges to the industry.[33] Specifically, the industry is not allowed to export military hardware and domestic defence expenditure is limited to approximately one per cent of GNP.[34] In view of these restrictions, continued reliance on defence contracts would appear inconsistent with MITI's strategy of developing strong export industries. Not surprisingly, therefore, the Japanese Government has attempted to foster civil programmes in tandem with the more extensive military ones.

In contrast to military projects, state support of civil programmes has not relied upon direct procurement; rather, the Japanese Government has tended to socialise risks through the underwriting of R & D costs. In terms of civil projects, MITI has set its sights on penetrating the commercial airliner market. The first effort in this direction was initiated in the late 1950s under the auspices of NAMC. Created under the Aircraft Industry Promotion Law (1959), NAMC was established as a consortium of major Japanese aircraft producers (consisting of MHI, Kawasaki, Fuji, Shin Meiwa, Showa, and Nihon) and tasked with the design and development of a medium-range airliner.[35] MITI and NAMC member firms jointly subscribed the necessary capital requirement, with the former contributing $11.6 million in start-up costs along with a commitment to underwrite debentures of $74.1 million. The outcome of this effort was the YS-11 twin-turboprop 60-passenger airliner. While NAMC was responsible for design and development work, production of the YS-11 was farmed out to the member firms with MHI handling final assembly and fuselage and equipment production, Fuji producing tail sections, Kawasaki building wings and engine nacelles, Shin Meiwa overseeing rear fuselage work; Nihon manufacturing the ailerons and flaps, and Showa responsible for honeycomb structures.[36] From the flight of the first production aircraft in October 1964 to the termination of production in 1974, 182 YS-11s had been delivered.[37] Although recording a loss of some $35 million over the course of the project, the YS-11 programme did realise a number of important benefits in terms of technological capabilities and, to a lesser extent, export market penetration. Whereas, industry exports in 1968 (the best year of the YS-11 programme) amounted to a meagre 18.8 per cent, approximately half of the YS-11s delivered were destined for the US market.[38] At the same time, however, the YS-11 experience also exposed the industry's weak marketing and support network. Commenting on the YS-11 programme, Kenji Uchino (an executive of Japan's Commercial Airplane Company) lamented, "To make the airplane is not that tough. Selling it is the real challenge."[39]

Cognisant of the importance of developing civil lines of business and given the institutional restrictions extant in the defence sector, NAMC began design work on the F-X commercial transport in the late 1960s. As a result, the YS-33 short-haul trijet was designed as a planned successor to the YS-11.[40] However, the YS-33 project was soon terminated as key elements of the Japanese aircraft industry preferred to concentrate their efforts on military contracts which provide a "relatively low risk haven" in comparison with commercial projects.[41] With the obvious need to generate civil activity, Japanese industry decided not to pursue the risky business of designing a complete airframe and instead opted to participate as a subcontractor and risk-sharing partner with established commercial transport manufacturers. Consequently, Kawasaki produced entry doors for Lockheed L-1011s, outer trailing-edge flaps for Boeing 747s, actuator transmissions for 727s, and inner flaps and wing ribs for the 737; while MHI built engine transport kits for 757s, inner trailing-edge flaps for 747SPs and assembled tail cones for DC-10s; and Fuji manufactured rudders for 747SPs.[42]

Meanwhile, the aforementioned F-X programme eventually evolved into a risk-sharing partnership with Boeing on its 767 transport. To this end, the Civil Transport Development Corporation (CTDC) was established (in much the same fashion as the NAMC) to manage Japan's 17 per cent interest in the 767 programme. MITI provided CTDC with an initial endowment of $87 million to undertake the project, and as a risk-sharing partner, CTDC was obliged to contribute $170 million towards 767 development costs.[43] In addition, MITI has pledged to underwrite production costs in order to allow Japanese firms to reduce their prices by 5-10 per cent and thereby make the 767 more competitive with the Airbus.[44] Production of fuselage panels, wing and fuselage fairings, cargo and entry doors as well as other airframe components is apportioned among member firms. Building on this experience, a consortium of Japanese firms under the aegis of the Japan Airplane Development Corporation (JADC) - an offshoot of the CTDC - entered into a second risk-sharing partnership with Boeing for the planned development of a 150-passenger airliner, the 7-7 (or alternatively the YXX in Japan).[45] Along with a 25 per cent share in the estimated $2 billion development cost, JADC is seeking a larger role in design, production, and marketing of the 7-7, relative to its status in the 767 programme.[46] As with other programmes, the Japanese effort is sponsored by MITI, which will underwrite the majority of R & D costs.

While MITI and industry ambitions in the civil market have been primarily focused on the airliner market, a number of important programmes have been undertaken in the business aircraft and helicopter markets. In terms of the former, MHI began basic design work on the MU-2 twin-turboprop in 1960, and the first aircraft flew in September 1963. By early 1971, roughly 85 per cent of the first 200 aircraft were destined for export markets, primarily the USA.[47] To further US market penetration, and following a decision by the Nixon administration to "permit government purchases of the MU-2 on the grounds that 65 per cent of the manufacturer's cost of production is spent in the US", MHI established an American subsidiary, Mitsubishi Aircraft International (MAI), to handle world-wide marketing as well as final assembly.[48] By March 1984 the firm had received orders for 745 MU-2s, of which 689 were exports.[49] MHI diversified its business aircraft product line in the early 1980s with the introduction of the MU-300 (Diamond I) turbofan. Like the MU-2, the MU-300 is shipped to San Angelo, Texas, for final assembly and the installation of engines and systems at MAI. As of July 1983, MHI had received orders for 61 Diamond I aircraft, of which North American sales numbered 48.[50] Japanese efforts in the area of rotary wing aircraft, though decidedly less pronounced than those in fixed-wing areas, have also been pursued. In typical fashion, initial efforts to familiarise the industry with the manufacture of helicopters were centred on licensed production of US designs, principally for JDA requirements. The only firm to undertake the development of an all new helicopter is Kawasaki. Following licensed production of Bell 47s, Boeing-Vertol KV-107s and Hughes OH-6s, Kawasaki entered into an agreement in 1972 with MBB for the joint development of a twin-engined multi-purpose helicopter in the 8-10 seat class. The resultant aircraft, the BK-117, entered the market in 1982 with orders reaching well over a 100. Production of the BK-117 is split between the two firms and sees Kawasaki responsible for airframe and landing gear manufacture, with both firms undertaking final assembly.

All told, the Japanese aircraft industry has grown rapidly since its rebirth in 1952. In large measure this growth has been spurred by state industrial policy and, in particular, through the use of military procurement. The JDA and MITI have integrated defence and industry requirements such as to ensure industrial growth in a pattern reminiscent of the American follow-on imperative. To facilitate technological development, the Japanese Government has sponsored licensed production programmes with established aircraft manufacturers. Building on product and process technology acquired and adapted from these programmes, Japanese firms have undertaken a variety of indigenous projects in the civil and military markets. At the same time, participation in licence and co-production programmes has slowly stimulated the development of important linkages. The fact that parts, component and equipment production accounted for $1.15 billion (or 51 per cent) of the industry's output in 1984 is ample testimony to that effort.[51] On the basis of the above, industry sales totalled $2.2 billion in 1984, a far cry from the $309.33 million recorded in 1971 (although employment growth has slowed considerably). Despite this laudable performance, the fact remains that the industry is overwhelmingly dependent on domestic military work, which has been increasing since the early 1970s and has generally exceeded 75 per cent during the recent period. Given the constraints on defence production in Japan, the dependence on defence work has meant that the industry's export mandate has remained largely unfulfilled. While low-risk defence production will carry the industry through the 1980s (on the strength of the P-3C, F-15, T-4, and a new fighter, the FXX), the Japanese aircraft industry does possess two important advantages which can potentially allow it to penetrate the more risky commercial export markets. On the one hand, the Japanese Government has firmly committed itself to supporting the industry into the future, and on the other, the major Japanese manufacturers are not inordinately dependent on aircraft production (with aircraft sales accounting for only 10-15 per cent of total sales).[52] In any event, industry growth will still rely on imports of foreign technology.

CANADA

The Canadian aircraft industry consists of approximately 100 firms and in 1982 accounted for $2.8 billion in sales (seventh in the world) and employed some 36,320 workers.[53] Approximately 77 per cent of these sales were exports, and the ratio of industry exports to imports was 3.11.[54] In terms of complete airframes and aeroengines, fully 88 and 69 per cent respectively of total sales were exports, the majority of which were destined for the USA, the country's major trading partner.[55] While most firms undertake Tier II and Tier III activities, there are three main Tier I firms. In particular, there are two airframe manufacturers, Canadair and DHC, which are nationalised enterprises held by the Canada Development Investment Corporation (CDIC). Both Canadair and DHC were foreign subsidiaries prior to the government's decision to take them over in the mid-1970s. The remaining Tier I firm is P & WC; a wholly-owned subsidiary of UTC of Hartford, Connecticut, and the nation's only aeroengine producer. In fact, P & WC is representative of the industry in Canada in as much as foreign firms tend to predominate. Indeed, more than half of the Tier II enterprise are subsidiaries of foreign corporations. Arguably, this structural characteristic has contributed to the rather dubious R & D record of the industry and its basically 'built-to-print' status, and directly led to the nationalisation of DHC in 1974 and Canadair in 1976. Another salient feature of the Canadian aircraft industry is the general absence of defence production among the Tier I firms.[56] In contradistinction to virtually all other aircraft industries, Canada's industry has had to evolve without the benefit of a relatively independent national defence procurement policy, a void which has had significant implications for the industry's development. In large measure, the industry's lacklustre R & D performance, and the abrogation of the independent Canadian defence policy are manifestations of the historical evolution of the North American political economy. The division of labour emerging out of this evolution sees Canada's primary role as a supplier of resources to the USA and, as a result, the nation's manufacturing sector remains dependent and under-developed. The aerospace industry, however, is one area where the Canadian Government has ostensibly pledged to forge a new division of labour.

The evolution of the Canadian aircraft industry may be divided into roughly three broad phases. The initial or formative phase ran from around 1915 to the onset of mobilisation for World War II. From the outset, and consistent with import substitution, foreign manufacturers established a marked presence in Canada. The first venture into aircraft production was the US Curtiss Company which, in 1915, established a subsidiary for the purpose of capturing British Admiralty orders. Boeing (US), Fairchild (US), Consolidated (US), Vickers (UK), and DH (UK) all established subsidiaries in Canada prior to World War II, and thus, "The aircraft industry ... evolved on a derivative basis with most research and design located elsewhere."[57] At the same time, Canada's traditional UK ties were giving way to continental ones. The preparation for war signalled the transition to the second phase of the industry's evolution, which extended to the early 1970s.

This phase was characterised first and foremost by the gradual erosion of Canadian production of complete airframes for defence markets. The need for additional aircraft production capacity prompted the Canadian Government to establish several new manufacturing operations. More importantly, however, the exigencies of war stimulated the crystalisation of a US-Canada defence pact along the precepts of a continental alliance. The initial step in this direction was the signing of the Ogdensburgh Declaration in 1940, which created the Permament Joint Board of Defence (PJBD), and was closely followed by the Hyde Park Declaration (1941) which extended continental defence strategy into the realm of production and articulated the position that, "in mobilising the resources of this continent each country would provide the other with the defence articles which it is best able to produce".[58] In terms of aircraft production, the result reflected the industry's established dependence on foreign inputs, as of the 16,000 aircraft made in Canada for the war effort, only one of the dozen principal types produced was an indigenous design, and all the aeroengines were imported. With the cessation of hostilities, the Canadian Government divested itself of its aeronautical ventures. The industry, however, continued to direct most of its output towards defence markets throughout the 1950s and 1960s. Not surprisingly, given the industry's technological status, licensed production of US aircraft was its trademark: the F-86 fighter (1949),

T-33 trainer (1951), T-34 trainer (1955) and F-104 fighter (1959) leading the way.[59] Despite this propensity, Canadian industry did maintain local design and production capabilities and this was best exemplified by the CF-100 produced by HS subsidiary, Avro Canada.) All the while, Canada-US defence links were moving towards formal integration. By 1957 this trend was formalised with the creation of the North American Air Defence Command (NORAD) held responsible for continental air defence. Concurrent with the integration of air defence, and arguably a result of it, Canada withdrew from autonomous military aircraft development. Thus the cancellation of the Avro Arrow supersonic fighter programme led not only to the demise of the last military aerospace design team in Canada, but to the purchase of all Canada's future combat aircraft from American sources. In recompense, and in order to maintain at least a semblance of Canadian military aircraft manufacturing (though not necessarily design) capability, the Canadian Government negotiated the Defence Production Sharing Agreement (DPSA) in 1959.

Under the DPSA, Canadian aerospace firms are able to direct their output to the needs of the Pentagon by way of free market access to US defence contracts, and thus receive reprieve from the 'Buy America Act'. In 1963, the two nations agreed to keep trade covered by the DPSA in a rough balance, and thereby, linked Canadian aerospace exports to the USA to sustained Canadian procurement of American military equipment. The ensuing period witnessed the continuation of licensed production (e.g. the CF-5 version of Northrop's F-5A), and the lucrative participation in the US Vietnam War effort. As indicated in Table 8.1, the peak of Canadian aerospace industry output and employment coincided with the peak of the Vietnam War in 1967-68. However, the acute dependence on US defence markets left the industry vulnerable, especially since much of its R & D had been abrogated under the DPSA. As Vietnam production wound down from the late 1960s, Canadian aerospace employment fell from 48,000 in 1967 to 25,000 in 1976. The composition of the industry's output told the story; whereas in the 1960s from 50-60 per cent of output was destined for defence markets, by the 1970s the proportion had dropped to below 40 per cent. Even licensed production of US aircraft ceased, as Canadair's (then a subsidiary of GD) CF-5 programme came to a close. Dwindling activity levels in the warplane field, coupled with difficulties encountered by the airframe firms in diversifying into civil markets, compelled state acquisition and, in so doing, ushered in the third and current phase of the industry's evolution.

The nationalisation of DHC and Canadair in many respects adopts the semblance of an industrial strategy in Canada. It arose not so much as part of a dirigiste industrial strategy, but rather, to secure manufacturing jobs and to maintain a Canadian presence in an important global industry. In terms of the latter, aerospace was viewed as a useful instrument for diversifying an otherwise largely resource-dependent economy. However, the government's ability to foster an indigenous industry was severely circumscribed as a consequence of its historical ties to the USA. In view of the importance of defence procurement to aerospace, the nationalisation and subsequent course of development of the industry emerged as a logical outcome of Canadian defence policy. Yet, as defence policy was subservient to US policy, so too became Canadian defence industry - and not least the aircraft industry. Thus, the subsequent development of the industry, under state auspices, would proceed along two basic lines: first, in the area of defence, the remaining policy instrument available to the Canadian Government was the negotiation of compensatory industrial offset agreements in exchange for the procurement of US military aircraft (and these will be discussed in the following section); and secondly, to concentrate indigenous aircraft production in the area of civil and commercial markets. This latter option is best exemplified by the strategy adopted by DHC; namely, that of strengthening its established lines of expertise in the STOL transport market. To this end, DHC furnishes a range of STOL types: the highly succcessful Twin Otter (19 passenger category), the recently developed DASH 8 (36 passenger class), and the DASH 7 (50 passenger class). In the case of Canadair, the Canadian Government saw the key to this firm's fortunes in the bizjet market. Paradoxically, while the government ostensibly promised to maintain a domestic design capability, it none the less saw fit to import a US design, that of William P. Lear's Learstar 600, as the basis for the Canadair Challenger programme.[60]

The industry's problems steadily mounted notwithstanding state ownership. In fact, the state's disenchantment became evident in its vacillating desire to, alternately, sell and retain its floundering enterprises. In 1981, however, the then Liberal Government seemingly issued a vote of confidence in the industry through its strategy document, which explicitly acknowledged aerospace as a leading industry in the nation's future;

Table 8.1 : Canadian Aerospace Industry Statistics

Year	Sales ($m)	Defence (%)	Exports (%)	Employment ('000)
1963	550	66.0	40.5	
1964	589	61.9	48.2	37.5
1965	541	61.9	43.6	37.9
1966	594	50.0	50.5	45.9
1967	680	54.0	59.1	48.1
1968	750	54.9	74.5	47.8
1969	695	52.7	71.5	44.4
1970	659	52.2	73.1	35.8
1971	596	48.0	71.0	28.7
1972	625	35.0	81.6	28.8
1973	662	32.9	77.9	31.7
1974	729	32.0	80.1	28.4
1975	785	32.0	79.6	27.3
1976[1]	800	36.0	77.5	25.3
1977[1]	872	39.0	73.6	27.4

Note: 1. Estimated figures.
Source: Canada, A Report by the Sector Task Force on the Canadian Aerospace Industry, (Department of Industry, Trade and Commerce, Ottawa, 1978).

> The third direction of growth is ... the innovative resources of Canadians in the development and exploitation of advanced technology and high productivity goods and services ... in manufacturing, engineering and service areas such as ... aerospace ... [that] can place ourselves [Canadians] at the forefront of technological change in selected world markets.[61]

The pronouncement could hardly have come at a more inopportune time as the global economy was amidst recession, interest rates were high, and civil aircraft markets were flat. Canadair alone lost $1.4 billion (largely attributable to the Challenger programme) on sales of $429 million in 1982.[62] DHC, for its part, did not fare much better, losing $226 million in the last seven months of 1982. While assuming responsibility for the losses, the Canadian Government has been pressed to inject a further $310 million and $240 million in new investment into Canadair and DHC.[63] Moreover, the Canadian Government was compelled to restructure Canadair and thus relieve the firm of its debt burden in order to instil confidence in the market so that the Challenger programme could at least continue.[64] All told, the government subsidised the two firms to the tune of $823.3 million per year (average figure) through the 1981-83 period.[65] In addition, under a Special Capital Recovery Program, the government conjured up, at a cost of $147 million, an order for 20 Canadair CL-215 water bombers in order to keep the production line active.[66] None the less, employment at Canadair dropped to a low of 4,200 in 1983, down from 7,000 in June 1982.[67] Obviously, the distinction between backing 'high-tech' winners and undertaking corporate bail-outs remains dubious, especially in view of the opportunity costs foregone.

Seemingly undaunted however, the Canadian Government again chased aerospace employment. This time, the government canvassed a number of foreign helicopter firms to locate a production (assembly) facility in Canada in order to capture a share of the country's large domestic market - and at the same time reduce the nation's import bill. Offering lucrative subsidies, the government successfully attracted Bell-Helicopter-Textron to Mirabel, Quebec (with the prospect of 3,700 jobs). In exchange for $275 million in state support (from the federal and provincial governments), Bell is to initially produce the Model 400 Twin Ranger. More importantly, the agreement calls for the establishment of a domestic design and production capability, initially through transfer of 'state-of-the-art' technology, which is to be followed by a Canadian designed and produced derivative of the 400, the 440. Concomitant with the development of the Model 440, the government has extended some $468 million (over ten years) to P & WC for the development and production of a new series of gas-turbines to power the aircraft (the PW 200 series).[68] In addition to the Bell venture, MBB was induced to locate an assembly facility in Fort Erie, Ontario (by way of $34.9 million in government support) to enable it to produce its BO105. Interestingly, both ventures are destined to produce civil products, thus making all complete airframe production in Canada dependent on civil markets. If the experience of Canadair and DHC is any indication, the result may be costly.

INDUSTRIAL OFFSET AGREEMENTS

In the past decade, major foreign defence sales have shown a marked propensity to involve compensatory co-production (as noted in Chapter 6) or 'offset' agreements. A US Treasury Department survey revealed that 144 contracts negotiated between American firms and foreign customers between 1975-81, were valued at $14.8 billion, but yet required $13.7 billion (91.9 per cent) worth of compensatory offsets.[69] Of these, aircraft contracts totalled $10.84 billion and were accompanied by $7.02 billion in offsets. Moreover, where co-production and offset agreements were primarily the preserve of AICs, the developing countries are beginning to demand industrial offsets in exchange for procurement of major warplanes. The recent acquisitions of F-16s by Turkey and Greece and F-18s by Spain are indicative of these new expectations. Relatively poor economic conditions, increasing financial constraints, and industrialisation desires have increased the pressure on governments to negotiate deals with ever increasing percentages of offset commitments, at times in excess of the cost of the purchase.[70] For example, in the Greek fighter competition, an official from a competing airframe manufacturer noted, "The Greeks have never asked for more than 100 per cent offset, but they have said they would not settle for less".[71] In the case of the four-nation NATO fighter replacement programme, Saab-Scania's proposal for its Viggen included direct and indirect industrial compensation in the neighbourhood of 200 per cent of the aircraft purchase costs.[72] In effect, compensatory industrial offset agreements have become a way of life for exporters of most major military aircraft.

Basically, co-production and/or offset agreements are struck between prime aircraft contractors and foreign governments, with the contractor's government also heavily involved. These agreements involve the specific geographic placement of work on contracts by prime aircraft manufacturers in exchange for major purchases of aircraft. The work allocated may be directly associated with the production of the aircraft being procured, or completely unrelated. In practice, the range of offset commitments extends across the spectrum of economic activity, including aerospace work, tourism promotion, and export marketing. From the buyer's perspective, co-production agreements are usually set within the nation's broader political-economic relationships with participating countries. If need be, the seller's government may support the sale through agreed purchases of goods from the purchasing nation or through the provision of preferential financing arrangements. From the selling firm's perspective, industrial offsets are concessions necessary to successfully compete for foreign aircraft sales. Finally, the rationale underpinning the negotiation of co-production agreements from the purchasing government's perspective may be loosely divided into two categories: economic and political. In terms of economic considerations, short and long term objectives may be discerned. In the short term, the expenditure of large sums of public funds provides an important and visible economic stimulus to the economy, particularly in terms of job creation and subsequent multiplier effects. When these funds are spent on foreign goods, such effects are lost on the local economy. Consequently, purchasing governments attempt to internalise these benefits to the domestic economy through offset demands. Of equal importance, compensatory offsets provide a means to overcome foreign exchange losses associated with the procurement of expensive weapons systems. In the medium to longer term, industrial offset packages are generally conceptualised within the framework of import substitution strategies. In this sense, budgetary allocations for major defence purchases are utilised as a policy instrument to foster industrial expansion. This is especially so with aerospace in view of its 'high tech' status. As such, these arrangements lean heavily towards facilitating transfer of advanced technology, promoting an indigenous design and development capability and creating a skilled labour force, all of which are expected to provide a base for future industrial strength. Finally at the political level, offsets are a means to generate public support for political initiatives (through employment creation) as well as to develop economic and political linkages to supplier nations. More ambitiously, these agreements are seen frequently as stepping-stones in furthering national sovereignty. To this end, Turkish President Kenan Evren exclaimed of the F-16 offset package, "It is impossible to defend this country by begging others for arms or purchasing weapons through credit. To overcome these problems it has become essential that we produce our own weapons.".[73] It should be pointed out, however, that the demand for offset participation imposes additional costs on the price paid for aircraft (relative to the off-the-shelf "fly away" cost), and thus diverts additional resources away from potentially productive uses. These increases arise (as indicated in Chapter 6) from additional transaction costs, transfer of technology costs (e.g. learning curve considerations), duplication of capital investment, the involvement of less efficient firms (to satisfy national objectives) and reduced economies of scale on the prime assembly line. The decision to demand offsets, therefore, must be weighed against the additional costs incurred in selecting this course of action. In the case of the NATO co-production of F-16s, the four nations involved incurred a 34 per cent cost penalty relative to a direct purchase.[74] In so far as defence spending is seen as a burden on the domestic economy, these penalties may be unacceptable.

In the aforementioned US Treasury Department survey, Canada had received the most offsets negotiated between the sampled US firms and foreign purchasers. Specifically, Canada had received industrial offsets valued at $4.66 billion on the 28 contracts included in the survey.[75] In Canada's two most recent purchases of military aircraft - the CP-140 (the Lockheed P-3 Orion) and CF-18 (the MD F/A-18) - significant offset industrial agreements have been involved. In large measure, Canada's propensity to engage in offset agreements with US corporations, and the tenor of those agreements, is a product of the country's political-economic evolution. Since the interwar years the country's economy has become heavily dependent on the United States, as manifest through trade patterns, large cross flows of foreign investment and an integrated defence structure.[76] By virtue of the latter consideration, Canada's aerospace industry has evolved on a derivative basis; largely (though not entirely) dependent on American R & D, and licensed producer of US combat aircraft. The tendency for licensed production of US designs was reversed, however, with the decision to procure 18 CP-140 maritime patrol aircraft "off-the-shelf" and promote Canadian industry through offset subcontract work rather than through airframe assembly. The offset benefit package was to extend from 1975 to 1994. It was conceived as follows:[77]

Phase 1 1975-1981: $213.2 million to be placed in Canada, including $94 million in direct orders, and $119.2 million in indirect offsets principally through arrangements with other Canadian companies for sales from Canada. Subject to a 10 per cent penalty if schedule not maintained.

Phase 2 1982-December 1993: $201.4 million to be placed in Canada, of which, $66 million in direct orders, and $135 million in indirect offsets arranged as above. Subject to a 5 per cent penalty if the schedule is not maintained.

Lockheed to place $168 million in subcontracts to Canadian companies if the company sells an additional 150 P-3 aircraft over the programme period. No penalty for non-performance.

The Canadian Government returned to the offset bargaining table a few years later with its New Fighter Aircraft (NFA) programme to replace its ageing fleet of CF-101s, CF-104s and CF-5s. The earlier CP-140 experience raised concerns about the distribution of offset work among the nation's provinces, as Quebec and Ontario received the majority of the 'targeted' work, although no regional breakdowns were specified in the contract. The regional dimension was elevated to priority status in the NFA programme and, in particular, the distribution of work between Ontario and Quebec was stressed. The NFA request for proposals was responded to by a number of firms including MD (F-18), GD (F-16), and Panavia (Tornado). The last entry really stood little chance, since Canada had been one of the original participants of the MRCA and subsequently dropped out, and because the country was so tightly integrated into the North American economy. Thus, the F-18 and the F-16 emerged as the front-runners and the chances of landing the contract rested on the size of offsets.

Ostensibly, the MD and GD proposals shared a number of similarities. For its part, MD presented a wide ranging $2.6 billion package to the Canadian Government based on an estimated sale of $2.34 billion, of which approximately $700 million was in the form of direct offsets to Canada (with possible final assembly and test of aircraft) and an additional $1.9 billion was manifested in indirect offsets covering aerospace-related programmes as well as non-industry benefits such as promoting Canadian tourism.[78] The GD offset package was valued at $2.84 billion.[79] Of this, $2.4 billion was to be in the form of offset benefits to Canadian industry (and expected to provide more than 20,000 jobs) while the remaining $500 million was to be in the form of Canadian industrial exports, generated through GD assistance. Significantly, the NFA programme was influenced by important national questions, including a government defeat, a federal election (1980) and the Quebec referendum on the independence option for that province. As the federal government's electoral fortunes were wholly dependent on Quebec and moreover, the Federal cabinet (and the Prime Minister himself) was dominated by

Quebecers, the issue then, was not only the nominal value of compensatory offsets, but where those were to be placed. GD read the political winds carefully and played up the regional distribution, implying in the Quebec press that the MD proposal was of limited benefit to that province.[80] Not to the outdone, and also sensitive to the Quebec question, MD astutely shifted the location of a proposed $60 million GE (F-18 engine manufacturer) blade and vane plant from Ontario to a part of Quebec experiencing economic hardship. [81] The move was an "11th-hour attempt to sweeten the offset pot" with MD adding an extra $300 million to its NFA offset package.[82] The operational principle guiding the Canadian Government through this process was an equitable distribution of offset benefits throughout Canada, largely based on the existing distribution of aerospace activity in Canada - Quebec and Ontario comprising 48 per cent and 41 per cent respectively. From the government's perspective the proposed offset packages broke down as follows:[83]

GD: total offset package $2.62 billion, of which Quebec was to receive $1.47 billion (56 per cent) over a 15 year period.

MD: total offset package $3.26 billion, of which Quebec was to receive $1.57 billion (48 per cent).

The MD proposal, therefore, benefited Quebec to a greater extent than the GD offer, was consistent with the government's operational principle, and potentially offered a better bargain to the country as a whole. Thus, the MD aircraft was selected, and Canada contracted for 137 of them at a cost of $3 billion. Yet MD's marketing acumen was evident not so much by what the company was proposing, but rather, by what it was not saying. Because no explicit regional quotas were specified, relative offset shares were largely contingent upon Quebec and Ontario firms bidding on potential contract work. The government position was that since Quebec had historically accounted for about 48 per cent of the Canadian aircraft industry it was reasonable to suppose that, other things being equal, its firms would capture a similar share of Canadian offset work. Ottawa's folly was to overlook the fact that two-thirds of Quebec's aerospace industry is accounted for by two firms - Canadair (a former GD subsidiary) and P & WC (a subsidiary of UTC). Canadair's preoccupation with civil work effectively precluded its ability to bid on major offset work. P & WC, on the other hand, was stymied owing to the fact that its parent was supplying the F-16 powerplant.[84] Hence, two-thirds of Quebec's aerospace industry was effectively removed from bidding on F-18 work, though seemingly neither Ottawa nor GD detected this.

All told, the offset package had a potential value of $3.3 billion (or about 110 per cent of the contract value) over a fifteen year period and called for 60 per cent to be committed to the aerospace and electronic sectors (of which $545 million was for the supply of navigational systems for MD cruise missiles, and a further $654 million was derived from MD purchases of Canadian-built jetliner wings from the company's Toronto subsidiary). A further ten per cent ($300 million) was to be in the form of high technology business, and the balance was to occur in the establishment of a blade and vane plant in Quebec ($60 million), an NC machining centre ($225 million) and in tourism promotion.[85]

Consistent with events elsewhere, the Turkish Government has utilised industrial offset agreements as a policy instrument to foster domestic development and expansion. As a means of enacting a long-range programme to create a national aerospace (and defence) industry, the Turkish Government has recently used its military purchasing power as a vehicle to acquire aircraft manufacturing technology from 'export hungry' aircraft producers. As a first step, the Turkish Government negotiated a comprehensive offset package in its recent $4 billion purchase of 160 GD F-16s.[86] With the expressed intent of creating a national aircraft and armaments production capability, the government and GD arrived at an arrangement which will enable Turkey to licence-build 152 F-16 C/Ds. Tusas Aerospace Industries Inc will be established as a joint "turn-key" operation by Turkey and US firms. Turkish Aircraft Industries Inc (along with other Turkish interests) will control 51 per cent of the new firm, while GD will maintain a 42 per cent interest and the aeroengine supplier will likely assume the remaining seven per cent.[87] For their part, the US firms are to provide $67 million in equity, equipment and technical assistance towards the scheduled $137 million investment.[88] As noted, the agreement calls for the licensed assembly of 152 aircraft with Tusas eventually responsible for aft and centre fuselage and wing production, sheet metal forming, structural bonding, tube assembly and plumbing, wire harness assembly and machining of selected parts, as well as final assembly of complete aircraft. The actual production programme calls for the phased build-up of Turkish participation, with the first aircraft assembled from knock-down kits supplied by GD, to be followed by the progressive expansion of manufacturing activity as Tusas proceeds down the learning curve. To accommodate production, a new 69,700 m^2 plant is to be constructed at an air base near Ankara, with the first aircraft expected to roll off the assembly line in 1988 and full production expected in 1990. Employment at peak production is set at about 1,500.

The second phase in the Turkish programme is tied to the scheduled replacement of Turkey's fleet of Douglas C-47 transport aircraft. Vying for the estimated $500 million contract to supply 52 aircraft are Spain's CASA (in co-operation with Nurtanio of Indonesia) with its CN-235, Aeritalia with the G.222, and DHC with its DHC-5D Buffalo.[89] In early 1985 while the decision was still pending, DHC had offered to transfer the entire Buffalo production line to Turkey, while Aeritalia had proposed an extensive co-production programme, a soft financing package including US Foreign Military Sales credits on US supplied inputs, and Italian assistance in getting Turkey into the EEC. Whether the Turkish Government's efforts are successful in nurturing a domestic aerospace industry remains to be seen. However, the Turkish case demonstrates the relative effectiveness of utilising state purchasing power to induce technology transfer and establish at least a nominal industrial capacity in a short period of time. In addition, savings in foreign exchange are also expected to ensue.

Whereas Turkey conceived of its industrial offset package as a means to establish its aircraft industry virtually from scratch, Spain's industrial offset package associated with the $3 billion purchase of 72 MD F-18s is seen as a means to expand its existing aircraft design, development and production capacity.[90] To this end, the proposed $1.8 billion offset package emphasises technology transfer to augment Spain's own efforts (through CASA) and calls for some co-production of F-18 parts, as well as important process technology transfer including carbon fibre epoxy bonding, aluminium honeycomb core carving, NC machining and ion-vapour deposition processes. By using MD and its F-18 as the vehicle for gaining process technology under the mantle of offsets, Spain is emulating the Australian example (recall Chapter 6).

ROMANIA

In 1968, the Romanian Government targeted the aircraft industry as high-priority economic activity, and established the Centrul National al Industriei Aeronautice Romane (CNIAR) as an umbrella organisation under the auspices of the Ministry of Machine Building Industry.[91] As a result, the nation's five aircraft manufacturing facilities: Craiova, Bacau, Brasov and two in Bucharest, were placed under the control of CNIAR. The restructuring was undertaken during Romania's fourth five-year plan of 1966-70, and was envisaged as a concerted part of the nation's postwar industrialisation drive, which, "has shifted in emphasis from the creation of a wide foundation of basic industries toward the development of technologically advanced secondary industries ...".[92] Upon entering World War II the Romanian economy was one of the least developed in Eastern Europe. In 1950, agriculture accounted for nearly 75 per cent of total employment, and 26 and 28 per cent of social product and national income.[93] Through a series of successive five-year plans beginning in 1950, the Romanian Communist Party (RCP) embarked on a long-term programme to transform the country into a highly industrialised economy. Underpinned by high rates of saving and investment, average annual growth of gross industrial production was 13 per cent over the entire 1951-75 period and, as a result, industry accounted in 1975 for 64.7, 56.2, and 30.6 per cent of social product, national income, and employment respectively.[94] To facilitate the transition to an advanced industrial economy, the RCP has undertaken to intensify research and technological development activities, concentrating on three themes; namely, improving the existing technologies and developing new production technologies and the associated equipment; improving the quality and diversification of production; and establishing export competitiveness.[95] To augment indigenous capacity, the RCP has made a deliberate effort to cultivate international economic and technical co-operation, particularly through licensing and technical assistance agreements. Consequently, Romania's external links began to veer towards developed market economies, "Further development of Romania's leading sectors - chemicals and machine building - required advanced technology, which could not be obtained from socialist countries".[96] It is in this context that Romania's aircraft industry has been nurtured since its targeting in 1968.

The selection of aircraft manufacture as a part of Romania's industrialisation drive did not arise simply as an ad hoc choice, rather the country's courtship with the industry dates back to the earliest days of aviation. Since that time, the Romanian Aircraft Industry (IAR) has produced some 90 different types of land planes, 80 of which were of indigenous design.[97] In fact, prior to World War II Romania was one of Europe's leading aircraft producers and was capable of military aircraft designs which were second to none in Europe. With the onset of war, the Romanian aircraft industry began extensive licence-production of Messerschmitt Bf-109G aircraft as well as production of indigenous IAR-80 and -81 high performance combat aircraft.[98] However, at the conclusion of the war, the Brasov factory was converted into a farm-implement production facility, with most aircraft manufacturing machinery and equipment transferred to the Soviet Union as the country's economic priorities shifted to the development of heavy industry and modernisation of the agricultural sector. Aircraft production for much of the post-war period was confined to gliders and light aircraft. While inheriting the semblance of an aircraft industry in 1968, much of its former prowess had eroded and Romania turned to the West to recoup its technological capabilities. Therefore, the desire to develop an industry capable of indigenous design and, ultimately, of promoting export-led development was expressed through contracts established after 1968 with Western aerospace firms.

As a point of departure, Romania signed an agreement with Britten-Norman to licence-produce the latter's Islander, a piston-engined light transport. Faced with capacity constraints, the agreement enabled Britten-Norman to meet its growing demand for Islanders while, at the same time, providing Romania with a launch project for its newly formed CNIAR as well as a means to acquire Western production technology. Islander production began at the Baneasa factory in 1969. The initial licence to produce 215 aircraft was subsequently extended in 1975, and by September 1984, 400 aircraft had been manufactured, of which 380 had been delivered to PBN.[99] As Islander sales have slowed, CNIAR had indicated its intention to build on the programme's experience, and begin design work on its own 20-40 passenger commuter transport/utility aircraft as a replacement for the Islander.[100] In actuality, the Britten-Norman agreement was facilitated through fellow UK firm, BAC, which arranged the deal as part of a compensatory offset package tied to the Romanian Government's purchase of BAC-111 airliners.[101]

A second set of licensing agreements aimed at

expanding CNIAR's product and technological base were signed with Aérospatiale. In the first of these agreements, beginning in 1971, Romania was granted a licence to produce the Alouette III helicopter (with the Romanian designation IAR-316B).[102] While providing for Romanian manufacture of various components, the Brasov plant is still required to import a fair amount of the aircraft's equipment, including its engine. As a follow-on agreement, Romania acquired the licence to produce 100 SA.330 (IAR-330) Puma helicopters in 1976. In contrast to the Alouette III programme, the Puma project extended Romanian participation in the aircraft's production, including the licence-production of the Puma's (Turboméca) Turmo IV engine and transmission at Turbomecanica, the Bucharest-based aeroengine manufacturer.[103] While originally conceived as an import substitution measure aimed at supplying the domestic market and Romanian Air Force requirements, the helicopter programmes are being promoted for export markets. This latter shift has been possible with the termination of Aérospatiale production of Alouette IIIs, thus enabling Romania to gain export exposure. Some 190 Alouettes and more than 100 Pumas had been produced at the Brasov plant by 1984, most of which were destined for the Air Force. In addition to forging links to Western aerospace industries, CNIAR has also maintained its COMECON ties in the aircraft industry with the licensed-production of the Soviet Yak-52 aerobatic trainer, some 500 of which have already been produced at the Bacau plant for distribution throughout the Warsaw Pact countries.

Arising out of Romania's business dealings with BAC has been the licence-production of the BAC-111, restyled the ROMBAC 1-11, production of which has since been terminated by the UK firm in favour of its new BAe 146 airliner. By way of offset commitments, ten per cent of 1-11 airframe components were manufactured in Romania for transfer to the UK assembly line. Subsequently, Romania struck an agreement in May 1979 with BAe for the series 475 version (under the Romanian designation 495) and the series 500 (redesignated the 560). Manufacture of the aircraft in Romania is to proceed through a phased seven-stage technology transfer process at the end of which, expected to be 1987, the complete aircraft will be almost entirely Romanian-made. To accommodate production of the ROMBAC 1-11, the Baneasa facility is being expanded to cover about 200,000 m^2 of floor space, and thereafter will concentrate its activities primarily on transport aircraft. The first of a scheduled production run of 22 aircraft rolled out in

September 1982 and was promptly delivered to the national airline, Tarom. As a part of the licensing agreement, BAe granted CNIAR exclusive worldwide marketing rights (with the exception of the UK) to the BAe 111. However, marketing of the 1-11 has proved difficult. On the one hand, the R-R Spey Mk.512 powered ROMBAC 1-11 is an old aircraft which is noisy and relatively fuel inefficient. Moreover, Romanian efforts to modernise the aircraft have been constrained by the country's economic crisis which is placing financial constraints on the technological upgrading of the aircraft. To this end, CNIAR is looking to replace the current R-R Spey engine with the quieter, improved thrust R-R Tay and is looking for Western partners to participate in a modernisation programme. On the other hand, Romania has no marketing experience in selling an aircraft as complex as the ROMBAC in a highly competitive environment. There are in fact a number of interrelated problems in this respect. First, the BAe 111 has been out of production for some time and the airlines are reluctant to acquire an aircraft which is not manufactured by an established firm which has proven its capability to provide global support. Secondly, there is concern over operating in the parochial atmosphere of a planned economy which is largely devoid of the discipline of Western markets. As one industry official commented, "We have been spoiled by having a planned economy domestically. When something is produced here, the consumer must purchase it. But this isn't true on the Western-style open airline aircraft market".[104] To overcome this marketing problem, CNIAR has conceded marketing tasks to the British aircraft broking company, DK Aviation, which will sell the 1-11 in Western Europe and Africa on a commission basis.[105]

Consistent with the pattern of development extant in the airframe sector of the industry, Romania has relied heavily on the transfer of Western aeroengine technology to establish an indigenous technology base, again principally through licensing arrangements. Turbomecanica began production in 1975, and since that time has produced several hundred powerplants. In order to augment the plant's production capabilities, Romania has imported new NC machines from Japan, West Germany and Switzerland to supplement home-produced equipment. With the objective of developing an independent aeroengine design and development capability, Turbomecanica has acquired its existing technological capability and quality control and assurance system through agreements with R-R, Turboméca and Aérospatiale.[106] In the first of these, Romania acquired the licence to produce the R-R Viper 632-41 which serves as the powerplant for the Romanian/Yugoslavian IAR-93A combat fighter. Following this agreement, Turbomecanica entered into agreements with the French for the production of main and secondary gearboxes and rotor heads for the Alouette III and Puma helicopters, as well as the Turmo 4C turboshaft engine. As an offshoot of the ROMBAC 1-11 programme, Romania acquired the licence to produce and assemble R-R Spey Mk.512 turbofan engines in 1980. Specifically, the agreement calls for the progressive expansion of engine component manufacture leading to full Romanian production by 1987, and provides for immediate final assembly and testing. Moving beyond licensed production, Turbomecanica has entered into a co-production agreement with R-R and Yugoslavia, which will see the firm responsible for the development of variable nozzle and burner sections of a planned afterburning version of the Viper.

While the thrust of Romania's aircraft industry development strategy has relied on licensed production programmes centred on the ROMBAC 1-11 project, the country has demonstrated an indigenous design capability. Thus complementing the spate of licensed production programmes are the production of Romanian developed airframes including: the IAR-825 Triumf turboprop aircraft (also available as the IAR-831 Pelican in a piston version) which is initially targeted for the Romanian Air Force (for about 100 aircraft) and is to be powered by P & WC PT6 and/or (Czech) Walter M601B engines; and the IAR-827 piston, and IAR-828 turboprop, powered agricultural aircraft which fulfil both domestic and export requirements. Further testimony to the existence of a domestic airframe design capability is Romania's recent development of the IAR-99 Soim jet trainer powered with the same version of the Viper as the IAR-93A.[107] Finally, as a means to maintain a balanced product base and to move away from complete dependence on Soviet-designed combat aircraft, Romania entered into a joint development/production programme with Yugoslavia. Originated in 1970, the agreement has led to the production of IAR-93 (or Orao in Yugoslavia) twinjet strike-fighters - the first combat aircraft adopted in Romania since World War II that is not a Soviet design. The Romanian production line is building 20 of the Viper 632-powered IAR-93As and 165 of the Viper 633-powered IAR-93Bs.[108]

Since the 1968 reorganisation, Romania's aircraft industry has built up a diversified product base and has correspondingly expanded its technological capabilities. The judicious selection of airframe and aeroengine licensing arrangements with BAe, R-R, Aérospatiale, Turboméca and Britten-Norman has considerably accelerated this process. Thus, in the space of 15 years employment has reached a respectable 25,000, and the industry maintains five firmly-established production facilities.[109] Over the course of the development of the industry, planners have looked to it as a leader in enhancing the country's industrial capabilities, in terms of quality control techniques, marketing in the world economy, and project management; as well as in stimulating important backward linkages in the economy - all with important balance of payment and employment implications. None the less, and common to virtually all nascent aircraft industries, technological dependence seemingly remains the order of the day. The country's recent economic problems have clearly demonstrated the constraints placed on the industry's development. Yet, one can hardly expect a country to establish itself in such a complex industry in such a short period of time. However, if Romania chooses to continue as a producer of complete airframe and aeroengines, it will inevitably have to ween itself away from its dependence on licensed production, and maintain a firm R & D commitment in its stead.

INDONESIA

Another NIC which has 'targeted' aircraft production as a part of its national industrial strategy is Indonesia. Following a decade of relatively slow growth during the 1960s, gross domestic product expanded at an average annual rate of 7.6 per cent throughout the 1970s, well in excess of other low-income countries.[110] In the 1970s growth of manufacturing output, averaging 12.5 per cent per year, provided an important impetus to industrial growth as a whole. None the less, the contribution of manufacturing to the nation's economy remained relatively small, constituting only nine per cent of GDP in 1978. Furthermore 98 per cent of Indonesia's exports were accounted for by fuels, minerals, metals and other primary commodities, while manufactured exports constituted a lowly two per cent.[111] By way of contrast, manufactured exports comprised 70 and 34 per cent of Romanian and Brazilian exports at that time.[112] To improve the situation, the Indonesian Government embarked on a programme to establish a national aircraft industry in the mid-1970s. Typical of the cases outlined so far, the industry was established with the intent of facilitating import substitution and diversifying the composition of national exports, while at the same time serving as a lead industry in a country with 'high-tech' ambitions. Although committed to private accumulation, the Indonesian Government (like Brazil) is not averse to direct participation in key national industries, as is the case for example in oil production. Indeed, on the basis of the investment of rents generated in the oil industry and appropriated by the state-owned oil company, Pertamina, the Indonesian Government established Pesawat Terbang Nurtanio (PT Nurtanio) as the aircraft manufacturer. By a government decree of 5 April 1976, PT Nurtanio was created out of the merger of LIPNUR (previously set up to prepare for the development of the industry) and the aviation activities of Pertamina. Created with the mandate to set up a fully-fledged and commercially viable aircraft industry, PT Nurtanio was placed under the tutelage of Dr. B. J. Habibie, an Indonesian who gained extensive aerospace experience as a vice-president at MBB.[113] Perhaps indicative of the industry's importance to national development plans, Habibie was subsequently appointed to the post of Minister of State for Research and Technology, as well as President of the Indonesian Agency for the Development and Application of Technology. In terms of industrial policy, the government has generously underwritten the costs of production, initially providing $170 million for the construction of a new manufacturing facility in 1975, and subsequently allocating approximately $100 million per year for working capital.[114] In addition, the government has attempted to underwrite the risks of production by requiring that Indonesian airlines and other aircraft operators purchase PT Nurtanio-built aircraft when these products fulfil user requirements. Furthermore, the government has not hesitated to use state procurement to ensure a minimum level of demand.[115]

At the time of its creation, PT Nurtanio's development was set within a ten-year plan, at the end of which the firm was to have significantly enhanced its design, development and production capabilities. Ostensibly, a number of development phases were discerned: Phase I called for the transfer of technology for the assembly and partial manufacture of established products as a means to move along the 'learning curve'; Phase II took the process a step further with the application of existing technology to the design and manufacturing of new products, as well as continuing to acquire foreign product and process technology through co-operative agreements;

and finally, a third phase envisaged the indigenous development of new aerospace technology.

While aircraft production was not completely alien to Indonesia, PT Nurtanio was essentially established without the benefit of any meaningful aeronautical production experience.[116] Hence, to gain familiarity with the production of aircraft the industry relied exclusively upon the transfer of foreign product and process technology in the formative phase. To launch production at its 500-employee Bandung facility, PT Nurtanio acquired the licences to produce the MBB BO105 helicopter and the CASA C-212 Aviocar turboprop commuter aircraft.[117] The selection of the BO105 (renamed NBO105) and C-212 (designated NC-212) was based on two general considerations. In the first place, the products met domestic transportation requirements and thus could displace imports. Secondly, the aircraft were of relatively simple design; an important consideration given the industry's technological and labour constraints. In order to augment PT Nurtanio's capabilities, the agreements were structured to allow the firm to take an increasing role in production. In both programmes, initial participation began with the simple assembly of knock-down kits provided by CASA and MBB, and a minimal level of local content.[118] On a step-by-step basis, locally manufactured airframe components accounted for a greater share of the total airframe, reaching approximately 80-90 per cent. Moreover, PT Nurtanio has since secured a contract to supply C-212 wings for CASA's main production line.[119] Behind import barriers, PT Nurtanio has sold 133 NC-212s and 130 NBO105s since production began in late 1976. Of perhaps greater significance, the firm has managed to realise 42 export sales (to Thailand, Bangladesh and Burma) for its NC-212. Consistent with its import substitution objectives, Nurtanio quickly signed a third licensing agreement in 1977 with Aérospatiale for the assembly of Puma and Super Puma helicopters with the purpose of supplying Indonesian military requirements from local sources.[120] As with the previous agreements, the deal called for the stepwise transfer of production technology so as to enhance the firm's capabilities while concomitantly diversifying its product base. Subsequently, PT Nurtanio has continued to maintain its cautious path of licensed production of established designs in order to expand its helicopter production capabilities. Stimulated by state orders for 36 helicopters, it entered into an agreement with Bell of the USA for the licence-production of Model 412s with initial deliveries expected in 1986.[121] Similarly, MBB and PT

Nurtanio extended their close ties; firstly, with the latter acquiring the licence for the manufacture of 100 BK-117 helicopters, principally destined to meet local demand, and secondly, through the joint participation in the development of a new light helicopter, the BN-109.[122] The BN-109 project appears well suited to launch PT Nurtanio's initial development helicopter programme, in as much as it demands minimal technological capabilities (in fact it utilises an automobile engine) and is relatively inexpensive.

Confident that it had accumulated sufficient production experience, PT Nurtanio began in 1979 the second phase of its ten-year plan, that is, the design and development of a new aircraft. In order to reduce programme risk, it combined with Spain's CASA to form Air Tech Industries, and the new enterprise was tasked with developing a 30-40 seat commuter/transport aircraft, the CN-235. As equal partners in the venture, the Indonesians assumed responsibility for the design and development of the aircraft's outer wing, rear and rear centre fuselage, empennage and cabin interior, as well as involvement with the hydraulic and flight control systems.[123] In addition, the agreement called for twin production lines in Spain and Indonesia and the establishment of a joint certification board. With limited experience in advanced development work, PT Nurtanio asked MBB for assistance with the flight-testing programme. In order to instil confidence in the project, the Indonesian Government made a commitment to purchase 100 CN-235s while the project was still in the design stage.[124] By March 1984, 110 firm orders had been received for the CN-235, with 22 destined for the Spanish airline Aviaco and four for the Royal Saudi Air Force.[125] What is more, well over half the options received were exports including aircraft for Thailand (20), Pakistan (10), Australia (9), Japan (6) and Burma (2).[126]

Although PT Nurtanio's airframe products are the backbone of its development, they are in fact only one aspect of a comprehensive strategy to develop the industry as a whole. Given the relatively weak state of the Indonesian manufacturing sector and PT Nurtanio's limited experience, the industry is confronted with technological and manpower (human capital) constraints. A number of programmes have been formulated to ameliorate these. Thus to meet growing demands for skilled labour, the firm established a training centre adjacent to its main production facilities, and is graduating about 300-350 persons per year (and is to increase this to 1,500 per annum).[127] To augment domestic capabilities, the company has formulated agreements with foreign concerns for personnel training and sends employees overseas to acquire needed skills.[128] Similarly, PT Nurtanio has utilised co-operative agreements with foreign producers to acquire process technology. Thus, for example, it signed a five year technical co-operation contract with Boeing. Under this agreement, the US firm is transferring CAD/CAM production technology to Indonesia, and is assisting with the improvement of production and quality control techniques.[129] In fact, the Boeing agreement was conceptualised as a means to qualify PT Nurtanio as a certified FAA (US) manufacturer and thereby allowing it to perform Boeing subcontract work (while at the same time allowing Boeing to capitalise on Indonesia's low wage rates, which are about 80 per cent less than those in the USA). Paralleling PT Nurtanio's efforts, the Indonesian Government has continued its support of the industry, investing $200 million for the construction of a new 380,000 m^2 integrated production facility which will house the company's expanded operations, and provide state-of-the-art machinery.

On the basis of a firm state commitment to develop an indigenous aircraft industry, PT Nurtanio has progressed steadily since its creation in 1976. Relative to its original objectives, company performance has been reasonably successful; contributing to the expansion of the nation's industrial base, providing 12,000 industrial jobs, manufacturing products consistent with import substitution, and is slowly evolving into an export industry. Rather than place heavy reliance on domestic military procurement to nurture its aircraft industry in the Brazilian and Romanian fashion, Indonesia is dependent on a protected domestic market which is largely civil in orientation. Its cautious dependence on foreign co-operation has minimised risks and facilitated the transfer of technology. Yet, while company performance has been laudable as a capital-intensive enterprise in an economy plagued by low incomes and high unemployment, its overall contribution to national development remains to be proven.

BRAZIL

The chapter will conclude with a review of the most promising case of NIC aircraft enterprise, that of Brazil. Prior to the Revolution in 1964, Brazil engaged in an extended programme (1947-63) of import-substitution-industrialisation. With the single-minded objective of promoting industrialisation, growth was rapid, averaging about eight per cent per year during the 1950s, and by 1962, Brazil's industrial base was capable of producing relatively sophisticated consumer goods and capital equipment. Following 1964, the political-economic foundations for Brazilian state capitalism and renewed expansion were being laid in the form of political stability through military state control over the political instruments and institutions, relative continuity in the economic policy environment, and the effective combination of a market-oriented economic philosophy with an active state role in terms of economic planning and management. In respect of the last point,

> While encompassing a myriad of specific policy measures, the overall economic philosophy has been twofold: (1) strengthening markets and employing the price mechanism to more efficiently allocate economic resources, and (2) engaging in active government intervention to improve policy effectiveness in meeting basic objectives and to stimulate growth where markets were judged to operate ineffectively.[130]

Indicative of this tendency is that, in 1969, the public sector accounted for about 61 per cent of total investment, while in the manufacturing sector, the state's market share had risen from 3.9 per cent in 1956, to 11.3 per cent in 1971. Brazilian federal and state governments have directly participated in industries deemed important to national industrial vitality. Accordingly, industrial expansion again became the leading edge of Brazil's development drive, with average annual industrial growth over the 1970-79 period reaching 9.6 per cent, while growth in manufacturing averaged 10.9 per cent (versus 8.7 per cent for GDP) per year over the same period.

Given the nature of aircraft production and its political-economic basis, Brazil's state capitalist commitment lent itself favourably to the establishment of a national aircraft industry. Begun in earnest in August 1969 with the creation of Empresa Brasileira de Aeronáutica SA (Embraer), the Brazilian aircraft industry was set up as an instrument of national policy. Specifically, Embraer was created with the intention of expanding Brazil's technological and industrial base, and as a means to ameliorate the nation's balance of payments position by way of displacing expensive imports and generating foreign exchange earnings through exports. Of equal importance, Embraer, as an outgrowth of the air force ministry, is a logical extension of the military's long term objective (dating as far back as the early 1900s) to develop an indigenous armaments production capability. The desire to obtain this capability emanates from the elite's geopolitical vision of Brazil as an intermediate (regional) power.

In nurturing its aircraft industry, the Brazilian Government has utilised the conventional array of industrial policy instruments including: the direct support of R & D and production initiatives; the judicious use of discretionary government expenditure, principally military procurement, to support production; the provision of sales support by way of liberal financing schemes; and the erection of trade barriers to create a captive domestic market and induce technology transfer. In terms of technology transfer, Baranson notes, "Its strategy of effectively closing entry to its markets for all but the foreign firm prepared to share front-end technology, to impart sophisticated design and engineering capabilities, and to instruct Brazilian nationals in managerial skills has been extremely successful."[131] With reference to state support, Brazil's dual commitment to a formidable state role in the economy and a respect for market forces is graphically illustrated in the case of Embraer, which was instituted to reflect both these concerns. On the one hand, the Brazilian Government supplied 23 per cent of the initial $19.5 million investment but retained control of the voting stock in order to direct the firm along state policy lines. On the other hand, the government relied upon the private sector to supply the lion's share of the capital investment, and provided tax concessions to stimulate support of the undertaking. The reliance on private capital has increased since this time, with 94.23 per cent of the subscribed capital held by private shareholders, although the government has retained its 51 per cent control of the voting shares.

With the aforementioned objectives in mind, the Brazilian aircraft industry has developed along three general lines: first, there has been an adamant commitment to indigenous designs; secondly, co-operative arrangements with foreign manufacturers have been used to acquire and expand technological capabilities and thirdly, industry output has been balanced between military and civil markets. From the outset, these themes have coloured the industry's evolution. The immediate impetus behind the creation of Embraer in 1969 was to bring into production the Bandeirante twin-turboprop light transport. The Bandeirante project began some years earlier at the Centro

Técnico de Aeronáutica (CTA) to fulfil a Ministry of Aeronautics specification calling for a general purpose aircraft. Under the design leadership of Max Holste, an established French designer, the first prototype flew in October 1968, and the first production aircraft flew in August 1972. As the lead programme at Embraer, the Bandeirante (designated the EMB-110 in its civil role and the C-95 for the Brazilian Air Force) was an unequivocal success, realising a number of important objectives. With some 428 aircraft delivered as of January 1984, the Bandeirante has provided Embraer with a long-term project, thus contributing to design (through successive derivatives) and production experience and the development of a skilled labour force. Catering to both civil and military markets, the EMB-110 has displaced Brazilian imports in both markets, serving initially as a replacement for US-made Beech C-45s used by the Brazilian Air Force and extending to other aircraft as well. In the civil commuter market, Brazil's 'law of similars', which blocks imports of products where similar domestic substitutes are available, has ensured Embraer with a captive market. Not entirely dependent on protectionist measures, the Bandeirante has scored admirably in export markets, with roughly 52 per cent of the aircraft destined for export to some 21 countries. Significantly, the Bandeirante increased its US market share from seven per cent in 1978 to 35 per cent in 1981, with some 115 aircraft delivered.[132] In a country burdened by a heavy foreign debt, such foreign exchange benefits are a valued commodity. Building on the Bandeirante programme, Embraer began design work on a second twin-turboprop transport in 1979, and had invested in excess of $200 million to bring the aircraft into the production phase.[133] Complementing Embraer's 19 passenger class Bandeirante, the 30 passenger class Brasilia (EMB-120) had secured 118 options by mid-1984, and is scheduled to enter the market in 1985. Export market penetration for the Bandeirante and the Brasilia has been facilitated by selling the aircraft with an attractive state-sponsored financing package: 15 per cent down and an extended low interest loan for the balance. Aside from the lead Bandeirante programme, a second project undertaken during the formative phase of the industry was the design and development of the Ipanema (EMB-200/210A) agricultural aircraft. The Ipanema project was initiated in 1969 in response to a Ministry of Agriculture proposal intended to meet domestic market requirements. Following its maiden flight in 1970, Ipanema sales totalled 484 as of December 1983.[134] Finally, rounding out the array of domestic designs aimed at meeting local requirements were the Embraer Urupema sailplane, and the Aerotec 122 Uirapuru and Neiva Universal Trainers, both of which were procured by the Air Force to replace foreign designs. Subsequently, Brazil diversified its civil product base with the design and development of the EMB-121 Xingu twin-turboprop general purpose transport (9 passengers) and advanced trainer. Intended to be the first in a series of pressurised turboprop twins, Xingu sales have been modest, numbering about 110 (mid-1984) since its introduction in 1977. Significantly however, the Xingu outcompeted the US Beech King Air C90 and Cessna 425 Corsair to capture a French Government order for 41 trainers for the Air Force and Navy.

While the thrust of Embraer's civil projects are centred on local designs, foreign exchange pressures and a desire to increase industrial capabilities led to a comprehensive licensing agreement with US based Piper Aircraft Corporation. On the heels of the 1973 oil shock, Brazil, representing the largest single export market for US general aviation manufacturers with 1974 sales of $600 million, sought to displace costly imports through import substitution.[135] Effectively closing the Brazilian market on the basis of the law of similars and through the imposition (in 1975) of a 50 per cent tax on imported light aircraft, Embraer acquired the licences to produce a series of single and twin-engined Piper aircraft. Production at Embraer's Neiva subsidiary is by way of a three-stage technology transfer process. Beginning with nominal assembly of completed structures and systems, and proceeding to systematically substitute locally-manufactured components, by the end of Phase-III, approximately 66 to 70 per cent of the aircraft will be of Brazilian origin - excepting those components which cannot be economically produced in Brazil. In addition to developing Tier I activities, the Piper programme is aimed at expanding Brazil's subcontractor base. After a decade of production (between 1975-85), the Brazilian aircraft industry manufactured greater than 1,800 Piper aircraft under licence, with important balance of payments implications.

Whereas indigenous design efforts were the focus of civil projects, Embraer looked towards a foreign design to familiarise itself in the production of military aircraft. Thus, Embraer acquired the licence to assemble the Aermacchi MB.326 Trainer and ground attack aircraft in May 1970. Renamed the Xavante (EMB-326), Embraer has since delivered 166 of the aircraft to the Brazilian Air Force, and even managed a number of export sales, including six to Togo and a further ten to Paraguay. On the basis of the production experience gained during the Xavante programme, Embraer began diversifying the military side of its operations relying on both domestic designs and co-operative and licensed production agreements. In terms of the former, independent efforts under the sponsorship of the Air Force have concentrated on the development of relatively simple trainer aircraft. Embraer began design and development work on a new basic trainer, the EMB-312 Tucano turboprop as a follow-on project to the Xavante. With an eye on both domestic and export markets, the Tucano gained initial support by way of an Air Force order for 118 aircraft with options for an additional 50. Brazilian sales were subsequently matched by an export coup whereby Egypt would manufacture 120 aircraft for its own and Iraqi use. Indicative of Brazil's ascendency in the world trainer market, the joint Egyptian/Iraqi purchase includes an extensive technology transfer programme with the Arab Organisation for Industrialisation responsible for final assembly as well as an increasing share of the aircraft's manufacture. The machine is also the subject of a licence-production pact with Shorts of the UK. In addition to the Tucano, the Air Force is also sponsoring the development of a cheaper piston-engined trainer, the Aerotec A-132 Tangará. Following funding of the prototype, the Air Force has indicated its intention to procure about a hundred of the aircraft which will provide sufficient impetus to launch production.

Aside from the independent design efforts for trainer aircraft, further development of Brazil's military aircraft production has been facilitated through co-operative efforts with foreign firms. To this end, since 1976 Embraer has been manufacturing components for the Northrop F-5E combat aircraft. However, "Since the early 1970s, Brazil has been trying to adopt a highly independent foreign policy, to defend its own interests rather than tying its international positions to those of the United States".[136] Thus, Brazil has looked largely to France and Italy for technology since these countries tend to impose fewer restrictions on recipient firms. As an extention of its earlier co-operation, Embraer entered into an agreement with Aeritalia/Aermacchi for the co-production of the AM-X light attack aircraft. The agreement calls for Brazil to underwrite about one third of the project's $420 million R & D costs (at a rate of $20 million annually) and will see Embraer assume responsibility for approximately 30 per cent of the aircraft's production, including development of the wing as well as undertaking final assembly. As a relatively inexpensive multimission aircraft, the AM-X is designed to meet stringent budget requirements in both countries with the Brazilian Air Force expected to procure an initial 79 machines. At the same time, the AM-X would appear well suited to Brazil's foreign policy objective; that of becoming a reliable supplier of inexpensive weapons within the Third World. In terms of technological development, the project will expand Embraer's exposure to the use of composite materials and NC machining. In respect to the former, Embraer has entered into a technology transfer agreement with the US Sikorsky firm involving the design and manufacture of composite material components for the AM-X and the Brasilia.

The agreement with Sikorsky is also intended as a building block for the development of a new lightweight helicopter. Brazil's initial entry into helicopter production was through the licence-production of established French designs. Specifically, the state government of Minas Gerais (with a holding of 52 per cent) and Aérospatiale (45 per cent) formed Helibras in 1977 as a part of a ten-year programme involving the assembly of SA-315B Lama (renamed the HB-315B Gaviao) and AS-350B Ecureuil (HB-350B Esquilo) helicopters. Again, aircraft production was initially tied to military procurement with the Brazilian Navy providing the initial launch order, while Brazil furthered its regional ties with subsequent sales to Chile, Bolivia and Venezuela. However, Brazilian ambitions extend well beyond simple licensed production of existing designs, as Ozires Silva (Embraer's managing director) emphasises,

> Embraer is not interested in assembling somebody else's helicopters in Brazil either under license or with a duplicate production line. What we are interested in doing is to build a new-generation helicopter that will not be competitive with the Sikorsky line and can be marketed not only in Brazil, but internationally.[137]

Financial and technological constraints, however, will necessarily demand co-operative programmes with foreign manufacturers if Brazil hopes to link military procurement and domestic production.

All told, the Brazilian aircraft industry has performed well in the years since the formation of

Embraer in 1969. Whereas the industry's output in 1969 amounted to a scant 30 aircraft, industry sales in 1979 reached $142.8 million with Embraer delivering 436 aircraft.[138] Moreover, nearly 50 per cent of these sales were in the form of exports, while the remainder reduced imports. Factory floor space has increased from 117,820 m² in 1978 to 238,000 m² by mid-1984, with employment increasing over the same period by nearly 70 per cent and totalling 7,300. On the basis of protecting the domestic market and integrating defence procurement with aircraft development, the Brazilian Government has successfully nurtured the industry. As a result, a number of objectives have been realised including the expansion of the economy's technological and industrial base, the reduction of the reliance on imported aircraft, and the development of an export industry. In addition, the expansion of Embraer's military aircraft production capabilities has furthered Brazil's geopolitical aims, as is evidenced by the destination of export sales. By the same token, Brazil is coming to depend on military programmes. To the extent that defence spending has negative consequences for national development, this course of development will impose political and economic pressures on the Brazilian Government. With intense competition in international markets and given the increasing tendency for export sales to be tied to offset agreements, returns on foreign sales will be diluted and therein will place additional onus on state support for the industry. Furthermore, continued export success will no doubt place increasing pressures on the government to decrease trade barriers, and thus open up the Brazilian market. Finally, despite the sizeable inroads made in the development of the industry, production is still highly dependent on foreign technology, especially in terms of aeroengines, avionics and advanced design.

NOTES AND REFERENCES

1. Raimo Vayrynen, 'Semiperipheral Countries in the Global Economic and Military Order', in Helena Tuomi and Raimo Vayrynen, (eds.), Militarization and Arms Production, (Croom Helm, London, 1983), pp.163-192. Quote is from p.167.

2. Concerning the structural changes emanating from technological change and the changing labour process see for example: I. M. Clarke, 'The Changing International Division of Labour Within ICI', in M. Taylor and N. Thrift (eds.), The Geography of

Multinationals, (Croom Helm, London, 1982), pp.90-116, A. Lipietz, 'Towards Global Fordism?', New Left Review, 132 (March/April, 1982), pp.33-47 and OECD, The Impact of the Newly-Industrialising Countries on Production and Trade in Manufacturing, (OECD, Paris, 1979). In respect to industrial policies, see F. Gerard Adams and Lawrence R. Klein (eds.), Industrial Policies for Growth and Competitiveness, (Lexington Books, Toronto, 1983).

3. Victoria Curzon Price, Industrial Policies in the European Community, (St. Martin's Press, New York, 1981).

4. Ibid, and Dennis Swann, Competition and Industrial Policy in the European Community, (Methuen, London, 1983).

5. F. Gerard Adams and C. Andrea Bollino, 'Meaning of Industrial Policy', in Adams and Klein (eds.), Industrial Policies for Growth and Competitiveness, 1983, pp.13-20.

6. See Gerald M. Meier, Leading Issues in Economic Development, (Oxford University Press, New York, 3rd edition,1976), and Michael Roemer 'Dependence and Industrialization Strategies', World Development, 9 (1981), pp.429-434.

7. World Bank, World Development Report, 1981.

8. Ibid, p.149.

9. F. Gerard Adams and Shinichi Ichimura, 'Industrial Policy in Japan', in Adams and Klein (eds.), Industrial Policies, pp.307-330.

10. Ibid, p.316.

11. OECD, The Industrial Policy of Japan, (OECD, Paris, 1972), p.15.

12. Interavia, 10, 1971, p.1151.

13. The absence of national armed forces emanated from the country's postwar 'peace' Constitution, which in Article 9 reads:

> Aspiring sincerely to an international peace based on justice and order the Japanese forever renounce war as a sovereign right of the nation and the threat of force as a means of settling international disputes.
>
> In order to accomplish the aim of the preceding paragraph, land, sea, and air forces, as well as other war potential, will never be maintained. The right of belligerency of the State will not be recognized.

Cited in Daniel I. Okimoto, 'The Economics of National Defense' in Daniel I. Okimoto (ed.), Japan's Economy: Coping with Change in the International Environment, (Westview Press, Boulder, Colorado, 1982), p.235.

14. The JDA makes decisions on the procurement

of aircraft based on mission requirements of the SDF. These procurement decisions are then passed on to MITI which then decides which firms will build JDA aircraft.

15. G. R. Hall and R. E. Johnson, 'Transfers of United States Aerospace Technology to Japan', in Raymond Vernon (ed.), The Technology Factor in International Trade, (NBER, New York, 1970), pp.305-358.

16. Jane's 1961-62.

17. G. R. Hall and R. E. Johnson, 'Transfers', p.325.

18. Ibid, pp.326-328.

19. Ibid, pp.352-3.

20. AW & ST, 4 February 1980, p.47.

21. AW & ST, 24 April 1978, p.16.

22. Jane's 1984-85.

23. AW & ST, 4 February 1980, p.47.

24. AW & ST, 12 June 1973, p.23.

25. AW & ST, 4 February 1980, p.42-43.

26. Jane's 1961-62. In addition to the LM-1 derivative, Fuji also developed the KM-2 two-seat primary trainer version under a SDF contract for 10 aircraft. Similarly, Fuji produced a STOL version of the L-19, which was previously produced under a Cessna licence.

27. Jane's 1971-72. The basic differences between the P2V-7 and P-2J is that the latter has a longer fuselage, as well as redesigned landing gear and turboprop (as opposed to piston) engines.

28. Interavia, 6, 1966, p.906.

29. Jane's 1984-85.

30. AW & ST, 18 March 1985, p.72.

31. AW & ST, 12 January 1970, p.59.

32. AW & ST, 19 April 1982, p.11.

33. AW & ST, 4 February 1980, p.53.

34. Both of the conditions have arisen from Japan's renouncement of the use of force to solve international disputes (see footnote 13). The one per cent ceiling on defence expenditure, while not constitutionally entrenched, has emerged through interplay of domestic political forces to such an extent that Diet attempts to exceed this level are considered tantamount to constitutional breach.

35. Jane's 1961-62. The YS-11 project was originally advocated by MITI in 1956, and placed under the Transport Aircraft Development Association in 1957.

36. Interavia, 6, 1966, p.906.

37. Interavia, 10, 1983, p.1094.

38. Interavia, 10, 1976, p.967.

39. Aerospace America, March 1985, p.61. Similar problems have confronted Romania's young aircraft

industry in its efforts to sell the Rombac 1-11 airliner.

40. Interavia, 18, 1970, p.974.

41. AW & ST, 19 January 1970, pp.69, 71, 73.

42. AW & ST, 1 September 1980, p.125; Interavia, 10, 1976, p.967.

43. AW & ST, 9 November 1981, p.164.

44. FI, 1 December 1984, p.1435.

45. Interavia, 10, 1983, p.1095. JADC was formed out of the CTDC to manage the YXX programme, while existing 767 work was taken over by the Commercial Airplane Company.

46. AW & ST, 23 January 1983, p.30; 19 March 1984, p.32.

47. Interavia, 10, 1971, p.1152.

48. AW & ST, 5 March 1973, p.9.

49. Jane's 1984-85. Since its introduction in the early 1960s 15 versions of the MU-2 have been offered, the most recent of which are the Marquise (6-11 passengers) and the Solitaire (6-9 passengers).

50. Interavia, 10, 1983, p.1096. In September 1983 MAI announced the development of a more powerful Diamond II using two P & WC JT15D-5 turbofans.

51. AW & ST, 25 March 1985, p.81.

52. For example, aerospace sales accounted for 12, 18.2, 4.4, 11.7 and 8.5 per cent of MHI, Kawasaki, Fuji, Shin Meiwa and IHI respectively for the fiscal year ending 31 March 1983. AW & ST, 20 June 1983, p.52.

53. Canada, Aerospace in Canada - Outlook and Strategy, 1983, p.1-1.

54. Ibid, p.3-2.

55. Ibid, p.3-7.

56. While DHC, Canadair, and P & WC tailor most of their output to civil markets, there are none the less military applications of their products, for example, P & WC supplies the engine for Brazil's Tucano military trainer.

57. W. McAndrew, 'The Early Days of Aircraft Acquisition in Canadian Military Aviation', Canadian Defence Quarterly, 12 (1982), p.42.

58. Cited in R. D. Cuff and J. L. Granastein, Ties That Bind: Canadian-American Relations in Wartime From the Great War to the Cold War, (Hakkert, Toronto, 1977), p.69.

59. Michael Rich et al, Multinational Coproduction of Military Aerospace Systems, 1981, Appendix A.

60. AW & ST, 12 April 1975, p.17.

61. Canada, Economic Development for Canada in the 1980s, (November 1981), p.2.

62. AW & ST, 20 June 1983, p.25.

63. Financial Post of Toronto, 17 March 1984.

64. AW & ST, 7 May 1984, p.95.
65. AW & ST, 3 September 1984, p.226.
66. Canada, Aerospace in Canada, p.4-8.
67. AW & ST, 7 May 1984, p.98.
68. Financial Post, 3 December 1983.
69. AW & ST, 9 August 1982, p.17.
70. AW & ST, 30 May 1983, p.111.
71. AW & ST, 25 October 1982, p.16.
72. AW & ST, 31 March 1975, p.20.
73. AW & ST, 12 November 1984, p.19. The Greek decision to split its procurement between the French Mirage 2000 and the US F-16 (in order to give the country greater political flexibility should the nation become involved in a conflict with Turkey) would also appear to vindicate the validity of sovereignty concerns in offset agreements. See Interavia, 9,1984, p.853.
74. Michael Rich et al, Multinational Coproduction, p.vii.
75. AW & ST, 9 August 1982, p.17.
76. Financial Post, 4 June 1983, p.18.
77. Financial Post, 15 April 1978 (supplement), p.20.
78. AW & ST, 26 November 1979, p.34.
79. AW & ST, 5 November 1979, p.48.
80. Financial Post, 17 May 1980, p.52.
81. Financial Post, 19 April 1980, p.12; 17 May 1980, p.51.
82. AW & ST, 31 December 1979, p.11.
83. Financial Post, 19 April 1980, p.12.
84. Financial Post, 4 June 1983, p.18.
85. Financial Post, 19 April 1980, p.12.
86. AW & ST, 12 September 1983, p.32.
87. AW & ST, 14 May 1984, p.26.
88. AW & ST, 12 November 1984, p.18.
89. AW & ST, 20 August 1984, p.22.
90. AW & ST, 6 June 1983, p.28.
91. Interavia, 8, 1983, p.859.
92. Andreas C. Tsantis and Roy Pepper, Romania: The Industrialisation of an Agrarian Economy under Socialist Planning, (World Bank, Washington, D.C., 1979), p.2.
93. Ibid, p.80.
94. Ibid, p.192 and p.80. Industry as defined in Romania includes mining and the extraction of hydrocarbons.
95. Ibid, p.514.
96. Ibid, p.466.
97. Jane's 1984-85, p.184.
98. AW & ST, 13 December 1982, p.62; AW & ST, 24 January 1983, p.52.
99. Jane's 1984-85, p.187; AW & ST, 28 April

1975, p.30. Britten-Norman was subsequently taken over by Fairey Engineering which went into receivership and was in turn taken over by Swiss-based Pilatus.

100. AW & ST, 8 November 1982, p.13.

101. Malcolm R. Hill, East-West Trade, Industrial Co-operation and Technology Transfer, (Gower Publishers, Aldershot, 1983).

102. Interavia, 8. 1983, p.859.

103. Ibid, p.862.

104. AW & ST, 13 December 1982, p.62.

105. Interavia, 8, 1983, p.861.

106. AW & ST, 20 December 1982, p.39.

107. Jane's 1984-85, p.187.

108. Ibid, p.124.

109. AW & ST, 3 January 1983, p.52.

110. World Bank, World Development Report 1981, p.136.

111. Ibid, p.150.

112. Ibid, p.151.

113. In fact, Habibie initially retained his Vice-Presidency at MBB while also serving as the head of PT Nurtanio.

114. Interavia, 12, 1981, p.1236.

115. AW & ST, 19 April 1982, p.71.

116. During the 1950s and 1960s Indonesia produced a number of aircraft types including: the Sikumbang, a single-seat counter-insurgency aircraft; the Belalong 85 basic trainer; the licensed production of the Polish PZL Wilga (renamed the Gelatik); and the Kepik and Manyang rotary-wing prototypes. In contrast, Romania and Brazil possessed at least a limited indigenous design and production capability.

117. AW & ST, 22 November 1976, p.20.

118. AW & ST, 26 December 1983, p.17; Interavia, 12, 1981, p.1236.

119. FI, 3 April 1982, p.783.

120. AW & ST, 26 December 1983, p.15.

121. Interavia, 10, 1984, p.1125.

122. AW & ST, 21 February 1983, p.25; FI, 19 May 1984, p.1334.

123. AW & ST, 19 April 1982, p.68.

124. AW & ST, 16 February 1981, p.33.

125. Jane's 1984-85, p.105.

126. Interavia, 10, 1984, p.1126.

127. AW & ST, 19 April 1982, p.69; FI, 26 February 1983, p.526.

128. For example, Nurtanio signed an agreement with FIAS, the aerospace personnel training establishment linked to France's GIFAS. Under this agreement Nurtanio will send senior factory inspectors and supervisors to France for training.

129. FI, 3 April 1982, p.783; 27 February 1983, p.526.

130. William G. Tyler, _Manufactured Export Expansion and Industrialisation in Brazil_, (J.C.B. Mohr (Paul Sieback) Tubingen, Germany, 1976), p.32.

131. Jack Baranson, _Technology and the Multinationals_, (Lexington Books, Lexington, Massachusetts, 1978), p.38.

132. AW & ST, 20 September 1982, p.115.

133. AW & ST, 1 August 1984, p.31.

134. The Ipanema programme began at Embraer's main facility and was subsequently transferred to Embraer's Neiva subsidiary in 1981. More than 500 aircraft had been built by the end of 1984.

135. _Interavia_, 12, 1984, p.1340.

136. Alexandre de S. C. Barros, 'Brazil' in J. E. Katz (ed.), _Arms Production in Developing Countries_, (Lexington Books, Lexington, Mass., 1984), pp.73-87; quotation from p.79.

137. AW & ST, 7 May 1984, p.17.

138. _Interavia_, 7, 1981, p.707; AW & ST, 31 March 1980, p.91.

Chapter Nine

CONCLUSION

Over the course of this century the manufacture of complete airframes has evolved from the pioneering visions of a few entrepreneurs to become an important component of the industrial fabric of contemporary AICs. The importance accorded the industry stems, on the one hand, from its economic attributes and, on the other, from its contribution to national defence. Indeed, it is owing to the latter reason that most AICs - and increasingly NICs as well - have attempted to foster an aircraft industry. Since defence falls within the purview of traditional state responsibility, government involvement in the industry is unavoidable. Moreover, as a so-called 'high tech' sector, the aircraft industry offers potentially sizeable benefits which are obviously brought out in the US aerospace sector's export, employment, and R & D performance. Thus, by virtue of the industry's strategic importance and its economic attractiveness, the 'targeting' of aircraft manufacture in industrial strategies has become commonplace.

Technological imperative is the industry's hallmark. Rendered possible by an interactive combination of demand-pull and technology-push innovations, market evolution and technical development have gone hand-in-hand. On the demand side, the industry was compelled to respond to the requirements of military and civil operators. In terms of the former, the exigencies of war and international tension forced the industry into making faster and more survivable aircraft. In terms of the latter, the industry had to deliver a product capable of competing with other modes of transport and ensuring airline profitability. On the supply side, technology-push innovations led to new opportunities in civil passenger and cargo transport. What is more, much of that inspiration came from antecedent military work. While subject to cyclical swings like other industries, the aircraft industry differs precisely because of its extreme dependence on military work. Consequently, the 'wave-cycle' of international tension is more of a regulator of the industry's activity levels than is the conventional business cycle. Coping with the downswings in the 'wave-cycle' is, in fact, a persistent problem of the industry. Refuge is frequently found in MIC arrangements or direct state control of aircraft manufacturers.

In as much as state support for the industry has been forthcoming to counter the perils of demand cycles, it has been equally forthcoming in underwriting R & D costs. A solid commitment to R & D is a prerequisite for market leadership in all aeronautical fields. Furthermore, with increasingly sophisticated aircraft has come inexorably rising development costs - to the extent, indeed, that this factor constitutes the fundamental constraint (and barrier to entry) confronting the industry. The relative paucity of airframe firms and the industry's concentrated market structure is an inevitable outcome of such a trend. In order to come to grips with this constraint, the state has been obliged to absorb the risk-burden associated with product innovation. Capital injections have been a common instrument for socialising risk, while, less conspicuously, state support is frequently extended through the provision of military R & D and procurement contracts. To be sure, governments may go further and both nationalise firms and compel them to undertake R & D and production on an international basis. As far as nascent aircraft industries are concerned, the principal way to overcoming R & D risks (and technological constraints) is to rely upon the transfer of product and process technology from established firms; primarily through licensed production programmes.

By way of conclusion, it is perhaps worthwhile to speculate on the future directions of the industry. As the 1980s unfold, US aircraft manufacturers continue to dominate the spectrum of civil and military markets: Boeing and MD in the jetliner field; Piper, Cessna and Beech in the general aviation market; and GD, Lockheed, Grumman, Northrop, RI and Sikorsky, among others, in military markets. In large measure, the technological and marketing advantages accruing to these firms derive from their ready access to the US market - the largest single source of demand for aircraft in the world. On the basis of a vibrant technological environment and the extended production runs afforded by the domestic market, US firms are bound to retain a dominant position in world export markets. Yet, such advantages notwithstanding, the dominance of the US aircraft firms in all market areas is not certain. For example, US pre-eminence in the large commercial aircraft area has come under increasing pressure. European nations, in particular, have made a concerted effort since the 1960s to overturn the virtual US monopoly on airliner production. The resultant Airbus series is posing a serious threat to the established market leaders, Boeing and MD. Evidence of this success is apparent from the doubling of the European share of the world market for short to medium-range jetliners between 1977 and 1982. None the less, the EEC share of the vital US market for this category of airliner amounted to only 6.2 per cent in 1982, while in the long-range category, the EEC share was less than one per cent. Notwithstanding such discouraging signs, the fact of the matter is that if European governments remain committed to supporting their aircraft firms, the outcome can only be the further erosion of American dominance of the world aircraft industry. It should be stressed, however, that this challenge will not be the exclusive preserve of the Europeans. The Japanese, for instance, have made it clear that they intend to enter the commercial airliner market. In a manner comparable to the Europeans, the Japanese favour aeronautical ventures which entail international co-production.

As well as competing directly with the Americans in civil markets, many countries have encouraged their aircraft enterprises to carve out market niches through product specialisation. This strategy has figured prominently in the development of newer aircraft industries in both the smaller AICs and the NICs as a whole. Especially noteworthy in this respect is the record of Brazil and the market penetration of its Embraer product, the Bandeirante. In a similar vein, a number of countries have scored notable successes: Canada (commuterliners), Japan (bizjets), Israel (bizjets), the Netherlands (light airliners) and Spain/Indonesia (light transports) come readily to mind. The fact remains, however, that these ventures rely, in varying degrees, on aeroengines and avionics produced by the major AICs. The signs suggest, in fact, that technological constraints confronting fledgling aircraft industries do not reside in the airframe sector as such, but, rather, in systems development, production and integration.

In so far as warplanes are concerned, the technological imperative will continue to push the aircraft industry to the 'fringe' of the art. By virtue of the correlation between technological sophistication on the one hand, and fiscal constraints of states on the other, the military market will become increasingly balkanised. At the upper end of the technological scale, the US lead will continue to be challenged by the Soviet Union. For their part, the major European countries will attempt to maintain an indigenous warplane design and production capability which will reside somewhere below that of the USA. In so doing, however, the Europeans will be forced to rely on co-operative ventures among themselves for most, if not all, of their new-generation military aeroplanes. As for other countries, the state-of-the-art in warplane technology is simply beyond their technological capabilities and, besides, is out of reach of their fiscal capacity too. They may, however, be able to gain some compensation from the design and production of less costly and less technologically-intensive alternative aircraft. Indeed, for the NICs, military procurement will remain one of the most effective instruments for nurturing indigenous aircraft production. To be specific, military procurement can be expected to provide, first of all, a basis for either independent or joint R & D and production programmes and, secondly, act as a means for acquiring foreign technology to augment national capabilities. With respect to the former, domestic procurement requirements have allowed neophyte aircraft industries to enter new product areas at minimal risk. Echoing the civil market, a number of smaller aircraft industries have attempted to fill market niches for military aircraft, especially for trainers and cheap fighters (e.g. Brazil's Tucano and AM-X respectively). The most important development in the military market of late has been the marked propensity of countries to demand compensatory offset packages as an integral part of foreign military aircraft purchases. Moreover, this trend is likely to intensify as escalating development costs force the major airframe firms in the AICs to rely increasingly on export sales. The technology transfer inherent in such offsets can only serve to upgrade the capabilities of NIC aircraft industries.

Whether for purposes of defence or as a supplier of transportation equipment, the industry will continue as an important component of national industrial strategies. In any event, the future development of the industry will be predicated on the twin concerns of fostering technological change and coming to grips with the lavish launch costs associated with modern aircraft. In terms of the former, the issue appears to be as much one of industrial capabilities as it is of political will. Tempering the political will, of course, is the ability to marshal the considerable resources necessary for aircraft programmes. Yet, the political will to establish this industry is boosted by the prospect of acquiring strategic benefits from the mere possession of an aircraft manufacturing capability. States will continue to induce and maintain aircraft industries even if that entails foregoing an element of national sovereignty in order to pursue co-production programmes. In other words, the highly 'nationalistic' aircraft industry is becoming, willy-nilly, a truly international business. The need to share crippling R & D and production costs leaves firms and their government paymasters no option but to foment collaborative aerospace ventures at both the national and international scale.

GLOSSARY

Aerofoil	Structure designed to obtain an aerodynamic reaction.
AIC	Advanced-industrial country
AIDC	Aero Industry Development Centre.
Ailerons	Moving surfaces to control the rolling movements of aircraft, usually on wing trailing edges.
Airframe	Aircraft without engines and systems.
All-up weight	Total weight of aircraft at take-off.
ATP	Advanced Turbo Prop airliner modification of BAe 748.
Autoclave	A high-temperature, high-pressure oven.
AW & ST	Aviation Week and Space Technology periodical.
AWACS	Airborne Warning and Control Systems.
BAC	British Aircraft Corporation.
BAe	British Aerospace.
BEA	British European Airways.
BOAC	British Overseas Airways Corporation.
Bonding	The joining of parts with adhesives.
CAD/CAM	Computer-assisted design and manufacturing.
CASA	Construcciones Aeronauticas SA (of Spain).
Centre section	The central part of the wing, often fused into the fuselage.
Cure	The process by which adhesives are hardened by chemical means.
DH	de Havilland.
DHC	de Havilland Aircraft of Canada.
DoD	Department of Defense.
EFA	European Fighter Aircraft.
Elevator	A horizontal control surface to regulate climb and descent of aircraft.
Empennage	The aircraft tail unit.
FI	Flight International periodical.
Fin	A fixed vertical aerofoil for stabilising the aircraft.
Flap	A control surface designed to increase the aircraft's lift or drag.
Fuselage	The body of the aircraft.
GAZ	Gosudarstvennye Aviatsionnye Zavody or State Aircraft Factory.
GD	General Dynamics Corporation.
GE	General Electric Company (US).
HAL	Hindustan Aeronautics Ltd.
HDH	Hawker de Havilland.
HS	Hawker Siddeley.
IAI	Israel Aircraft Industries.
IHI	Ishikawajima-Harima Heavy Industries.
In-line Engine	Cylinders arranged in a row rather

	than radial or rotary pattern.
Leading Edge	Edge of an aerofoil which first comes in contact with the air in flight (opposite to the trailing edge).
LTV	Ling-Temco-Vought; aerospace component which has variously been called Chance Vought, Vought Corporation and LTV Corporation.
MBB	Messerschmitt-Bolkow-Blohm.
MD	McDonnell-Douglas Corporation.
MHI	Mitsubishi Heavy Industries.
MIC	Military-Industrial Complex.
MITI	Ministry of International Trade and Industry (Japan).
MRCA	Multi-role Combat Aircraft.
MTU	Motoren-und-Turbinen-Union München.
Nacelle	Separate enclosure on the aircraft for containing objects or crew.
NASA	National Aeronautics and Space Administration.
NC	Numerically-controlled machine.
NIC	Newly-industrialising country.
P & W	Pratt & Whitney component of UTC.
P & WC	Pratt & Whitney Aircraft of Canada.
PBN	Pilatus Britten Norman.
PZL	Pantswowe Zaklady Lotnicze or State Aircraft Factory (Poland).
R-R	Rolls-Royce.
Radial engine	Radial arrangement of cylinders around crankshaft which are stationary as opposed to those in a rotary engine.
RDT & E	Research, development, test and evaluation.
RI	Rockwell International Corporation.
Rudder	Vertical control surface for guiding the aircraft in horizontal flight.
SABCA	Société Anonyme Belge de Constructions Aéronautiques.
SNECMA	Société Nationale d'Étude et de Construction de Moteurs d'Aviation.
Spar	A spanning part of the wing.
Spoiler	An air brake.
SST	Supersonic Transport.
Stabiliser	An aerofoil used to provide stability.
STOL	Short Take-off and Landing.
Undercarriage	Landing gear and wheels.
UTC	United Technologies Corporation.
VFW	Vereinigte Flugtechnische Werke.
VTOL	Vertical Take-off and Landing.

REFERENCES

ACDA, World Military Expenditures and Arms Transfers 1972-82, (Arms Control and Disarmament Agency, Washington, DC, April 1984).

Adams, F. G. and C. A. Bollino, 'Meaning of Industrial Policy' in F. G. Adams and L. R. Klein (eds.), Industrial Policies for Growth and Competitiveness, (Lexington Books, Toronto, 1983), pp.13-20.

__________ and S. Ichimura, 'Industrial Policy in Japan' in F. G. Adams and L. R. Klein (eds.), pp.307-330.

Adams, G. The Politics of Defense Contracting: The Iron Triangle, (Transactions Books, New Brunswick, 1982).

Angelucci, E. The Rand McNally Encyclopedia of Military Aircraft 1914-1980, (Rand McNally, Chicago, 1980).

Armitage, M. J. and R. A. Mason, Air Power in the Nuclear Age, (University of Illinois Press, Urbana, 1983).

Atwood, J. L. North American Rockwell: Storehouse of High Technology, (Newcomen Society, New York, 1970).

Baranson, J. Technology and the Multinationals, (Lexington Books, Lexington, Mass., 1978).

Barros, S. C. 'Brazil' in J. E. Katz (ed.), Arms Production in Developing Countries, (Lexington Books, Lexington, Mass., 1984), pp.73-87.

Baxter, N. D. and E. P. Howrey, 'The Determinants of General Aviation Activity: A Cross-Sectional Analysis' in G. P. Howard (ed.), Airport Economic Planning, (MIT Press, Cambridge, Mass., 1974), pp.177-190.

Bowyer, M. J. F. Action Stations 6: Military Airfields of the Cotswolds and the Central Midlands, (Patrick Stephens, Cambridge, 1983).

Boyd, A. The Soviet Air Force since 1918, (MacDonald and Jane's, London, 1977).

Cao-Pinna, V. 'Regional Policy in Italy' in N. M. Hansen (ed.), Public Policy and Regional Economic Development, (Ballinger, Cambridge, Mass., 1974), pp.137-179.

Clarke, I. M. 'The Changing International Division of Labour Within ICI' in M. Taylor and N. Thrift (eds.), The Geography of Multinationals, (Croom Helm, London, 1982), pp.90-116.

Cook, C. and J. Stevenson, The Atlas of Modern Warfare, (Weidenfeld & Nicolson, London, 1978).

Corlett, J. Aviation in Ulster, (Blackstaff Press, Belfast, 1981).

Cuff, R. D. and J. L. Granastein, Ties That Bind: Canadian-American Relations in Wartime From the

Great War to the Cold War, (Hakkert, Toronto, 1977).

Cunningham, W. G. The Aircraft Industry: A Study in Industrial Location, (Morrison, Los Angeles, 1951).

Degrasse, R. W. 'Military Spending and Jobs', Challenge, vol. 26 (1983), pp.4-15.

Dorfer, I. Arms Deal: The Selling of the F-16, (Praeger, New York, 1983).

EEC, 'The European Aerospace Industry: Trading Position and Figures', EEC Commission, Staff Working Paper, Sec.(80), 1237, Brussels, 23 September 1980.

Endres, G. G. World Airline Fleets 1977, (Airline Publications & Sales, London, 1977).

Erickson, R. A. 'The Regional Impact of Growth Firms: The Case of Boeing, 1963-1968', Land Economics, vol. 50 (1974), pp.127-136.

__________ 'The Spatial Pattern of Income Generation in Lead Firm, Growth Area Linkage Systems', Economic Geography, vol. 51 (1975), pp.17-26.

Estall, R. C. and R. O. Buchanan, Industrial Activity and Economic Geography, (Hutchinson, London, 4th edition, 1980).

Evans, H. Vickers: Against the Odds 1956-1977, (Hodder and Stoughton, London, 1978).

Fabian, F. M. 'The Soviet Industrial Base' in L. D. Olvey, H. A. Leonard and B. E. Arlinghaus (eds.), Industrial Capacity and Defense Planning, (D. C. Heath, Lexington, Mass., 1983), pp.65-69.

Fearon, P. 'The Formative Years of the British Aircraft Industry, 1913-1924', Business History Review, vol. 43 (1969), pp.476-495.

__________ 'The British Airframe Industry and the State', Economic History Review, vol. 27 (1974), pp.236-251.

__________ 'The Vicissitudes of a British Aircraft Company: Handley Page Ltd Between the Wars', Business History, vol. 20 (1978), pp.63-86.

Freeman, R. Thunderbolt: A Documentary History of the Republic P-47, (MacDonald and Jane's, London, 1978).

Gansler, J. S. The Defense Industry, (MIT Press, Cambridge, Mass., 1980).

Gardner, C. British Aircraft Corporation: A History, (B. T. Batsford, London, 1981).

Gibbs-Smith, C. H. The Aeroplane: An Historical Survey of its Origins and Development, (HMSO, London, 1960).

__________ Aviation: An Historical Survey from its Origins to the End of World War II, (HMSO,

London, 1970).
Gordon, M. R. 'Are Military Contractors Part of the Problem or Part of the Solution?' in L. D. Olvey et al (eds.), Industrial Capacity and Defense Planning, (D. C. Heath, Lexington, Mass., 1983), pp.93-102.
Gorgol, J. F. The Military-Industrial Firm: A Practical Theory and Model, (Praeger, New York, 1972).
Gunston, Bill The Encyclopedia of the World's Combat Aircraft, (Salamander Books, London, 1976).
________ Jane's Aerospace Dictionary, (Jane's, London, 1980).
Hall, G. R. and R. E. Johnson, 'Transfers of United States Aerospace Technology to Japan' in R. Vernon (ed.), The Technology Factor in International Trade, (NBER, New York, 1970), pp.305-358.
Halpenny, B. B. Action Stations 4: Military Airfields of Yorkshire, (Patrick Stephens, Cambridge, 1982).
Hartley, K. and W. S. Corcoran, 'Short-run Employment Functions and Defence Contracts in the UK Aircraft Industry', Applied Economics, vol. 7 (1975), pp.223-233.
Hayward, K. 'Politics and European Aerospace Collaboration: The A300 Airbus', Journal of Common Market Studies, vol. 14 (1976), pp.354-367.
Higham, R. 'Quantity vs Quality: The Impact of Changing Demand on the British Aircraft Industry, 1900-1960', Business History Review, vol. 42 (1968), pp.443-466.
________ Air Power: A Concise History, (St Martin's Press, New York, 1972). Hill, M. R. East-West Trade, Industrial Co-operation and Technology Transfer, (Gower Publishers, Aldershot, 1983).
Holloway, D. 'The Soviet Union' in N. Ball and M. Leitenberg (eds.), The Structure of the Defense Industry, (St Martin's Press, New York, 1983), pp.50-80.
Hornby, W. Factories and Plant, (HMSO, London, 1958).
Jane's All the World's Aircraft, (Jane's, London, various years).
Johnston, R. J. 'Congressional Committees and the Inter-State Distribution of Military Spending', Geoforum, vol. 10 (1979), pp.151-162.
Jones, D. R. 'The Beginnings of Russian Air Power, 1907-1922' in R. Higham and J. W. Kipp (eds.), Soviet Aviation and Air Power: A Historical View, (Westview Press, Boulder, Colo., 1977), pp.15-33.

Kaldor, M. 'Technical Change in the Defence Industry' in K. Pavitt (ed.), Technical Innovation and British Economic Performance, (Macmillan, London, 1980), pp.100-121.

________ The Baroque Arsenal, (Hill and Wang, New York, 1981).

Kanter, A. Defense Politics: A Budgetary Perspective, (University of Chicago Press, Chicago, 1975).

Kennedy, G. Defence Economics, (Duckworth, London, 1983).

Koistinen, P. A. C. 'The "Industrial-Military Complex" in Historical Perspective: World War I', Business History Review, vol. 41 (1967), pp.378-403.

________ 'The "Industrial-Military Complex" in Historical Perspective: The Inter War Years', Journal of American History, vol. 56 (1969-70), pp.819-839.

Kolodziej, E. A. 'France' in N. Ball and M. Leitenberg (eds.), The Structure of the Defense Industry, (St Martin's Press, New York, 1983), pp.81-110.

Kucera, R. P. The Aerospace Industry and the Military: Structural and Political Relationships, (Sage Publications, Beverly Hills, Calif., 1974).

Kurth, J. R. 'The Political-Economy of Weapons Procurement: The Follow-on Imperative', American Economic Review Papers and Proceedings, vol. 62 (1972), pp.304-311.

Lancaster, J. 'Piper Aircraft's Vero Beach Plant: An Analysis of Locational Determinants in Light Aircraft Manufacturing', The Southeastern Geographer, vol. 7 (1967), pp.22-33.

Lee, A. The Soviet Air Force, (Harper & Brothers, New York, 1950).

Lewis, P. The British Fighter since 1912, (Putnam, London, 4th edition, 1979).

Lipietz, A. 'Towards Global Fordism?', New Left Review, vol. 132 (March/April 1982), pp.33-47.

Lowi, T. J. 'Towards a Politics of Economics: The State of Permanent Receivership' in L. N. Lindberg et al (eds.), Stress and Contradiction in Modern Capitalism: Public Policy and the Theory of the State, (Lexington Books, Toronto, 1975), pp.115-124.

Mansfield, E. The Economics of Technical Change, (Longman, London, 1968).

McAndrew, W. 'The Early Days of Aircraft Acquisition in Canadian Military Aviation', Canadian Defence Quarterly, vol. 12 (1982), pp.35-43.

McDermott, P. and M. Taylor, Industrial Organisation and Location, (Cambridge University Press, Cambridge, 1982).
Meier, G. M. Leading Issues in Economic Development, (Oxford University Press, New York, 3rd edition, 1976).
Miller, R. and D. Sawers, The Technical Development of Modern Aviation, (Routledge and Kegan Paul, London, 1968).
Molson, K. M. and H. A. Taylor, Canadian Aircraft since 1909, (Putnam, London, 1982).
Mondey, D. (ed.), The Complete Illustrated Encyclopedia of the World's Aircraft, (A & W Publishers Inc., New York, 1973).
Nobbs, R. L. 'A Note on Aerospace Collaboration', Journal of Common Market Studies, vol. 14 (1976), pp.368-371.
Nocifora, E. 'Poles of Development and the Southern Question', International Journal of Urban and Regional Research, vol. 2 (1978), pp.361-378.
OECD, The Industrial Policy of Japan, (OECD, Paris, 1972).
_____ The Impact of Newly-Industrialising Countries on Production and Trade in Manufacturing, (OECD, Paris, 1979).
Okimoto, D. I. (ed.), Japan's Economy: Coping with Change in the International Environment, (Westview Press, Boulder, Colo., 1982).
Peck, M. J. and F. M. Scherer, The Weapons Acquisition Process: An Economic Analysis, (Harvard University Press, Cambridge, Mass., 1962).
Penrose, H. British Aviation: The Pioneer Years, (Putnam, London, 1967).
Phillips, A. Technology and Market Structure, (D. C. Heath, Lexington, Mass., 1971).
Plowden Report, Report of the Committee of Inquiry into the Aircraft Industry, (Cmnd. 2853, HMSO, London, 1965).
Price, V. C. Industrial Policies in the European Community, (St Martin's Press, New York, 1981).
Purcell, C. W. (ed.), The Military-Industrial Complex, (Harper & Row, New York, 1972).
Rae, J. B. Climb to Greatness: The American Aircraft Industry, 1920-1960, (MIT Press, Cambridge, Mass., 1968).
Rallo, J. 'The European Community's Industrial Policy Revisited: The Case of Aerospace', Journal of Common Market Studies, vol. 22 (1984), pp.245-267.
Rayner Report, Government Organisation for Defence Procurement and Civil Aerospace, (Cmnd. 4641, HMSO, London, 1971).

Rich, M. et al, Multinational Coproduction of Military Aerospace Systems, (Rand Corporation, Santa Monica, Calif., October 1981).
Robertson, B. British Military Aircraft Serials, (Patrick Stephens, Cambridge, 1979).
Roeme, M. 'Dependence and Industrialisation Strategies', World Development, vol. 9 (1981), pp.429-434.
Rossi, S. A. 'Italy' in N. Ball and M. Leitenberg (eds.), The Structure of the Defense Industry, (St Martin's Press, New York, 1983), pp.214-256.
Schmookler, J. Invention and Economic Growth, (Harvard University Press, Cambridge, Mass., 1966).
Scott, J. D. Vickers: A History, (Weidenfeld and Nicolson, London, 1962).
Sealy, K. R. The Geography of Air Transport, (Hutchinson, London, 1966).
Simonson, G. R. 'Missile and Creative Destruction in the American Aircraft Industry, 1956-61', Business History Review, vol. 38 (1964), pp.302-314.
Singh, P. Aircraft of the Indian Air Force, 1933-73, (The English Book Store, New Delhi, 1974).
SIPRI, Yearbook, (SIPRI, Stockholm, various years).
Spencer, F. A. 'A Reappraisal of Transport Aircraft Needs 1985-2000: Perceptions of Airline Management in a Changing Economic, Regulatory, and Technological Environment', NASA Langley Research Center, Hampton, Virginia, 1982.
Stone, I. F. 'Nixon and the Arms Race' in C. W. Purcell (ed.), The Military-Industrial Complex, (Harper & Row, New York, 1972), pp.221-235.
Straszheim, M. R. The International Airline Industry, (The Brookings Institution, Washington, DC, 1969).
Swann, D. Competition and Industrial Policy in the European Community, (Methuen, London, 1983).
Taneja, N. K. Airline Traffic Forecasting: A Regression Analysis Approach, (D. C. Heath, Lexington, Mass., 1978).
____________ Airlines in Transition, (D. C. Heath, Lexington, Mass., 1981).
Taylor, M. J. 'Industrial Linkage,"Seed-bed" Growth and the Location of Firms', University College London, Geography Occasional Paper 3, September 1969.
Taylor, T. Defence, Technology and International Integration, (St Martin's Press, New York, 1982).
Trebilcock, C. The Vickers Brothers: Armaments and Enterprise, 1854-1914, (Europa Publications, London, 1977).
Tsantis, A. C. and R. Pepper, Romania: The

Industrialisation of the Agrarian Economy under Socialist Planning, (World Bank, Washington, D. C., 1979).
Tyler, W. G. Manufactured Export Expansion and Industrialisation in Brazil, (J. C. B. Mohr, Tubingen, 1976).
Tuomi, H. and R. Vayrynen, Transnational Corporations, Armaments and Development, (Gower, Aldershot, 1982).
Vayrynen, R. 'Semiperipheral Countries in the Global Economic and Military Order' in H. Tuomi and R. Vayrynen (eds.), Militarization and Arms Production, (Croom Helm, London, 1983), pp.163-192.
Warford, J. J. Public Policy toward General Aviation, (The Brookings Institution, Washington, DC, 1971).
Whynes, D. K. The Economics of Third World Military Expenditure, (University of Texas Press, Austin, 1979).
Williams, G. et al, Crisis in Procurement: A Case Study of the TSR-2, (RUSI, Whitehall, 1969).

INDEX

For Product Safety Concerns and Information please contact our EU representative GPSR@taylorandfrancis.com
Taylor & Francis Verlag GmbH, Kaufingerstraße 24, 80331 München, Germany

www.ingramcontent.com/pod-product-compliance
Lightning Source LLC
LaVergne TN
LVHW020642300926
849161LV00004B/781

* 9 7 8 1 1 3 8 6 3 2 7 3 8 *